Roy Jenkins

Roy Jenkins

A BIOGRAPHY

John Campbell

St. Martin's Press   New York

Copyright © by John Campbell 1983

All rights reserved. For information, write:

St. Martin's Press, Inc., 175 Fifth Avenue, New York, NY 10010

Printed in Great Britain

First published in the United States of America in 1983

ISBN 0-312-69460-1

Library of Congress Cataloging in Publication Data

Campbell, John.
    Roy Jenkins, a biography.

    Bibliography: p.
    Includes index.
    1. Jenkins, Roy. 2. Statesman—Great Britain—Biography. 3. Great
Britain—Politics and government—1945-   . I. Title.
        DA591.J46C35 1983   941.08'092'4   [B]   83-10927
                ISBN 0-312-69460-1

To Robin

Contents

Illustrations

Preface

The idea of writing a biography of Roy Jenkins first came to me in the autumn of 1981; but I think that, subconsciously, I had been nursing it for almost twenty years before that. It happens that I was brought up as his near-neighbour, living two doors away from him in Ladbroke Square. Though my parents barely knew him (my mother was quite friendly with Mrs Jenkins over the garden wall) he was the first politician I was aware of as I grew up; and I gradually realized that he was the one with whose public positions I most often agreed. Here I must declare a political interest. For ten years before 1981 I was one of that vast frustrated constituency who found no representation in the Conservative or Labour parties but, as a lukewarm Liberal, was just waiting, impatiently yet confidently, for the realignment of politics that we knew must come; when the SDP was eventually formed, our dominant reaction was relief that at last the break had come. To that extent, this book is undisguisedly partisan. At the same time, I am a professional historian: my two previous books (the second not yet published) were impeccably academic, and though this one had necessarily to be written more quickly and more journalistically, I would claim that it is still a historian's book. Mr Jenkins has very kindly helped me from the moment I first approached him by providing me with press cuttings and factual information, and encouraging friends and colleagues to speak freely to me; but he has not looked over my shoulder as I wrote, nor attempted to influence me in any way at all. He positively declined to read my text until it was beyond a stage where he could be tempted to suggest changes. I am grateful to him equally for his help and for his restraint. I believe that I have represented his views correctly, but there may be points, particularly in the final pages, which he would make differently. The interpretation of his career and the responsibility for any errors is of course entirely my own.

One word about sources: I am very conscious of having relied heavily, in Chapters Five and Six, on the Crossman Diaries, and am grateful to

Hamish Hamilton Ltd and Jonathan Cape Ltd for permission to quote from them. I remember writing in the *New Statesman* some years ago of the danger that the sheer bulk and quotability of Crossman would pose for future historians: I might have been warning myself. I can only say that I have tried to use them with caution; but in a period for which there is as yet little other contemporary evidence, beyond the press, and of which the political memoirs so far published (except perhaps for Douglas Jay's) are entirely useless, he was impossible to ignore. In mitigation of any possible distortion, I plead the fact that Mr Jenkins himself, reviewing the second volume in the *Observer* in 1976, described the Diaries as 'surprisingly accurate'. Nevertheless I am sorry that I did not see Barbara Castle's imminent diary for the same period – or indeed Mr Jenkins' own occasional journal, which he withheld, understandably, for his memoirs.

Otherwise I have been able to supplement published recollections with a number of useful interviews with friends, colleagues and relations (though not as many as I should have liked, had I had more time), as well as two or three conversations with Mr Jenkins himself and Mrs Jenkins (to whose importance in his life I am conscious of having done scant justice). I am particularly grateful to the following for giving some of their time to talk to me: Leo Abse MP; Lord Balogh; Hon. Mark Bonham Carter; Ivor Bulmer-Thomas; Rt. Hon. Sir Ian Gilmour MP; David Ginsburg MP; Lord Harris of Greenwich; Norman Hart; Oliver James; Mrs Pita Karaka; Robert Maclennan MP; Professor David Marquand; Matthew Oakeshott; Hayden and Laura Phillips; Rt. Hon. William Rodgers MP; Madron Seligman MEP and Mrs Seligman; Dick Taverne; Don Touhig (Editor of the *Monmouthshire Free Press*); Mrs Kathleen Tuck; and Philip Williams. Also for more casual conversations with Christopher Brocklebank-Fowler MP; John Grigg; Christopher Layton; Anthony Lester; Mrs Sybil Marchmont; and Roderick Mac-Farquhar. I should like to thank Mrs Jenkins and Celia Beale for help with pictures.

Among my own friends, I am grateful to Paul Addison for his invariably wise advice; to Ian Chisholm for several conversations about the Home Office; to Kathleen Burk for free use of her unrivalled library of contemporary political history; and to Esmée Roberts and Jill Ford for putting me up extraordinarily conveniently on the edge of the Glasgow, Hillhead constituency for several days in March 1982. I am grateful to many friends and relations, but particularly to my mother-in-law, Mrs Olive McCracken, and my aunt, Mrs Joyce Jackson, for supplying me with recent cuttings from papers I might otherwise have missed.

I should especially like to thank Robert Baldock of Weidenfeld for putting the book through the press with such (to me unprecedented) speed.

Finally, I am deeply grateful to my wife, Alison, for her unfailing support, encouragement and occasional correction, reading each day's production as it fell from the typewriter and proof-reading under extreme pressure of time; and to our daughter Robin, for giving me the necessary incentive to write faster than I have ever written before.

John Campbell
Ladbroke Square, London
February 1983

ONE

From Pontypool to Oxford,
1920–1945

A characteristically British controversy surrounds Roy Jenkins' origins. To his critics, particularly on the left of the Labour party – often themselves guiltily middle-class and public school educated – it has always been intensely galling that this superior figure should have been born and raised in the very heart of the Labour movement. The son and grandson of miners, brought up in the South Wales coalfield during the depression, his father actually imprisoned for his part in the General Strike – what would not Michael Foot or Tony Benn give for such a pedigree?

The response of those who cannot match it has always been – even before Jenkins left the Labour Party – that he has betrayed this proud inheritance. Some allege only a political betrayal – one more in the line of good working-class boys seduced by power and money to forget the class from which they sprang. Others, like Leo Abse, the present Labour member for Pontypool and mischievous amateur Freudian, see a deeper psychological betrayal: the true and somehow more authentic Welsh, working-class, Labour allegiance which Jenkins derived from his father was overborne, early in life, by the corrupting influence of his anglicized, social-climbing, petty-bourgeois mother, leaving Jenkins in adult life rootless and *déclassé*.[1]

There is just enough truth in this simplistic analysis to make it plausible, though all the evidence is that Jenkins' transcending of the most narrow class stereotypes troubles his class-obsessed critics a great deal more than it worries him. But the reality, when his origins are examined a little more closely, is that Roy Jenkins is quite clearly and comprehensibly the product of his background and the child equally – and with no great conflict – of both his parents.

He was born into the Labour movement, certainly; but he was born very firmly into a Labour élite. There was never any question of Roy going to work down the mine. By the time he was born, on 11 November

1920, his father, Arthur Jenkins, had left manual work far behind him:
he was a full-time trade union official, chairman of the Pontypool
divisional Labour party and a Monmouthshire County Councillor. He
became an Alderman in 1926, a Justice of the Peace, Vice-President of
the South Wales Miners' Federation, a member, on and off, of the
National Executive of the Labour Party, and in 1935 MP for Pontypool
– a position he could probably have had very much earlier if he had
been the type of man to push for it. By any reckoning he was a very
remarkable man.

Educated at the Varteg Board School only up to the age of twelve, he
had gone straight down the pit, but at eighteen won a miners' scholarship worth £30 a year which enabled him to go to Ruskin College,
Oxford (he was always thereafter proud to call himself an Oxford man),
where he won other scholarships and was able to go on for ten months
at the Sorbonne (where he learned to speak French much better than
his son ever did, laid the foundations of a deep knowledge of continental
mining conditions and made contacts with European socialists which
he retained all his life). Thus equipped, he returned to the mines in
1909, became Secretary of the Pontypool Trades Council in 1911,
Deputy Miners' Agent for the Monmouthshire Eastern Valleys branch
of the South Wales Miners' Federation in 1918, and Agent in 1921.

When he was elected to the National Executive of the Labour Party,
he characteristically resigned after a couple of years because it took him
too much away from Pontypool, but bowed to pressure later to go on
again. When he went into Parliament, he was a model constituency
member until 1940, when Attlee rather surprisingly appointed him his
PPS and took him into the very heart of the wartime Government. Attlee
much later recalled the older Jenkins as one of the three 'most unselfish'
men he had ever met in politics.[2] He had a modesty rare in a successful
politician, and an even rarer gentleness: he was never heard to lose his
temper, or even raise his voice. Several obituary tributes echoed that of
the *Daily Herald*: 'This gentle and sensitive son of Wales seemed ... more
the poet or the student than the man of action.'[3] He was, in short, no
ordinary miners' leader, but (as James Griffiths, President of the South
Wales Miners' Federation, called him) 'one of Nature's gentlemen'.[4]

'It is given to some men', the *South Wales Argus* commented when he
died, 'to rise above Party and to do incalculable good in a community
sense – to hold certain principles, yet to have a breadth of vision and
magnanimity of spirit which carry them into the realm of common
service. Such a man was Alderman Jenkins.... Kindly, considerate,
temperate in all things, he never spared himself in the service of the

people.... Few men have achieved so much for a constituency – and, in his case, for the wider area of South Wales and Monmouthshire.'[5]

The young Roy thus grew up with a father who was a highly respected local dignitary – not at all in the sort of household where to be Labour was to be in revolt against society. Despite the setback of 1931, and despite the unemployment of the thirties and the failure to achieve the nationalization of the mines, Labour was marching steadily towards power. Arthur Jenkins was among the leaders of a confident generation who fully expected to see the dawn in their lifetime and did not expect to have to break any heads to bring it about. Though an intelligent and highly cultivated man, he was not an intellectual: his idea of socialism was simply a practical improvement in the conditions of life of working people. 'He was deeply conscious', as the *South Wales Argus* put it, 'that the wheel of social progress revolved slowly, but he tried to give it impetus.'[5] Of the direction and inevitability of progress he had had no doubt. The political faith which the young Roy unquestioningly imbibed – not so much with his mother's milk as with his father's innumerable cups of tea – was that the Labour party was the vehicle of progress: gradual perhaps, but certain, peaceful and constitutional. (On a bleak hillside above Abersychan there is still a working men's pub proudly named The British Constitution.) It is in this light that the famous incident of Arthur's imprisonment must be understood.

During the General Strike in May 1926 (when the TUC pulled all its members out in support of the miners) there was an affray between a crowd of locked-out miners and the police outside a colliery at Blaenavon, a few miles up the road from Abersychan. All the evidence is that Arthur Jenkins, as the men's leader, went to try and cool things down: it would have been out of character for him to do anything else. But the police arrested him and charged him with inciting the riot: in the overheated atmosphere of the moment he was sentenced to nine months in jail. Such was the outcry, however, and the weight of petitions bearing witness to his pacific character, that he was released after only a few weeks. The continuing interest of the story lies in the fact that Roy was not told the reason for his father's absence until several years later: he was told that Arthur had gone to Germany to look at mines, and he remembers being puzzled by the cheering crowds that greeted him on his return. To those who think that a boy of his background should naturally have been brought up as a good class warrior with an animus against the bosses and the police, this very understandable tempering of the truth towards a child of five is evidence of an early smothering of proper socialist attitudes with a concern for petty-bour-

geois respectability which explains all the adult Roy's subsequent de-
viations from true socialism. He was brought up – by his mother, it is
alleged – to be ashamed of his father's imprisonment when he should
have been proud of it. In practice, he cannot as a schoolboy in Abersychan have long remained unaware of the truth. But the wish not to talk
about the incident was entirely characteristic of Arthur. He was not
proud of it himself. It was certainly not that he was ashamed: to the end
of his life he nursed a grievance against the inspector who arrested him.
But he did not want to be a martyr, and he did not want his son to grow
up with a chip on his shoulder: fighting the police was not his idea of
socialism. There was in this matter no conflict between Arthur and
Hattie Jenkins: Roy's later indifference to the class war is the very
reverse of a betrayal of his patrimony. There are those in Pontypool
today who will still shake their heads in disbelief that a man whose
father had been in prison could have implemented, as Home Secretary,
the Mountbatten Report on prison security. But they are wrong to see
any inconsistency. Roy was brought up very firmly in the Labour
tradition, but in a confident Labour tradition of civic responsibility and
peaceful progress.

There is no doubt that Hattie Jenkins – born Harriet Harris – whom
Arthur had married in 1911, did regard herself as socially a cut above
most of her husband's colleagues. She was not of a mining family herself,
but was the daughter of the manager of a local steelworks. Most of those
who knew her find it hard to deny that she was a bit of a snob, though
the family explain that impression by shyness: where Arthur had a
warmth and ease of manner with all sorts of people, she appeared rather
formidable. In private, she was ebullient, even dominating. But she took
little part in Arthur's constituency politics; she never went to his meetings, nor did she associate much with other Labour women. Her preferred society was rather of the level of the local doctor and solicitor;
her most conspicuous public service was to 'work like a Trojan' for the
annual hospital bazaar. During the 1939–45 war she did a lot of Red
Cross work, and after Arthur's death she became a JP. She was unquestionably ambitious, both for Arthur – she liked him bringing important
people to the house – and later for Roy. But her role in the partnership
was much more that of the traditional Tory member's wife than the
tea-making and constituency-visiting role usually assigned to Labour
wives.

There are some obvious points of resemblance between Roy Jenkins
and his mother. For one thing she was physically somewhat plump,
unlike Arthur who was always very slight: as he has grown older, Jenkins

has visibly taken after her. Then, too, she hid a kind heart behind a rather grand manner: his shyness takes the same form. His ill-disguised lack of interest in the chores of politics does not derive from Arthur. In many respects, Hattie fits admirably the cliché of the ambitious mother who is the driving force behind an only child. But it was unquestionably Arthur whom the young Roy revered, Arthur whose career he set out to follow, and Arthur from whom he took his political bearings on the Labour right, his magnanimity and moderation, his internationalist outlook, his sense of historical perspective and his love of books.

The house in which Roy Harris Jenkins was born, on Armistice Day, 1920, just two years after the ending of the Great War, was small but well-built, bow-fronted and gabled, one of a terrace of six imposingly elevated above the main street through Abersychan (it backs into a steep hillside). Abersychan itself is a straggle of houses a couple of miles up the valley from the main centre of Pontypool. When he was two, they moved two hundred yards down Snatchwood Road into a larger, yellow-brick but stone-faced house in a terrace of nine, with a garden at the back and a basement where there was room for a ping-pong table. The front parlour was Arthur's office, where a stream of people could call to see him without going into the rest of the house. In this house they employed a live-in maid – not unusual in quite modest homes at that time, but something Hattie had been used to, and a mark of some social standing. In 1935, around the time that Arthur went into Parliament, the family moved again to a much larger house on the edge of Pontypool itself, a solid white-painted house standing on its own in a substantial garden. (All three houses, confusingly, were called Greenlands, the name of Hattie's childhood home, which they carried around with them at every move.)

Roy was brought up, then, not in any sort of affluence but in a secure degree of middle-class comfort. All three houses were filled with books: he has estimated that his father must have owned between five hundred and a thousand.[6] He was an only child, and this was important: he was not spoiled – Hattie was a strict parent, and expected instant obedience – but he was never short of anything he needed. He was certainly not short of love and attention. The family was in fact an unusually close one, the three of them enjoying a degree of intimacy and equality that is very rare, and perhaps only possible with a single child. They all had private nicknames: Arthur was Jumbo, Hattie was Pony and Roy was Bunny. Not only did Arthur and Hattie call one another Jumbo and Pony, but so did Roy. The first time their long-serving maid, Kathleen Tuttle, heard him call his father Jumbo she thought he was being rude, but she soon realized that this was his normal form of address. Roy was then ten. (He had a pet name for Kathleen too – Kathlet – though he would not have used it in front of his mother.)

He had, by the standards of South Wales in the 1920s, a fairly sheltered childhood, but he was not a solitary boy: he had plenty of friends, who came to Snatchwood Road to play in the sandpit in the garden, and later table-tennis in the basement. Nor was he brought up entirely as an only child. He had two elder girl cousins, the daughters of Hattie's sister, who had lost her husband: Sybil and Connie Peppin were always around, particularly in the school holidays, and the families always went away together in the summer to Swansea or Porthcawl. In 1932 their mother died, and Connie came to live with Arthur and Hattie while Sybil went to another aunt. From the age of eleven Roy had for practical purposes an elder sister, though he seems to have treated her, with a boy's assumed authority, as though she were the younger: she joined *his* games, playing cricket in the garden or going trainspotting. She would have been the Indian to his Cowboy if 'Aunt Hat' had not abhorred games with guns. In adult life they have remained very close – closer than many a real brother and sister.

He went first to school at a primary school called Pentuin, a mile or so from home: Hattie used to pay a girl to take him there and back, which may be the origin of some of the rumours still current in Pontypool of a rather cossetted little boy. But one piece of gossip, maliciously retailed, can be interestingly explained. The fact is remembered that young Roy sometimes went to school in gloves, which was thought very cissy: he did, but only in the strawberry season, when he was allergic to strawberries and had to wear cotton gloves to prevent him coming out in a rash!

When he was ten, rising eleven, he went on to Abersychan County School. The choice was somewhat surprising, since there was a clear disparity in esteem between the two major schools in the area, and West Monmouth School, in Pontypool, was considered the better. Kathleen Tuttle, for one, would have expected Hattie to wish to send Roy there. It may be that she wanted to keep him closer to home (Abersychan was just up the hill at the back of the town within walking distance). It is unlikely that Arthur was influenced by the thought that it might be politically damaging for him to send his son to the 'snob' school: he believed too passionately in education, and was actually a Governor of West Monmouth. Perhaps that was the reason. Anyway, Roy went to Abersychan, where he did well at first, but rather less well later on.

He was not a particularly bookish boy. He had abundant physical energy, was good at games and mad on cricket, though he excelled, perhaps significantly, at individual rather than team sports: he won prizes for swimming, and used to go bicycling a lot. His academic work he accomplished, even at this age, with little visible effort. Hattie was very firm that he could do nothing else until he had finished his homework, so he acquired the habit, which he has never lost, of getting through work quickly to free himself for pleasure. At fourteen, he passed with credit six School Certificates (English, Geography, French, Mathematics, Physics and Chemistry), and added Latin the following year; at sixteen he gained Highers in History and Geography (principal subjects) and English (subsidiary subject). But he was not being stretched sufficiently to fulfil his father's ambition that he should go to Oxford. Perhaps he would have done better at West Monmouth. To spur him on to greater effort, he was sent for three terms to University College, Cardiff, to polish up his History and particularly his French.

Those who believe that Jenkins is ashamed of his background and deliberately blotted out the memory of Wales once he had got to Oxford, attach great significance to his omission of these three terms from his *Who's Who* entry. In fact he used Cardiff merely as an extension of school – a sort of sixth-form college – to bring him to the necessary standard to get into Oxford: he was less than seventeen when he went there, had to travel the twenty miles there and back each day by bus and, though he made two friends with whom he is still in touch, was not in a full sense a member of the university. Having won his place at Balliol, he left Cardiff before the end of his third term to spend some months in France. Even so – as he wrote only recently in a memoir for the college magazine – he looks back 'with both nostalgia and gratitude for a period of awakening interest.'[7] Only the most puritanical Welsh fundamentalist could criticize a clever boy of his background for looking ambitiously to Oxford. In any case, the determination that he should try was much more strongly his father's than his own: since his own days at Ruskin – 'then only a ship moored alongside the University'[7] – Arthur had nursed a romantic idealization of the dreaming spires. He had only been able to go, briefly, with a miners' scholarship. Though Roy, despite two attempts, did not win a scholarship, Arthur was now earning enough (£600 a year as an MP, plus £90 from the Miners' Federation) to pay for him out of his own pocket. No-one thought in 1938 that such upward social mobility from father to son was a betrayal of socialism; on the contrary, it was part of the march of labour that the opportunities of Oxford should be open to the sons of trade unionists. Arthur was intensely proud of his son.

Jenkins went to Oxford, as his father wished, with no chip on his shoulder, but firmly Labour in his allegiance. A distinct stage in his life was now over: Oxford was the gateway to wider horizons, in which he would leave Pontypool far behind. The question must be asked, because they sometimes seemed in later life to have left so little mark, what he had drawn from these eighteen formative years in South Wales, living among great poverty but not in it. One curious legacy is perhaps that fastidiousness which has always been remarked as one of his character-istics. His critics would put this down to a sense of social superiority, instilled by his mother and confirmed by Balliol. It can better be explained by embarrassment at the consciousness of his own good fortune, a desire not to intrude upon or claim a share of a suffering that was not his own. He has never made the political capital that he could so easily have done out of his background, because he knows that it would be fraudulent in one who comes, not from the true working class but from what he has called the 'Labour squirearchy'. What was possible for his father, who had raised himself by his own efforts, was not possible for him, who had been raised on his father's shoulders. He grew up with a strong inherited belief in the urgency of progress towards an order of society in which injustice should be mitigated or abolished; but it was an intellectual belief, or perhaps rather an inbred assumption, rather than the product of searing personal experience. He did not, as a boy, help with Arthur's constituency work, or go canvassing, any more than Hattie did. He was deliberately distanced from that. As soon as he was old enough to form an ambition, he knew that he too should go into politics, which meant without question Labour politics. But his would be – had to be, by the nature of his upbringing – the high Oxford road, not the trade union and local authority low road.

Despite this diffidence about assuming a class identity that he could not wear with conviction, Jenkins never had any doubt that he belonged in the Labour party. This political self-confidence distinguished him in later years from other Oxford-educated socialists in the Wilson Cabinets – Denis Healey, Tony Benn, his friend Tony Crosland – in all of whom one can detect a certain straining to prove their Labour identity at critical moments by self-consciously siding with 'the workers'. The strength Jenkins has always drawn from his roots is that he feels no need to strive for a spurious proletarianism. During the revisionist controv-ersies of the 1950s and early 1960s, when there began to be murmurs that he was really a Liberal, it never occurred to him that his loyalty to the Labour party could be in doubt: born and raised in the party, he did not have to keep making obeisance to party myths and traditions which he thought exhausted. Politically, it might have been wiser if he had, but he never saw Labour as an exclusively working-class party, and always protested against it becoming so. It can be traced as a fundamental attitude in the formation of the SDP that it does not idealize the working class as holding the monopoly of political virtue.

A further question is whether Jenkins today thinks of himself as being Welsh. During the Hillhead by-election, in 1982, he took rather suddenly to insisting that he was not an Englishman, when his apparent Englishness seemed likely to be a serious handicap with the Scottish electorate. But he has more often described himself as a borderer, taking advantage of Pontypool's position in the very last valley in Wales. In practice he thinks of himself as British. Leo Abse would maintain that he has deliberately rejected Wales and suppressed his whole Welsh inheritance, as a result of Pontypool's rebuff when he sought to succeed to his father's seat in 1946: he claims that when he (Abse) arrived at Westminster in 1958 as the member for Pontypool, Jenkins could not bear even to look at him! But Oxford and the war had already taken him out of Wales, and it is very doubtful if he wanted to succeed to Arthur's seat, where he could never have been more than his father's son. He had no traumatic reason to turn his back on the scenes of a singularly happy childhood; but the introverted Welsh culture of pub, rugby club and chapel had never meant anything to him – why should it? It was his father who gave him wider horizons, and his limited visual sense was not excited by the bare, brooding landscape of the valley. Those in Pontypool today who still hold that no good man would ever leave, only exemplify the parochialism he was glad to leave behind. Transplanted into a wider field of opportunity, rather than rootless, Jenkins' life only really began to flower when he got to Oxford.

Oxford has been the nursery and forcing house of aspiring politicians of every generation going back at least to Gladstone's day in the 1820s. Whatever the academic claims of Cambridge, it is overwhelmingly from Oxford that the governing élite of the country has reproduced itself. The rise of the Labour party interrupted the tradition only briefly. The pioneers, naturally, had not been to university at all. The London School of Economics made a stab at becoming Labour's university between the wars. But by the time Labour came fully into its inheritance after 1945, its younger leaders were increasingly Oxford men, and very often dons, like Hugh Gaitskell, Douglas Jay, Patrick Gordon Walker, Richard Crossman and Harold Wilson. In 1976 five of the six contenders for the party leadership – Foot, Jenkins, Healey, Crosland and Benn –

had been at Oxford (though exceptionally, on this occasion, it was the outsider, James Callaghan, who won). The situation in the Conservative party is, less surprisingly, no different: the last Tory leader not to have been to Oxford was Winston Churchill.

But if the dominance of Oxford is remarkable, the pre-eminence within the political élite of a single college, Balliol, is even more so. Three strands make up the Balliol tradition: brains; an unusually democratic admissions policy that mixes the brightest from the state schools with the best of the public schools; and a strong ethos of public service. The first two combine to produce the third. Amid the upper-class frivolity of so much of Oxford – particularly between the wars – Balliol was a serious college, self-consciously training up the next generation not only of Cabinet Ministers but of Ambassadors, Permanent Secretaries and Bishops. This was the ideal college for the young Jenkins – as it was for the organ scholar from Broadstairs, three years ahead of him, 'Teddy' Heath – where his background would be least of a handicap. Here he found his model for life. The archetypal Balliol man is still the Liberal Prime Minister, Asquith – the son of a Yorkshire wool merchant, honed and polished into the classical image of the scholar-statesman, Olympian, enlightened, effortlessly superior. In his late thirties Jenkins wrote Asquith's biography, and cultivated an explicit affinity with him. But twenty years earlier, from the first moment he arrived in Oxford, he had already slipped smoothly into the Balliol mould.

'Life', it has been said, 'is one Balliol man after another': the famous joke is only a mild exaggeration. Within his own college, Jenkins was able to meet and get to know several of those who would be the rivals and antagonists of his political life in the House of Commons over the following forty years – not only Ted Heath, but also Denis Healey, Julian Amery, Maurice Macmillan and Hugh Fraser; later on Mark Bonham Carter (Asquith's grandson) who became a particularly close friend. Very different men, they all perceptibly carry the Balliol impress – that air of aloof superiority and an inability to suffer fools.

Michaelmas term 1938 was an unsettled but politically exciting moment to go up. War was already in the air. No freshman could have any confidence that he would be able to complete his degree. It was only a couple of weeks before that Neville Chamberlain had flown back from Munich with his famous piece of paper bearing Hitler's signature, proclaiming 'peace with honour'. But Chamberlain's peace never looked more than a breathing-space, dishonourably bought at the expense of Czechoslovakia. No sooner had Jenkins taken up residence than Oxford in general, and Balliol in particular, were in the thick of the national debate. In a highly-publicized by-election the Master of Balliol, the philosopher A.D. Lindsay, stood as an Independent with Labour and Liberal support against the policy of appeasement. The National Government was defended with spirit by the young Quintin Hogg; he held the seat, but his majority was halved. The same term Heath, the most prominent young Conservative in Oxford, made a sensational *démarche* at the Union, bitterly attacking the Government, which won him the Presidency the following term. For Jenkins, the transition from the obscurity of the valleys to the brilliantly spotlit Oxford scene must have been intoxicating. He worked for Lindsay, and 'almost certainly' voted for Heath.[8]

With his background and political ambition, it was inevitable that his life in Oxford centred on the Union. Looking back, he now regrets that he spent so much time at the Union, neglecting the range of other opportunities which Oxford offered. But at the time, politics were his whole life, his friends all political. Balliol dominated the Union even more than usual. The Presidents elected in Jenkins' first five terms were all from Balliol: they included Heath, Hugh Fraser and, in the Hilary term of 1940, Madron Seligman (now a member of the European Parliament), with whom Jenkins shared a room in Trinity when Balliol had to move next door to allow Chatham House to be evacuated from London. The previous term the elected President had gone to the war: the acting President was another who has remained a lifelong friend of Jenkins – Sir Nicholas ('Nico') Henderson, recently British Ambassador to the United States. Jenkins waited until his second term before making his debate in this arena: then he spoke three times. His maiden speech ('very fluent . . . quite good', according to *Isis*)[9] was on a general motion condemning the domestic policy of the National Government. In his second, he summed up for the Noes against the motion that 'This House welcomes the breaking down of traditional party lines': he took the approved Labour position against Cripps and Bevan, who were calling for a Popular Front against Hitler. In his third, he joined in deploring the Government's recognition of General Franco. At the end of that term he stood for election to the Library Committee, but did not get on: *Isis* did not yet pick him out as a 'Union prospect'. In the Trinity term, he took another approved Labour position against immediate conscription, and failed again to be elected to the Library Committee.

In his second year he made much more impact. The war had now begun, and several of the elected officers had joined up: Jenkins was co-opted to the Management Committee. More important, he was gaining in self-confidence, discovering his characteristic style. The first time that David Ginsburg, who came up to Balliol that year, heard him speak at the Union he took him for a peer's son, even though speaking for the Labour party! Ginsburg was another who became a close friend and political associate – Labour MP for Dewsbury from 1959 and one of the first to join the SDP in 1981. He and Jenkins found a shared interest in good food and wine. At home in Pontypool there was rarely drink in the house: tea was Arthur's stimulant, and if wine was sometimes provided for visitors he barely touched it. At Oxford, Jenkins developed a taste which was to become a major component of his future image: claret. (Ginsburg still remembers Jenkins introducing him, when they were both undergraduates, to Chateau Margaux.) Neither came from wealthy backgrounds: but Arthur somehow made sure that Roy could afford to live up to the level of his friends and indulge his increasingly expensive tastes.

The most important friend Jenkins made in his second year was the man with whom his political career was to be most inextricably entwined for the next thirty-seven years, Tony Crosland. Crosland was then in his third year at Trinity College, reading 'Greats'. Jenkins himself described the beginning of their friendship in an obituary tribute in 1977:

> I first saw Tony Crosland in 1938 or early 1939. He was 20, and I was 18. The gap seemed bigger. He was a very impressive undergraduate, showing every sign of intellectual and social self-assurance. He was immensely good-looking, and even in those days rather elegant. He wore a long camel-hair overcoat, and drove a powerful low MG known as the Red Menace. I, like many of his near-contemporaries, admired him from afar, and was rather intimidated.
>
> Then, one winter's evening a few months after the outbreak of the war, he came to my rooms, probably on some minor point of Labour Club business, and having settled it, remained uncertainly on the threshold, talking, but neither sitting down nor departing for nearly two hours. His character was more ambivalent than I had thought, but also more engaging.
>
> Thereafter, I saw him nearly every day for the next six months until he left Oxford.[10]

Once formed, the friendship between Jenkins and Crosland was an exceptionally close one, which is what gave such a sharp edge to their later rivalry. Susan Crosland, in her recent life of her husband, completely underestimates the intimacy of their early relationship: either the truth did not accord with her purpose, or Crosland himself – for his own reasons – had not talked much of it to her. In fact, for those first six months of 1940 they were never out of each other's company. They moved into digs together at 2 St John Street, and were continually together at the Union and the Labour Club. An unusual feature of the relationship was that Crosland soon became equally close to Jenkins' parents. His own upbringing had been very different – middle-class, materially comfortable but very strict: his parents were Plymouth Brethren. By becoming a socialist, Crosland was in revolt against his family. In Arthur and Hattie Jenkins, when Roy took him to stay, he found the sort of family he would have liked to have. Hattie in particular he adopted almost as a second mother; he wrote regularly to her from Italy when he was serving with the Parachute Regiment during the war. But he had also the greatest respect for Arthur as a Labour MP solidly rooted in the working-class movement. Arthur's example and fatherly advice had considerable influence in bringing Crosland back from the wilder shores of intellectual socialism, with which he flirted at Oxford, to the mainstream of the Labour party. Still more with Roy, from the moment they became friends, Crosland had endless arguments about socialism, theoretical and practical. From different starting points, they came gradually to a common view. For Jenkins it was easy. He was not, in the speculative sense, an intellectual, as Crosland was, attracted by ideas for their own sake. He did not come to socialism through books or in revolt against his parents or his class, but was raised in it and took unaltered from his father a simple faith, uncomplicated by feelings of class guilt, in progress towards social justice by state action. He was a natural loyalist: generally speaking, what the National Executive laid down at any moment as Labour policy was to be defended against mavericks like Cripps and Bevan (who were both expelled at this time). Crosland, outwardly more brilliant but personally much less secure, came rather enviously to respect his younger friend's certainty: undoubtedly he envied the working-class roots on which that certainty was based. (In his later years he made it a guiding principle that the Labour party should not evolve too far from its roots: one of the points of contention between them in the 1970s was that he felt that Jenkins had personally and politically done exactly that. Like other middle-class socialists, Crosland tended to idealize the working class.) It would be wrong to suggest that Crosland cultivated Jenkins for his parents rather than himself, just because he liked going to stay in Pontypool: their friendship was already close before he ever went there. But he continued to go frequently, whenever he got leave during the war, whether Roy could be there at the same time or not. It is a passage in the life of Tony Crosland which his next biographer should not overlook.

Jenkins and Crosland were the leading speakers, on opposing sides, in a Union debate in November 1939 on the Nazi–Soviet Pact and the partition of Poland: 'This House considers that recent Soviet policy has not been in accordance with socialist principles.' The report in the *Oxford Magazine* (*Isis* was suspended during the war) commented on their respective styles, as well as on their arguments:

> Mr R.H. Jenkins (Balliol) ... stated that he was a socialist, but that he thought a country's policy should not necessarily be guided by what Marx would have thought or Lenin would have done. He was not prepared to accept the dictates of Moscow as infallible reason. Socialist principles will never be served by the forcible annexation of a country or a part of a country. Mr Jenkins made, as usual, a very sound and sensible speech; but he should try and get his arguments home by using more emphasis and thrust at the right moments.
>
> Opposing the motion, Mr C.A.R. Crosland (Trinity) related his version of how the breakdown of Anglo-Soviet conversations occurred, and the resulting German-Soviet pact was concluded. The odd thing was that Russia had negotiated with the British Government for so long. The German-Soviet pact had been made in self-defence, after the Poles had refused to allow Russian troops on their soil. This was the best speech Mr Crosland has made in the Union. His *sang-froid* was useful against interruptions.[11]

At the end of this term, Jenkins was elected Secretary of the Union, and Crosland Treasurer. They were never in contention for the same office, because Crosland was always one jump ahead. For the Trinity term of 1940, Jenkins was overwhelmingly elected Librarian, but Crosland was defeated for President – the penalty, perhaps, of continuing to take a pro-Soviet line. When the Finnish Ambassador came to plead for aid for his country – a popular cause during the 'Phoney War' – Crosland staged a demonstration against him, hanging down a banner from the balcony reading 'Hands Off Russia'. But Crosland's fellow-travelling had its limit. In the Labour Club, matters came to a head between what would nowadays be called the 'hard left' who followed the Moscow line against the 'imperialist' war, and the mainstream loyalists like Jenkins who supported the war, though *not* the Chamberlain Government. In April the left-dominated Universities' Labour Federation, to which the Oxford University Labour Club was affiliated, was expelled by the NEC. The Oxford moderates, marshalled by Patrick Gordon Walker, who was then a don at Christ Church, then moved to disaffiliate from the ULF and apply to re-affiliate directly to the Labour party. They were defeated by 182 votes to 108; (prominent among the neo-Communist majority were Edmund Dell and Leo Pliatzky who, a quarter of a century later, was Permanent Under-Secretary at the Treasury when Jenkins was Chancellor of the Exchequer!). But the moderates were prepared and immediately broke away to form a new club, loyal to the NEC, the Oxford University Democratic Socialist Club, which within a few days had more members than the old Labour Club had ever had. G.D.H. Cole was President, Crosland the first Chairman and Jenkins Treasurer; the next year Jenkins, and then Ginsburg, were Chairman in turn.

This was Jenkins' first collision with the hard left. The episode makes an interesting pre-echo, forty years before its time and on a minor scale, of the formation of the SDP. Indeed much the same process has been repeated by two subsequent generations of Social Democrats in conflict with the left during their Oxford careers – by Bill Rodgers, Shirley Williams and Dick Taverne in 1950, and again by Alec McGivan and Matthew Oakeshott in 1976. On the latter occasion, Jenkins became President of the breakaway club.

At the end of May 1940 Jenkins stood for the Presidency of the Union. His opponent was James Comyn of New College (a lawyer, now a judge). The presidential debate was on the motion 'That without a great growth of Socialism, this war will have been fought in vain.' As guest speakers, Jenkins had on his side Kingsley Martin, the editor of the *New Statesman*, and Philip Noel-Baker MP, who deputized for Attlee. (It was a useful service that Jenkins could do for the Union, through his father, that he could secure top Labour names as guests: the previous term he had got Arthur Greenwood for Seligman.) Comyn had only the Liberal barrister A.S. Comyns Carr. In 'a fluent and well-prepared speech', Jenkins proclaimed Labour's vision:

> Nazism was a religion: we too must fight inspired by belief in a new world order. The League of Nations had failed because of Capitalism's inherent tendency towards war. Capitalists had brought Hitler to power: a Socialist Germany was vital for European peace. The power of the international financier must be destroyed if social justice was to be won.[12]

Jenkins won the debate easily. It was no handicap being Labour in Oxford in 1940. But he lost the Presidency by 117 votes to 112. He was desperately disappointed. At the time it seemed a most serious setback to his career. Today he feels ashamed at this 'egocentric misjudgement' at a moment when the German tanks were rolling through France. So disappointed was he, however, that he stood again the following term, which was unusual. His opponents at this second attempt were an Indian, I. J. Bahadoorsingh, and Roger Gray (also now a judge). On another clear party motion 'That this House does not want to hear of the Conservatives again', Jenkins made a characteristically practical case for Labour as the vehicle of progress:

> [He] attacked the Treasurer's [Gray's] attitude in making an abstract defence of Conservatism. He asked the House to base its verdict on past deeds of the Conservative party rather than the Treasurer's aspirations. The past deeds conclusively showed that twenty years of virtual power had only succeeded in destroying post-war hope of better things to come. Conservative power began with a victorious Britain and ended, he hoped never to be resurrected, with a Britain discredited and distrusted in the world. At home, their idea of justice was the Means Test; abroad, the strengthening of their potential enemies. Mr Jenkins was, as usual, sincere and impressive, and he concluded by addressing what was almost a personal appeal to the Treasurer to jettison the vanquished Conservatives and take his place with the victorious progressives.[13]

Aided by Nye Bevan, Jenkins and Bahadoorsingh again carried the debate. But in the contest for the Presidency Bahadoorsingh got 94 votes to his 85, and picked up more of Gray's redistributed second preferences for a comfortable victory, 123–96. Jenkins was not then the Labour man who appealed to Tories. Bahadoorsingh probably picked up the Empire vote; or maybe there was a revolt against Balliol. More seriously, perhaps Jenkins had not yet displayed quite the force of personality expected of a Union President. He was physically slight, a little shy, still young for his age and somewhat narrow in his interests: not enough of an exhibitionist. His friends, canvassing in his support, urged him to make more of his background, his personal knowledge of the poor. Scrupulously he refused, eschewing 'sob stuff': that was not his way. As a result, Jenkins was left nursing a second rebuff to his most cherished ambition.

He determined to get a good degree instead. He was reading PPE – Politics, Philosophy and Economics – with the emphasis very much on economics. A.D. Lindsay, he recalled years later, tried to teach him philosophy 'very unsuccessfully ... I was a very bad philosopher'.[6] The tutor who did make an impression on him was the Hungarian-born economist, Thomas Balogh; nearly thirty years later, tutor and student were respectively economic adviser to the Cabinet and Chancellor of the Exchequer. Balogh used to tease Jenkins by attacking Attlee, forcing him to justify his loyalty (his father was by now Attlee's PPS). But for his first two years Jenkins was too preoccupied with the Union and the Labour Club to do much serious work, though he read and absorbed the prophets of modern socialism, Cole, Laski and Evan Durbin. Then

Balogh told him firmly that if he did not take care he would fail. So in the classic manner he applied himself for his last two terms, discovering the formidable capacity for hard and rapid work when necessary which has been the foundation of his success in government, and surprised himself by winning a First.

On coming down from Oxford in the summer of 1941, Jenkins was not immediately called up, but got a job for a few months at the American Embassy in London – a job which marked the beginning of the close interest in the United States which he has cultivated ever since. America was not yet in the war, but President Roosevelt was doing all in his power, through the Lend-Lease scheme, to help Britain by all means short of hostilities. Jenkins was already a great admirer of Roosevelt, and after Pearl Harbor quickly became, as he has remained, a strong believer in the central importance for Britain of the American alliance. It was in 1941 that Churchill quoted Arthur Hugh Clough – 'But westward, look, the land is bright': Jenkins has continued to quote the same line on appropriate occasions ever since.

Early in 1942 he joined the Royal Artillery and underwent training as a gunnery officer. He was commissioned in July, and posted with the 55th (West Somerset Yeomanry) Field Regiment, first in camp on Salisbury Plain, later in Somerset and Sussex. He was by all accounts a quiet but efficient young officer, deriving intellectual satisfaction from mastering the technicalities of gunnery but keeping himself very much to himself. Every week a copy of Hansard arrived for him, which he would disappear to his tent to read.

To the relief of his cousins Connie and Sybil, who thought the very idea of him shooting anybody too incongruous to be imagined, Jenkins never saw active service. In 1943 he was plucked out of his regiment and seconded on intelligence work to Bletchley, the now famous, then highly secret centre for deciphering German codes. He was promoted to the rank of Captain, and remained there for the rest of the war with some three hundred other eggheads and boffins hand-picked from the universities. Jenkins might not have seemed at first sight the most obvious choice: but the recruiting sergeant was A.D. Lindsay, who knew what he was doing. The work suited the particular bent of his intellect admirably – a fact which casts a useful light on the nature of that intellect.

Unusually for one who, at school, excelled in the arts subjects rather than the sciences, and is today thought of as a literary man, Jenkins is highly numerate. As a small boy he was a great trainspotter, and he still enjoys working out complicated timetables. He has no mechanical sense at all (he is hopeless with his hands); but he loves numbers and uses them with a precision which in everyday conversation can be maddening. Even in telling the time, he will say that it is 'fourteen minutes past six' rather than 'nearly quarter past'. He knows exactly how long it takes to drive from A to B, and in consequence never catches a train with more than a minute to spare – but never misses it. This accuracy was the basis of his Oxford success in economics. He was never a creative economic thinker, but he could grasp ideas rapidly and see his way through complex figures with unusual clarity. This was, of course, the quality which, thirty years on, and allied by then to good political judgement, made him an outstanding Chancellor of the Exchequer. One of Jenkins' greatest attributes as a politician is that he is a superb problem-solver. Problem-solving, in its purest sense, was what Bletchley was all about.

Jenkins found deciphering German codes intellectually fascinating, but unnervingly abstract: the satisfaction of solving a puzzle seemed utterly remote from the serious business of winning the war. In fact, of course, the cracking of the 'Ultra' code was absolutely vital. But his war is another part of his life, like his childhood, that he does not talk about very much. He had a comfortable and interesting time, while his friends and contemporaries were fighting and, in some cases, dying.

Not being away at the war meant that these were not years out of his life, as they were for so many – including Tony Crosland, who joined up before he had finished his degree and went back to Oxford (to read PPE this time) after the war (when he succeeded in becoming a rather elderly President of the Union). While at Bletchley, Jenkins could look to his future. On the one hand, he was able to attend selection conferences in pursuit of a Parliamentary seat which he might be able to win in the postwar General Election. (Crosland, when invited, could never get home leave.) On the other, he was able, without too much difficulty, to carry on his courtship of the girl who, before the end of the war, had become his wife.

Jennifer Morris was the daughter of Sir Parker Morris, Town Clerk of Westminster. He had previously been Deputy Town Clerk of Salford and Town Clerk of Chesterfield, before attaining the pinnacle of the Town Clerk's profession in 1929. He was knighted in 1941 for his civil defence work; but he is best remembered for his work in raising housing standards after the war. When he retired from Westminster in 1956, he became chairman of the Housing Standards sub-committee of the Macmillan Government's Central Housing Committee, whose 1961 report laid down minimum standards in floor space, ceiling height etc., known as the Parker Morris standards. His daughter inherited both his ability and his social concern.

Jennifer went up to Cambridge in 1939, where she read History at Girton and became chairman of the university Labour Club. She was a clever, energetic girl who might easily have had a political career in her own right; but, as she says now, 'One politician in the family was enough.' She met Roy Jenkins at a Fabian Summer School at Dartington Hall in August 1940. None of his friends can remember that he had had any serious girlfriends before this, but he fell immediately for her, and she for him, and they very quickly became engaged – to the extreme irritation of Tony Crosland, who was acutely jealous. They were not in a position to get married for the moment, but managed to see quite a lot of one another – at first on visits between Oxford and Cambridge, later whenever Roy could get leave. Jennifer worked for the Hoover company for a year when she left Cambridge, then became a civil servant in the Ministry of Labour until 1946, when she joined the social research organization, Political and Economic Planning. Despite three children and the special demands of marriage to an ambitious politician, she has always kept up a career of her own, at least part-time. At the same time she has been a superb wife who has supported, soothed and steeled Jenkins through the doubts and crises of a turbulent career.

They were married in January 1945, in the Savoy Chapel – Jenkins wearing his uniform as a Captain in the Royal Artillery. The groom and his parents lunched beforehand with a few friends – including David Ginsburg and the historian Asa Briggs, whom Jenkins had got to know at Bletchley – at Boulestin's off the Strand, which has remained one of his favourite restaurants. As the war in Europe came to an end the newly married couple settled down in a small flat in Marsham Street – just five minutes from the House of Commons – to face the austerity and the rationing, the hopes and the opportunities of postwar Britain.

TWO

Industrious Apprentice, 1945–1953

As the war ended, Jenkins had only one ambition – to join his father in the House of Commons as quickly as possible.

He had every advantage. There had not been a General Election for ten years, and the constituencies had instructions from Transport House to clear out their dead wood and look for younger candidates. Not only was Jenkins conveniently available to attend selection conferences: he was the obviously able son of a respected father, with a good record in student politics (chairman of the National Association of Labour Students); he had joined the Transport and General Workers' Union, and was a member of the Fabian Society. He had excellent contacts with Attlee and other Labour leaders, and evidently took his politics very seriously: he even offered to pay his own expenses. Yet he did not find it easy to win a nomination. He came closest at Aston, Birmingham, but lost out to Woodrow Wyatt, allegedly because he declined the agent's offer to put him up but preferred to stay the night in a hotel. He concentrated his efforts in the Midlands, because the Labour regional organizer there was very helpful. Eventually he was nominated for Solihull, on the south-east edge of Birmingham, one of the safest Conservative seats in the country, with a majority in 1935 of over 31,000, so secure that at a subsequent by-election Labour had not even put up a candidate. Jenkins fought this unpromising territory hard, however – showing for the first time the power of sustained effort which belies his Balliol manner – and actually persuaded himself that he could win. In fact he cut the Conservative majority to 5,000, taking 21,647 votes against 26,696, with a swing of over 20 per cent against the national average of 11.8 per cent.

He had done well, but he had lost. In that historic landslide that gave Labour 393 members in the new House of Commons against 213 Conservatives and 12 Liberals – not only an absolute majority for the first time but, so it seemed in the excitement of the moment, a permanent breakthrough – he felt that he was the only socialist who had not won. Amid the exhilaration of victory, Jenkins feared that he had missed the bus. He was despondent not to be one of the generation of new members ushering in the millennium.

Instead he had to look for a job. He found one in the City, working for the Industrial and Commercial Finance Corporation, a semi-philanthropic body set up immediately after the war by the Labour peer Lord Piercey to channel investment into new businesses. This was useful practical experience for a hitherto purely academic economist who as an undergraduate had uttered conventional anathemas on international finance. If it was not exactly socialism – to lend to the likes of Charles Forte the money to found his catering empire (though his ultimate reward was to be a knighthood from a Labour Prime Minister) – only the most rigid doctrinaire could hold working for the ICFC to be unsuitable employment for an aspiring Labour MP. Though privately funded and independent of the Government, the ICFC was the acceptable face of capitalism, an expression of the postwar climate of Keynesianism, putting City finance to work for the economic growth that Labour needed.

Nevertheless Jenkins did not enjoy working in the City. His eyes were still fixed on Westminster, and his spare energies engaged in promoting himself in Labour politics as best he could, exploiting his father's connection with Attlee for all it was worth. Soon after the Labour Government was formed he conceived the idea, first of editing a selection of the Prime Minister's speeches (published as *Policy and Progress* in 1947), then of writing an 'interim biography' of him. Personally and politically Attlee was the least-known premier the British people had ever elected: there was a gap in public knowledge to be filled. Attlee was at first characteristically reluctant; but having once agreed he was exceptionally helpful, providing unpublished material and photographs, answering Jenkins' questions and even allowing him to rummage unsupervised through his papers. The book was published in June 1948, to respectful reviews; but it was very much a young man's first book – earnest, uncritical and a trifle pedestrian. Admittedly Attlee is a difficult subject for the most skilled pen to bring vividly to life; but Jenkins was not yet the writer he has since become.

There are only occasional flashes in *Mr Attlee* of his mature urbanity. But there are autobiographical sidelights. A singularly snide reference to Lloyd George's contribution to the fall of Neville Chamberlain ('Lloyd George was an expert in arranging for the removal from office of wartime Premiers')[1] reveals that he was already a partisan Asquithian. Significantly he describes Asquith as the Prime Minister 'most comparable in character' to Attlee.[2] Admiration of these two temperamentally conservative men who presided over the most progressive administrations of the century has been a guiding light of Jenkins' career; it is one reason why he has never thought criticism of his own lifestyle relevant to his politics. In his developing view of British political history, Attlee was the inheritor of the Asquith tradition: it is this tradition which he has in his own career sought to represent, and latterly to lead.

In April 1946 Arthur Jenkins died, aged sixty-one. In the 1945 Government he had become Parliamentary Secretary under Ellen Wilkinson at the Department of Education; but failing health forced him to resign after less than three months. It was 'an open secret', according to the *Western Mail* and other Welsh papers, 'that he was meant for a place in the Cabinet', had his health allowed;[3] an alternative view is that Attlee, having been used to him for so long in the capacity of PPS, actually underestimated his ability. At any rate, when he died on 25 April 1946, two weeks after an unsuccessful operation for a long-neglected prostate condition, it was as a tireless worker for his constituency that he was mourned. Only a few weeks before, though he had already had one operation, he had been the leading speaker at a conference in Pontypool aimed at bringing new industries to the eastern valley to replace the jobs that were being lost in coalmining; he laid particular emphasis on providing jobs for the disabled and for older men. At the very end of his life he came out of hospital especially to vote for the National Insurance Bill: it would have passed anyway, but he wanted to be present to vote in person. The death of a man revered in South Wales as a secular saint left a very big gap to fill in the Pontypool constituency.

Hattie was determined that the only man who could take her husband's place was Roy. This placed him in a dilemma. He desperately wanted a seat in Parliament; but he knew that if he were selected to succeed his father, he would be expected to live by his father's example; and he knew that he was not his father. His interests and his ambitions were different: he did not want to conduct his career in Arthur's shadow. Yet he could not deny his mother's dearest wish. He allowed his name to go forward, and found some support.

What better memorial could Arthur Jenkins have, demanded one former councillor in the local paper, than that his constituents should send his son to the House of Commons 'to carry the torch that his father lit nearly fifty years ago on Varteg Hill?' But another correspondent voiced the contrary view. 'I know it would not be Arthur Jenkins' wish that we should, out of sympathy, reconstitute the old practice of hereditary representation.... If Mr Roy Jenkins is to be the Member for Pontypool, it must not be because he is the son of an illustrious father.' He should be fairly and democratically considered on his merits.[4]

In fact he was rejected, partly, it may be, on principle; partly perhaps because in the suavely anglicized young man who appeared before them the members of the selection conference did not recognize their former member's son; but largely, it was said, to spite Hattie, whose unpopularity in the local party was now visited on Roy. Could she have been persuaded to go away for a fortnight, one of his supporters was later quoted as saying, they might have got him in. 'But with her touting him from door to door I'm afraid his chances were very much reduced.'[5] For her sake, he was hurt; no doubt, having once entered the contest, he felt some disappointment at being rebuffed, in favour of a local solicitor and county councillor named Granville West, by 134 votes to 76. If so, he very quickly recognized that the result was for the best. Away from Pontypool he could continue to grow into his own man. In another constituency he could start from scratch. It is fantasy to suggest, as Granville West's successor Leo Abse does, that his rejection by Pontypool scarred Jenkins' soul and turned him bitterly against his heritage. The life of the eastern valley never meant much to him in the first place – which was precisely why the local party turned him down, and why they were absolutely right to do so.

Not for two years did he get another chance – two years which gave him just the time he needed to complete his Attlee book. Then, in April 1948, the Labour member for Central Southwark was forced by illhealth to resign. Jenkins put in for the nomination to succeed him, and was selected. The catch was that the seat was due to disappear at the next General Election. A narrow wedge of run-down housing stretching from the Elephant and Castle down the Walworth Road towards Camberwell, the constituency had been heavily bombed during the war, and much of its former population evacuated. Even on paper the electorate was now only 27,000, and less than half that number had voted in 1945, when Labour had won by 9000 votes against 3000. Central Southwark offered to a new MP no more than a toehold in the House of Commons: whoever won the nomination had to promise not to challenge the sitting member for North Southwark (the Minister of Labour, George Isaacs) for the enlarged constituency. Nevertheless Jenkins thought that two years would be time enough for him to make a name that would help him to something more secure. Rather as he was in very different

circumstances thirty-three years later, he was impatient to get into the
House without delay.

At the selection conference he won the backing of the local committee
with a characteristically polished speech combining a becoming modesty with socialist conviction and a display of economic expertise. He
had found his voice: to anyone familiar with Jenkins' mature style, the
phrasing and rhythms are unmistakeable. It is a speech worth pausing
over, since it offers the most candid snapshot, at the moment of his entry
into full-time politics, of how he presented himself and what he thought,
in 1948, the Labour party was for.

After an elegant expression of regret at the passing of the constituency
and a tribute to the retiring member, he made four personal points.
First, he would have been mad not to point out that 'although I have
been lucky enough to receive a first-class university education', he was
not brought up 'in an atmosphere detached from the harsher facts of
life'. In South Wales he had seen dole queues longer than they had
known in South London. Second, 'I was brought up in a family that
had its whole being in Labour politics. . . . I know how important a part
of an MP's job lies not in Westminster, but in Pontypool or in Central
Southwark or wherever his constituency may be.' Third, though not a
local candidate, he lived only a mile from the Elephant and Castle, 'and
it is a mile which it would be my intention to cover very frequently';
while his wife, 'who shares to the full my interest in politics', would be
'equally willing to play her part'. Fourth, he had already fought, in
Solihull, one hard campaign in a difficult area.

These points made, he went on to give his view of the situation facing
the country three years into the life of the Labour Government. Its
achievement was emphatically one to be proud of: conditions of life for
ordinary people in Britain since the war had been better than in any
comparable country. 'If one compares the legislative record of this
Government with that of almost any previous administration one real-
izes how big is the step towards social equality and a decent ordering of
the nation's resources which we have taken since 1945.' The social
security system, the National Health Service, 'the rehabilitation of the
coal industry', 'the reorganization of the country's transport' – 'each
one of these measures would in normal times be sufficient to ensure a
Government's claim to reforming fame.' Moreover all this had been
accomplished 'at a time when Britain's economic position in the world
is worse than it has been for generations, and when it is tending to
deteriorate still further.'

'Of course, the hard fact is' – here speaks the future Chancellor of the

Exchequer – 'that we have been living well above our national income during the last few years.... We have, as everybody knows, failed to balance our international currency payments.... But the fact that we are short of dollars, the fact that we have a balance of payments problem, the fact that we cannot buy imports, is in no way the result of having a Labour Government. If anything the reverse is true.' The deficit had already been developing before the war, and had been greatly aggravated by it. Even so, 'if world prices had not moved against us, we would be almost paying our way today.'

The problem for the next few years was simple. With or without the help of Marshall Aid, 'we must balance our account'. But the grim economic situation need not be an electoral handicap to the Labour party.

> If times are difficult and many goods are scarce, it is more than ever essential that the Labour Party policy of fair shares for all should be supported. If we face a period of possible economic crisis, then let us ensure that it is the socialist solution of increased production and a planned allocation of resources which is applied, and not the old Tory solution. For don't let us forget that the Tories have a solution of a sort to our present economic difficulties. By creating a certain amount of unemployment, by allowing a slashing of wage rates to follow from this, by applying all the old deflationary methods, by ending scarcity by the illusory method of taking purchasing power away from the pockets of the people, they might cut down the volume of our imports, not because people didn't need them but because people couldn't pay for them. But we don't want that. I am pretty sure that the people of Central Southwark don't want that. I am pretty sure that the people of the country as a whole don't want it....

If selected, he thought he should fight a successful campaign in Central Southwark on these lines – 'a campaign which would give us a great victory at the polls and which would also make a contribution to the task of educating the people to the facts of our economic situation, and thus strike a blow in the vital battle for production, with which is bound up the whole future of our movement and of our Government.'[6]

If there was some initial surprise at Labour's choice of candidate, Jenkins quickly began to get a good press as the national papers gathered for the campaign. 'Mr Jenkins', the *Manchester Guardian* reported, 'is a tall young man with a rather shy manner. But he warms up on the platform and has the Welsh flair for oratory.'[7] More perceptively, the *Observer* suggested that oratory was not really his style:

> A Labour meeting here is apt to be quiet. The audience appears to listen with polite inattention. When, as happened the other night, some citizen

shouts an interruption, everyone turns round in mild amaze, as if the cry
had come from the back pew in church. In these uninspiring circumstances
Mr Jenkins deals soberly with the larger issues, as becomes Mr Attlee's man.
Patiently struggling against a training which inclines him to speak above
the local heads, he stands as counsel for the defence of a Government which
might be accused of failure and calls for an impressive acquittal.[8]

He held meetings nearly every night, at which he was supported by
an impressive line-up of Cabinet and junior ministers and MPs, including
Hugh Dalton, James Griffiths, Edith Summerskill and Douglas Jay,
Bessie Braddock and the young MP for next-door Bermondsey, Bob
Mellish. His Tory opponent was an energetic local man named Greenwood – local in the sense that he had long been active in local politics:
Jenkins rather punctured his claim by pointing out that he actually
lived in Hampstead, six times further away than he did himself! Greenwood tried hard to bring the campaign down to the level of the parish
pump; he alleged that the Labour council intended to close a local
market, and claimed that East Street market was more important to
the people of Southwark than the United Nations. Jenkins was able to
deal loftily with this spectacular parochialism and kept firmly to his
national theme, that the eyes of the country – indeed the world – were
on Southwark, looking for a big vote of confidence in the Labour
Government. Full employment was his trump card, illustrated in leaflets
showing a long queue outside the Labour Exchange in Walworth Road
before the war, contrasted with a recent picture of the same building
with no queue. Other photographs showed the dapper young candidate
talking with building workers and old age pensioners; the back page of
his election address featured Jennifer asserting that 'the housewives and
mothers of Southwark stand solidly behind Labour's policy of fair shares
for all.' Repeatedly Jenkins damned the Tories as the party of unemployment which would tackle Britain's difficulties by cutting the
living standards of the working class. 'The leopard does not change its
spots.' In his eve-of-poll speech he ridiculed a Tory poster which showed
a tug of war – the Labour party plus Communists plus Fascists against
the Conservative party plus the people.

Poor Tories! They still believe that they are the people and those who vote
against them are just the riff-raff. But what is the truth? It is that the Labour
Government is the greatest bulwark against totalitarianism of any sort, both
in this country and in Europe as a whole. It offers freedom with social
justice, it offers an end to industrial unrest and to the long dole queue, which
are the most dangerous breeding grounds of totalitarianism.

That is why its success is so important to other countries. That is why people all over the world are watching it, almost with bated breath.[6]

Polling day was 29 April. Jenkins held the seat quite comfortably – Labour did not drop a single by-election between 1945 and 1951 – but his share of the vote was down.

Roy Jenkins (*Labour*)	8,744
J. M. Greenwood (*Conservative*)	4,623
Labour majority	4,121

Greenwood claimed that a similar swing throughout the country at a General Election would give the Conservatives a working majority; but Jenkins was well pleased. 'The result shows that the majority of people do appreciate the way the Labour Government is trying to solve our problems.' He had fought a good campaign. He had served the Government well, and himself at the same time. However precarious his tenure, he was at twenty-seven the youngest member of the House of Commons. He had got his foot on the bottom rung of the ladder.

The new MP took his seat the following Monday, 3 May 1948, with no less a figure than the Prime Minister acting as one of his sponsors (the other was an assistant whip). It was a generous gesture on Attlee's part to the son of his old PPS; at the same time it was a questionable asset for Jenkins – about to become known as Attlee's biographer when his book hit the shelves in June – to be regarded in the Parliamentary Labour party as the leader's protégé, rather than his own man. For his part, however, Jenkins did nothing to modify the common view of him as a devout loyalist. From his first speech he threw himself energetically into the task of defending the Government in its multiplying economic difficulties, against both the Conservatives and, when necessary, the Labour left.

He waited exactly a month before making his maiden speech on 3 June, on the Committee stage of the Finance Bill following Stafford Cripps' first Budget. Though he hardly knew him to speak to, Cripps, in Jenkins' own words, 'exercised a considerable fascination over me' at this time.[9] Twenty years later that fascination increased, as Jenkins found himself as Chancellor facing the same inexorable necessity of subordinating other aims of policy to the urgent priority of shifting national resources into exports. One feature of Cripps' 1948 Budget made a particularly lasting impression on him: a special once-for-all tax on investment income over £250. In his own first Budget in 1968 he imposed a very similar levy. He devoted his maiden speech to defending Cripps' tax against Conservative howls of outrage. Freshly elected by some of the poorest people in the country, he asserted the importance of the Government being seen to place the burden of sacrifice on the strongest, not the weakest, backs:

> I know hon. Members opposite pretend to be rather shocked by the thought that the Government are influenced by considerations of this sort. They regard it as playing politics, but I and the majority of members on this side of the Committee do not regard it as playing politics. It is not a question of that, but a question of righting the balance and putting rather more on the shoulders of the rich, who were looked after so well by successive Conservative Governments, and putting less on the shoulders of the poor, who were not so well looked after by the same successive Conservative Governments. If the Labour Government abandoned this policy in its financial plans it would not only be politically foolish but morally wrong and socially unjust. Therefore, I submit, it would have been virtually impossible for the Chancellor to carry out the general design of his Budget without some additional impost on the rich.[10]

All maiden speakers are congratulated by those who follow them. But Sir Arthur Salter was exceptionally complimentary in his praise of Jenkins' maiden effort: 'I can say with complete sincerity that I have hardly ever heard an hon. Member speaking for the first time in this House, and without notes, who has spoken so charmingly and with such clarity as the hon. Member for Central Southwark. I say that with no less sincerity because I take a diametrically opposite view from him.'[11] Another Conservative expressed envy at Jenkins' 'self-confidence, fluency and logicality'.

He spoke a second time in July, balancing gratitude for Marshall Aid with a recognition that it would not by itself solve Britain's problems. ('I believe that it would be churlish not to stress the first point, and that it would be unbelievably foolish not to stress the second.')[12] In November, he made another intervention, his longest speech so far, in support of the Government's Iron and Steel Bill. Characteristically and significantly, he argued the case for nationalization on grounds that were determinedly non-doctrinaire: the fact was simply that the money to finance the steel industry could no longer be found privately.

> With the steel industry we have reached the point when nationalization is the natural next step. It is an industry in which I believe the money must come from public or semi-public sources. It is an industry in which free competition is dead. It is an industry in which even the party opposite

admits there must be a good deal of State control. Now, when that position is arrived at – public money, State control, no competition – who are the doctrinaires? Those who want to take the natural and logical step and put the thing under public ownership as well as under public control, or those who despite all these things insist on saying that it must still remain under private ownership?[13]

In February 1949 Attlee appointed Jenkins PPS to the Secretary of State for Commonwealth Relations, Philip Noel-Baker; but this brief experience (it lasted only a year) of the lowest form of ministerial life did not prevent him speaking as often as before on the economic matters that he had made his speciality. In this field he was already making his mark. It is striking how early and how authoritatively he got into the debate on Cripps' second Budget in April 1949, speaking very much like a future Chancellor; he then stayed on through the debate to make pointed interjections during the speeches of the Government's critics, like the Communist Phil Piratin. He was assiduous in his attendance and participation in the debates on the Finance Bill that summer, showing himself a skilful and effective debater, at once elegant in the Oxford Union manner and thoroughly combative. He continued to take his greatest pleasure in portraying the Tories as the true doctrinaires, unable to credit Cripps' success in turning round the balance of payments deficit because it conflicted with their prejudice that socialism must be damaging.

> They insist upon believing [he declared in the debate on the 1950 Budget] that if we have high taxation, comparative equality of wealth, and what the hon. Member for Chippenham [David Eccles] often calls over-full employment, we are bound to get stagnation of effort in production and external difficulties. They believe that because they want to believe it and because they have always believed it. The directly contradictory evidence of the facts makes no difference at all to the outlook of these doctrinaire politicians.

The reality was that the Labour Government 'has not only had important welfare effects through redistributing our income.... It has also been peculiarly efficient.'[14]

By the time he made this speech, Jenkins was no longer MP for Central Southwark, but the member for Birmingham, Stechford. He made the transition quite smoothly, being adopted in the autumn of 1949, a few months before the General Election which Attlee called in February 1950. Stechford was a new constituency created by the same redistribution process which had abolished Central Southwark: a third of its electorate was taken from Solihull, where Jenkins had fought unsuccessfully in 1945, but the complexion of the new seat seemed certain to be Labour. To win the nomination, Jenkins had to beat the sitting member for Birmingham, Duddeston, whose seat was also disappearing; but his age, his promise, his record in the House and the Solihull connection gave him the edge. He made the constituency, rather than the House of Commons, his priority for the next five months, getting himself thoroughly known in every ward: and when the General Election came, he won comfortably.

Roy Jenkins (*Labour*)	33,077
Miss E. Pitt (*Conservative*)	20,699
S.W. Haslam (*Liberal*)	2,789
	Labour majority 12,378

Stechford was as different from Southwark as another urban Labour seat could be. Southwark was a doomed but still vital community, its small electorate crowded together in crumbling tenements ripe for redevelopment. Stechford was an anonymous stretch of new housing estates on the eastern edge of Birmingham, predominantly inhabited by prosperous car workers. If Southwark was a traditional Labour seat in which any of the early pioneers would have felt at home, Stechford epitomized the new world of Labour, less interested in the brotherly ideals of socialism than in the size of the pay packet and increasingly, as the 1950s went on, the washing machine, the family car and the package holiday in Spain.

Jenkins represented Stechford for twenty-six years, until he went to Brussels in 1976. Its character clearly affected the development of his political thinking over the next two and a half decades. Yet he acquired little love of the place (as opposed to some of the people in it). He became a conscientious spokesman for the interests of Birmingham as a whole (in 1955 he was elected leader of the city's nine Labour MPs) and wrote occasional articles in such journals as *The Sphere* rather glumly dissecting its distinctive qualities. ('A certain civic dignity ... good theatres and good shops. But compared with European cities of roughly equal size, Milan or Marseilles or Munich, it lacks pulsation at the centre. It is essentially a place where people live and people work, rather than where people congregate.'[15] But he could never find much personality in Stechford to identify with or romanticize (as, for instance, Tony Crosland romanticized and identified with Grimsby). He held constituency 'surgeries' monthly; but so far as constituency functions went, both he and Jennifer found that there was simply not so much going on as in Southwark – fewer clubs, fewer churches, fewer activities of any sort requiring their attendance or patronage. Jenkins' reputation as a poor constituency member partly reflects his own shy nature and wider political interests, but in part also the nature of the constituency.

He fought Stechford in 1950, against the returning Tory tide which cut the Labour Government's overall majority down to six, on much the same platform as Southwark two years before – full employment, high production and fair shares, the need to maintain Labour's social advances and not allow the Tories to take advantage of the country's economic difficulties to reverse them. At the selection conference, however, when he was speaking to a committed Labour audience and looking further ahead than the election immediately coming up, he went rather further than this and listed three specific, much more radical, steps which the next Labour Government should take towards creating 'a more genuinely equal and democratic society': a capital levy, to spread the ownership of wealth more widely; the destruction, or at least the absorption into the state system, of the public schools; and moves towards industrial democracy, first of all in the nationalized industries. He concluded with a statement of the ultimate purposes of socialism, as he understood the term, of which a great deal more would be heard in the next ten to twelve years.

> I am by training an economist. Day-to-day politics ... are becoming more and more an affair of economics. But do not let us for that reason begin to think that socialism is something solely concerned with economics. It is nothing of the sort. Economic policies, measures of nationalisation, these are only the means to an end. The end is the creation of a society in which everybody can live full, contented and worthwhile lives, working in a decent atmosphere and living in good houses and pleasant surroundings. This is the end, and we must never lose sight of it. I think that so far we have made fairly good progress in the right direction, but that we still have a long way to go. It is our task in the Labour movement to see that we get there.[16]

Jenkins' most personal cause at this time, however, was the capital levy. In his maiden speech in the House of Commons in 1948 he had welcomed Cripps' once-for-all tax, but regretted that it was not to be repeated. The following year, when he was fortunate enough to be called to speak for the first time at the party Conference at Blackpool, he made the same point, hoping that Cripps had not ruled out a general levy; and in his speech on the 1950 Budget he called again for a capital tax to reduce 'the gross inequality of property ... which still persists and which I believe to be totally incompatible with a truly democratic society.'[17] In 1951 he published his own detailed scheme as a *Tribune* pamphlet entitled *Fair Shares For The Rich*. (Surprising as it may now seem, Jenkins had been writing regularly for *Tribune* for the previous three years – serious, generally cautious, articles on economic and financial matters.)

The title, *Fair Shares For The Rich*, has been misrepresented in recent years by those who wish to show that Jenkins never belonged in the Labour party, as though it were an appeal for clemency to the rich. On the contrary, it was a call not merely for the reduction but for the *abolition* of large private fortunes, by taxing them on a scale rising from 50 per cent between £20,000 and £30,000 and up to 95 per cent over £100,000. To minimize the shock, the Government might pay back to the former owner, for his lifetime, the income he would have got from his capital. But the essence of Jenkins' scheme was a swift, sharp act of confiscation; death duties and capital gains tax he discussed and dismissed as ineffective, because too slow. Anticipating Conservative uproar, he argued that *all* taxation was confiscation; and – reflecting his growing historical interest in the pre-1914 Asquith Government – compared his proposals with Lloyd George's famous 'People's Budget' of 1909, which precipitated the House of Lords crisis. For the Tories to suggest that the redistribution of wealth by democratic means was impossible, he asserted, was a far more sinister threat to democracy than any tax, in 1950 as it was in 1910. Thus at the most radical point in his career, when he was advocating a measure which he would today be the first to regard as extreme, Jenkins explicitly placed his proposals in the Asquith tradition of liberal reformism.

Fair Shares For The Rich concludes with an important passage on nationalization which anticipates much of the 'revisionist' Labour position of the later fifties. With the abolition of great private fortunes, Jenkins argued, it would be no longer possible for 80 per cent of industry to remain in private hands. 'There will simply not be enough rich people to own it.'

A large capital levy therefore implies an extension of nationalisation. But it will be nationalisation for a different object, and therefore of a different pattern, from that which we have seen in the past five years.

The coal industry, the railways, gas and electricity, were all brought under public control because it was thought necessary to take the particular industry, to reorganise it, to impose a certain structure upon it, and to run it as a unified whole. These nationalisation measures were essentially planning measures. They called for the control of whole industries, and they called for the control of particular industries. It would have defeated the whole object to have taken merely one of the main-line railway companies, or to have substituted catering for coal.

After steel, the position will be different. Future nationalisation will be more concerned with equality than with planning, and this means that we can leave the monolithic public corporation behind us and look for more intimate forms of ownership and control. It will not matter if a large number of public bodies – municipalities, co-operatives and the like – and not merely the central Government, participate in the ownership. It will not matter if only sections of industries are publicly owned, so that they have to meet competition from the sections remaining in private hands. It will not matter if only a part of the shares of a particular company, and not necessarily a controlling part, are in the hands of a public body. It will indeed be positively desirable that all these things should occur, for the widest possible diffusion of control and responsibility is an essential aim of democratic socialism.[18]

Fair Shares For The Rich was an important statement of the philosophy of the 'new right' which was beginning to emerge in the Labour party in 1950-51, as the triumphant consensus of 1945 fragmented in recrimination and uncertainty where to go next. The scope and form of future nationalization was the central, symbolic issue. The obvious target industries had all been nationalized between 1945 and 1950. Labour fought the 1950 election committed, rather unconvincingly, to adding sugar and cement to the public sector; but the rift was already opening up between the pragmatists of the right who recognized that further nationalization, unless clearly justified on practical grounds, was not an election winner, and the fundamentalists on the left who would contemplate no dilution of the aim of a fully socialized economy. Under the influence of Herbert Morrison, Labour went into the 1951 election with no further specific commitments to nationalization, merely a list of criteria by which future candidates for takeover might be assessed. Morrison represented the old right of the party, which wanted only to consolidate the gains made since 1945. The radical right, under the growing influence of Hugh Gaitskell (who succeeded Cripps as Chancellor in October 1950) sought a more subtle way forward on lines first explored in the writings of Evan Durbin, Hugh Dalton and Douglas Jay before the war, which were to receive their fullest development in Tony Crosland's *The Future of Socialism* in 1956. They proposed that there should be no more nationalization of whole industries on the Morrisonian model of huge public corporations, but that the public sector should be extended piecemeal, not towards the Marxist goal of a 100 per cent socialist economy, but within the framework of a mixed economy, in the name of a non-doctrinaire socialism that placed its highest priority on equality.

Hugh Gaitskell was to become, over the next dozen years, the most controversial figure in the Labour movement since Ramsay MacDonald. Jenkins was his friend, his disciple and his political heir. Their relationship was to be the dominating fact of the next decade of his life; it continued to be the association by which many in the party judged him for years after Gaitskell's death. Before Gaitskell became Chancellor, Jenkins does not recall that they had ever spoken to one another. But Attlee's promotion of the 44-year-old Wykehamist from outside the Cabinet (he had been Minister of State for Economic Affairs, deputizing for Cripps during the latter's illness) to fill the second position in the Government when Cripps was obliged to resign, dramatically widened and personalized the developing split within the party. Aneurin Bevan, the standard-bearer of the left, was personally affronted not to get the Treasury himself; he conceived a violent animosity towards the 'desiccated calculating machine' who, he thought, personified the take-over of the Labour party by middle-class intellectuals dedicated to subverting it from the path of true socialism. Looking for an issue to dramatize the clash of personalities, principles and ideology, Bevan found an ideal one in Gaitskell's 1951 Budget. To pay for the war in Korea which, in the climate of the Cold War, he regarded as an inescapable obligation on Britain, Gaitskell required expenditure cuts across the board, not excluding the health service, whose costs had vastly exceeded Bevan's estimates. Charges were imposed for NHS false teeth and spectacles, breaking the principle of a service free at point of treatment. Bevan resigned, followed the next day by Harold Wilson (President of the Board of Trade) and John Freeman (Under-Secretary at the War Office). Bevan's resignation was the watershed from which the division of the Labour party through the 1950s flowed. Jenkins chose his side without hesitation. There was some speculation that as a regular contributor to *Tribune* he might follow Bevan. But his old instinctive loyalty to Attlee and the Cabinet majority was now reinforced by warm admiration for Gaitskell, with whose ideas about socialism and the future direction of the party he was in complete agreement. 'Mr Bevan', he told a meeting in Birmingham, 'tried to hold a pistol at the head of the Cabinet. That was wrong.'[19] Jenkins, if he would not yet have called himself a Gaitskellite, was ripe to become one.

In October 1951 Attlee went to the country again, for no better reason than that the Government was exhausted and too demoralized by its divisions to stagger on with a tiny majority. Labour actually won more votes than ever before or since; but the Liberal party put up only 109 candidates, and most of their share of the vote (9 per cent in 1950,

$2\frac{1}{2}$ per cent in 1951) went to the Conservatives, who finished up with fewer votes than Labour but twenty-six more seats. By this ambiguous verdict the 77-year old Churchill returned to office, flanked by Eden and Butler to represent the modern face of Toryism. Labour went into opposition not altogether sorry to shed the burden of six strenuous years while it regained its ideological bearings, confident that the interruption of the march of progress would be only brief. No-one – certainly not Jenkins – imagined that this was the beginning of the longest period of single party rule since the 1820s, that the Conservatives would win two further General Elections by increased majorities under a succession of Prime Ministers, or that Labour would not taste office again for thirteen years.

In the short run, however, opposition gives far more opportunity to the ambitious young backbencher than he can ever enjoy while his party is in power. Jenkins had held Stechford comfortably, his majority only slightly reduced by the absence of a Liberal. He now had the security of a safe seat and had got used to the procedures of the House. Over the next two or three years he knuckled down industriously to stake his claim to office when Labour's turn came again. He became a member of Gaitskell's Shadow team of economic specialists – not a frontbench spokesman but a backbench guerrilla, persistently harassing the Chancellor, Rab Butler, with questions and amendments, fighting his Finance Bills clause by clause through committee; but also doing a great deal of detailed background work to provide the ammunition for Gaitskell's attacks. The notion of 'Butskellism' – the idea that Chancellor and Shadow Chancellor were not seriously divided over political objectives – is a myth. 'Economic debates during this period', Jenkins wrote some years later, 'were conducted at a higher level and with more interest on both sides than in any other period since the war. Gaitskell's annual reply to the Budget became a regular parliamentary *tour de force*, listened to with rapt attention by a packed House.'[20]

Working with Gaitskell on these speeches was an invaluable apprenticeship for a future Chancellor; it gave Jenkins an understanding of the nuts and bolts of economic policy which stood him in good stead later on. It was also the experience which consolidated political admiration into friendship, and convinced Jenkins that Gaitskell had the qualities of a leader. 'He worked closely with a group of four or five lieutenants, one or two of whom had distinctly uncompromising personalities. Private relations were very close amongst the group, and Gaitskell could be treated with as much mocking but friendly disrespect as anyone else. But in matters of work his authority was effortless.'[20]

Another of Gaitskell's little group was Tony Crosland, who had
entered the House of Commons at the 1950 election for the insecure
Labour seat of South Gloucestershire and was drawn quickly into
Gaitskell's circle. At the time of Bevan's resignation, he wrote in *Tribune*
a trenchant defence of Gaitskell's controversial Budget.[21] Thrown together again, Jenkins and Crosland resumed their Oxford friendship
almost, if not quite, where it was broken off in 1940. They were still
temperamental opposites: Crosland casual and cavalier, lax in his
attendance at the House, riotous in his private life, Jenkins much more
earnest, precise and diligent. But they stimulated one another intellectually; and they were henceforth linked inseparably in the party's mind
as Gaitskell's most promising young protégés.

In the early fifties Gaitskell was deliberately shedding his donnish
image to come forward as the leader of Labour's new right. At the 1952
Conference, at Morecambe, the party swung, as always after an election
defeat, sharply leftwards: Morrison and Dalton were voted off the NEC
and replaced by Wilson and Dick Crossman, making six out of seven
Bevanites elected in the constituency section. Gaitskell came nowhere.
Jenkins was among those who encouraged him to speak out, writing the
day after the Conference ended to assure him that the local leaders in
Birmingham 'who were rather wobbly beforehand, have been so
shocked by Morecambe as to be driven hard our way.'[22] Two days later
Gaitskell made an outspoken attack on the 'mob rule' and Communist
infiltration of the Conference, and virtually declared war on Bevanism
as a disruptive and irresponsible force within the party. Attlee asserted
his authority sufficiently to have the Bevanite group in the House of
Commons disbanded; but the bitterness remained.

In the struggle that was now joined, Jenkins was an unapologetic
partisan, and a firm supporter of disciplinary measures against left-
wingers who persistently voted against the party whip. In December
1953 he explained the right's position candidly to Crossman:

'They – I mean we – feel that every speech, every action must now be
considered as part of the power fight within the Party. That's why we hate
Bevanism. Before it began one could have free speech. Now one can't afford
to'. He repeated several times, 'We on the right feel that every force of
demagogy and every emotion is against us. In the constituency parties,
which are now Opposition-minded, the Bevanites have it all their own way.
I suppose one must wait for the tide to turn, as it slowly did in the 1930s,
away from the Opposition-mindedness of 1931 to constructive policies'.
I asked him why he felt it was so terribly important to defeat the Bevanites
and he said, 'The electorate is extremely Conservative-minded and we can

never win except with the kind of attitude represented by the right-wing leadership'. He also added that, for people like himself and Tony Crosland, the very existence of the Bevanites and their popularity was the major factor in making him loyal to Gaitskell. In the sort of hopeless fight that Gaitskell was waging, one had to stand by him.

What was interesting about the whole talk, which lasted for an hour and a half, was Roy's feeling that they were battling against the tide in the constituencies, that they must hang on for dear life. He also repeatedly emphasized that, just because the Bevanites were so strong, Gaitskell was more and more forced to rely on forces such as Arthur Deakin [General Secretary of the TGWU], which made him even further to the right than he would naturally be.[23]

It was above all the left's opposition-mindedness which Jenkins found abhorrent. He was and is, by temperament and conviction, a man of government, interested, not dishonourably, in power and the practical uses of power – not in the emotional satisfaction of empty protest. The division in the Labour party after 1951 was to him a simple difference between, on the one hand, serious politicians whose concern was, first, to get back into office, and second, to give a better life to the mass of the people in the country, according to certain principles but recognizing the constraints of the real world and ready if necessary to make hard choices between shades of grey; and, on the other, a muddle of essentially frivolous play-actors, some warm-hearted romantics, others narrow-minded ideologues, temperamentally suspicious of the compromises of power and only concerned to preserve their sense of righteous indigna-tion. His fear was that the self-indulgent posturing of the left would prevent the right from getting back into power to resume the practical pursuit of social progress.

Pursuit of Progress was the very characteristic title of a short book which Jenkins had published earlier in 1953 in which the frustration he expressed to Crossman found more polished form. (The *Times Literary Supplement* unkindly commented that it might as well have been called *Pursuit of Office*:[24] but the point of the book was that the one was dependent on the other.) Subtitled *A Critical Analysis of the Achievement and Prospect of the Labour Party*, it represents his mature political credo after five years in the House. Its form is historical, tracing the two streams in Labour thinking back to the utopian MacDonald and the realist Henderson before 1914. The chapters concerned with domestic policy broadly repeat the analysis and prescription Jenkins had already offered two years before in *Fair Shares For The Rich* (and also in an essay, *Equality*, which he contributed to *New Fabian Essays*, edited by Crossman, in 1952 – an important volume to which several of the other emerging 'revisionists', Crosland, Denis Healey, Austin Albu and John Strachey, also contributed). There is some retreat from his earlier drastic proposal to abolish private wealth at a stroke; redistribution might have to be spread over a generation, but the aim is the same. Similarly Jenkins no longer writes of abolishing the public schools, but only of making education such a priority that the state system will be able to absorb them. But while he takes a superior swipe at 'those who regard the nailing of one's colours to the mast of nationalization, without much regard to what it is designed to accomplish, as an infallible proof of robust radicalism',[25] his commitment to greatly increased public ownership within a mixed economy is unchanged.

> It is quite impossible to advocate both the abolition of great inequalities of wealth and the acceptance of a one-quarter public sector and three-quarters private sector arrangement. A mixed economy there will undoubtedly be, certainly for many decades and perhaps permanently, but it will need to be mixed in very different proportions from this. . . .[26]
>
> Whether this will require a thirty per cent, a fifty per cent, or a seventy per cent public sector it is difficult to say. The answer will become clearer as the goal is approached. But the whole concept obviously demands a much more vigorous and far-reaching nationalisation policy than would be likely to follow from the application of nothing more than the three tests laid down in *Labour and the New Society* [the party's 1951 manifesto].[27]

It is on foreign policy that Jenkins directly confronts the utopians. This was where the left, in the right's view, most dishonestly ran with the hare while hunting with the hounds, and persisting in defiance of all the evidence in taking the rosiest view of the Soviet Union while grudging the least show of gratitude, friendship or common interest with the United States, and demanding that Labour adopt a distinctively 'social-ist' foreign policy. For Jenkins, one of the Labour Government's greatest achievements was Bevin's clear alignment of Britain with the United States in NATO, quickly putting aside, in the face of the Russians' crushing of democracy in Eastern Europe, the naive 'left can talk to left' attitude with which it had come to power. The Bevanites had never in their hearts accepted this alignment, and now that Labour was back in opposition, hankered to commit the party to a neutral posture between the two superpowers. Jenkins believed the idea of a 'socialist' foreign policy to be a delusion, based on an outdated view of Britain's impor-tance in the world – 'the essential foundation of utopianism. . . . a subconscious faith in the omnicompetence of British policy'[28] – and a refusal to accept that a Labour Government in its foreign policy was not sovereign but had to deal with the world as it was, not as it would like it to be. A party that hoped soon to be again the Government could not base its foreign policy on wishful thinking; Labour must make up its mind, between the Soviet Union and the United States, which was the democracy and which the tyranny. Which, if one felt no enthusiasm for either, showed the greater propensity to evolve towards welfare social-ism? With the United States, he argued, there was at least hope, while as her ally Britain had some influence on her; with the Soviet Union there was none, and a neutral Britain would have no influence on either.

Neutralism, Jenkins asserted, was no policy at all, merely a craven abstention from the battle of life which could have no appeal to a progressive party.

> Neutrality is essentially a conservative policy, a policy of defeat, of announc-ing that we have nothing to say to which the world will listen, and that we must therefore try to contract out of history and look inwards and backwards rather than outwards and forwards. Neutrality could never be acceptable to anyone who believes that he has a universal faith to preach. And those countries which have successfully adopted it in the past have paid the price of becoming little islands full of frustrated hedonists. Switzerland and Sweden are as ideologically sterile as they are physically undevastated.[29]

Here, for the first time in his writings, is sounded a theme which was to become increasingly dominant over the next twenty-five years. In 1953 the idea of the European Common Market was no more than a twinkle in Jean Monnet's eye, and Jenkins would not yet have supported Britain's joining it; but this passage shows him already seeking the right international vehicle for her constructive idealism.

Having once rejected neutralism, Jenkins continued, and accepted that Britain had a role to play in the world – a role commensurate with her real power – Labour must drop its continued hostility to the defence expenditure necessary to keep it up. The phenomenon of the Defence Secretary, Shinwell, being voted off the NEC in 1951 to salve the party's sense of guilt at possessing armaments at all, was a shameful example of Labour's wishful thinking getting in the way of realism. It was a proper and honourable part of the Labour tradition to be suspicious of the *use* of force; but it was flying in the face of reality to pretend that to exercise influence does not require its possession. If Labour was to be a Govern-ment party, he insisted, and not a permanent Opposition, the leadership must face the task of educating the rank and file to give informed and positive backing to its foreign policy, even at the risk of a split and a temporary loss of support.

It is better that this fairly remote eventuality should be faced than that differences should continue to go unresolved, that habits of thought should continue to grow further apart, and the greater danger be run of the destruction, by schism, perhaps for a generation, of the whole progressive movement in the country.[30]

'The whole progressive movement in the country'; that was what Jenkins believed, above all, Labour now was, and should take care to remain. In the last two chapters of *Pursuit of Progress*, entitled 'The Swinging Pendulum' and 'A Party of Advance,' he expressed perfect satisfaction with the working of the two-party system. The pendulum *would* swing, as in 1950–51, and *should* swing; the country needed periods of consolidation between periods of advance, and Labour itself needed periods of reflection to prepare the next instalment of advance. Unstated but implicit was his confidence that the pendulum would swing back again in 1955. There was no need for the left to think in terms of revolution: the experience of 1945–51 had disproved the fears of the thirties that the capitalist establishment would never allow a socialist programme to be carried through. The opposite danger concerned Jenkins more at this date – that Labour would itself try to be simultaneously the party of advance *and* the party of consolidation, losing its radical edge in the attempt to be all things to all men. Its purpose should not be to try to win all the time; nor need it set an ultimate goal. 'The first duty of a party of the left is to be radical in the context of the moment, to offer a prospect of continuing advance, and to preserve the loyalty of those whose optimistic humanism makes them its natural supporters.'[31]

Reading 'The Swinging Pendulum' – the chapter was republished on its own in Jenkins' *Essays and Speeches* in 1967 – it is at first sight ironic that it should have fallen to the same Roy Jenkins, in his 1979 Dimbleby Lecture and the subsequent formation of the SDP, to lead the first determined attempt to break the two-party system since Lloyd George in the 1920s. But Jenkins has never fundamentally changed his view of politics. What had happened by the end of the 1970s was that the two-party system had already broken down because Labour, by becoming a doctrinaire socialist party, had thrown away 'the loyalty of those whose optimistic humanism' had formerly made them its natural supporters. 'Optimistic humanism' has always been what Jenkins' politics have been about. In 1953 he still very often called it 'socialism', but just as often 'radicalism', 'progress' or 'reform': the terms are interchangeable. The essential political divide, in his philosophy, is temperamental rather than doctrinal, between the fatalistic pessimism of Toryism and the liberal-socialist-radical creed of optimism – the belief, not in the perfectibility of man (that belongs to the millenial revolutionaries), but in the possibility of society being improved. It is a very simple philosophy, and an essentially practical one. 'Hope and realism' was what Jenkins offered on becoming leader of the SDP in 1982; the specific content of his policies may have shifted with the years, but the same two words have described his political programme all his life.

In the 1950s there was more solid ground for realistic optimism than there is today. On all sides, ideology was in decline. Even under a Conservative Government there was full employment and rising prosperity for all; the Tories showed no inclination to undo Labour's gains. It was reasonable to look forward to a continuing steady improvement in the health, wealth and happiness of the British people. The gap between the parties, though real, was narrow.

> The British economy is most unlikely ... to relapse into uncontrolled capitalism. It is equally unlikely ... to stand still. The effective choices are between development towards democratic, participant socialism and development towards a highly-privileged managerialism, which may be economically efficient, but which will be unacceptable to those who believe in the rights and freedom of all individuals.... Economic efficiency any Government must try to achieve. A socialist party, while accepting and fully discharging this primary task, must distinguish itself by its approach to matters which lie beyond it.[32]

An exceptionally percipient reviewer of *Pursuit of Progress* in the *Times Literary Supplement* thought Jenkins too complacent both about the steadily improving future and specifically about the ability of the liberal reformists to keep control of the Labour party.

> For if there is peace, accompanied by an American slump with two million unemployed in Britain, will not the Utopians and the nationalizers and the Russia-lovers and all the rest of them once again seek a more radical transfer of power than Mr Jenkins proposes? And even in a less extreme hypothesis, are not Mr Jenkins and the Oxford economists of the Labour movement unduly self-content in a dangerous world?[24]

Time was to prove that they were; but not just yet.

THREE

Widening Horizons, 1954-1964

Somewhere around 1953-54, a change came over Jenkins' life. Up to this point he had been a rather intense young man in a hurry, determined on a political career to the exclusion of other interests, desperate to get into the House of Commons and, once there, to make his mark as a hard-working and serious-minded candidate for advancement. By 1953 he had succeeded: the publication of *Pursuit of Progress* signalled to anyone who had overlooked his backroom beavering for Gaitskell, the emergence of a distinctive new voice among Labour's rising generation. He could now afford to relax, change down a gear, give more time to his private life and widen his political horizons. He did not, of course, cease to be a highly professional and ambitious politician; but it is from about the middle fifties that there begins to take shape the public persona familiar in the seventies and eighties – the well-rounded, unhurried, even indolent-seeming man of the world, biographer and *bon viveur*, cultivated, fastidious and rather grand. The industrious apprentice of 1950 was, by 1960, being regarded at Westminster as something of a dilettante, with too many outside interests to devote himself seriously to politics. Only in the years after 1964 could it be recognized that the previous decade of diversification had been just as important as the specialized apprenticeship in the education of a formidably well-equipped politician.

Relaxation came first in response to the claims of a growing family. By 1954 he and Jennifer had three young children – Charles (born in 1949), Cynthia (born 1951) and Edward (born 1954). They had moved in 1949 from the flat in Marsham Street to a larger one in Cornwall Gardens, South Kensington. Then in 1954 they moved again to what was to be the family home for the next twenty-three years – 33 Ladbroke Square, a tall early Victorian terrace house in North Kensington, just by Notting Hill Gate. Though the area was not then as fashionable as it has since become, but rather run-down and dilapidated, number 33 was a fine house with large elegant rooms, high ceilings and moulded cornices. His cousin Pita Karaka (the former Connie Peppin) remembers very well the excitement when Roy and Jennifer first moved in: on four floors with a basement (to say nothing of a large wine-cellar), it was a very substantial residence for a 33-year old MP. Better than anything else, the move to Ladbroke Square symbolizes Jenkins' expanded horizons. Here he was able to entertain in some style a widening circle of friends, political and increasingly non-political – small, intimate dinners and larger parties with dancing afterwards. (Hugh Gaitskell, a regular guest, was a great dancer, though it was not particularly Jenkins' *forte*.) In his study on the first floor, overlooking the narrow garden, he wrote his books.

In the square opposite the house – the largest private garden in London – Jennifer was the moving spirit in getting a tennis court built, and from now on tennis became Jenkins' principal form of weekend exercise. Even in those days, he did not cut an athletic figure on the court: his walk is a somewhat flat-footed waddle, and he habitually wears his sleeves buttoned to the wrist ('like an Indian spin bowler', as one of his friends has said). His serve is a most original production, left-handed and very quick, as though he were trying to catch the ball unawares.* But the intense competitiveness which he brings to everything he does makes light of shortcomings of style. 'Suddenly', as Ian Trethowan noted in a perceptive profile in *The Times* in 1967, 'he will thrash some unoffending tennis ball with unexpected ferocity. The Englishman in him may just be playing for a little gentle exercise. The Celt, one suspects, wants to win.'[1]

Intellectual relaxation – as well as a useful way of supplementing his parliamentary salary – Jenkins found in writing. The books that he wrote between 1953 and 1964, and particularly the subjects and the period that he chose to write about, tell a great deal about him and provide a fascinating coded commentary on his own career. He had not read much history while at Oxford, still less political biography. During the war, he recalled in a lecture to the Royal Society of Literature in 1971, he was able to repair 'some of the more obvious gaps' in his reading of English fiction.

> Then, at the end of the war, I found myself enjoying one of those periods of paid, but almost complete unemployment which have always been an occasional feature of army life. In the late summer and autumn of 1945 I decided to try to repair ... the biographical gap as well.

* If Jenkins were ever to reach No 10, incidentally, he would be the first left-handed Prime Minister in British history.

With characteristic single-mindedness, once he had set himself the task, he proceeded to read 'in rapid succession' the standard lives – mostly in two or more volumes – of Gladstone, Joseph Chamberlain, Salisbury, Lord Randolph Churchill, Rosebery, Balfour, Harcourt, Campbell-Bannerman, Asquith, Grey, Curzon, Lansdowne and Austen Chamberlain.[2]

This crash course provided a very solid foundation of familiarity both with the genre and with the late Victorian/Edwardian period of political history. His own first book, however – his biography of Attlee – fell outside this period and was more a part of his apprenticeship in Labour politics than relaxation. In 1952 he was invited to write the biography of Ernest Bevin. Significantly, he refused. (The commission went instead to Alan Bullock, who has not yet finished it.) First, Bevin's life was too closely bound up with controversies still very much alive in the Labour party to be much of a hobby. Secondly, as he wrote in a review of Bullock's first volume in 1960, 'Bevin . . . was neither a light man . . . nor an elegant one, and there is much to be said for a biographer who reflects some of his subject's attributes.'[3] On the score of elegance, if not of lightness, Jenkins did not feel close enough to the crude heavyweight figure of Labour's greatest trade unionist. Some will see in this refusal a shrinking from the reality of the Labour party. But as a summer holiday and weekend escape from Labour's feuds, Jenkins can be forgiven for preferring to slip back into the Edwardian Liberal party.

His first historical book was not in fact a biography, but *Mr Balfour's Poodle*, a short narrative account of the House of Lords crisis of 1911, published by Heinemann in 1954. This actually grew out of contemporary politics, since in 1949, soon after Jenkins had entered the House of Commons, the Attlee Government had passed another Parliament Act to reduce to only one year the delaying powers left to the House of Lords in 1911. Jenkins had demonstrated then his familiarity with the previous struggle – his first article for *Tribune* was a look back to 1911, and he had engaged in a number of exchanges on the subject in *The Times* and elsewhere. The 1949 Parliament Act – forced through only after the Lords had rejected it the year before – was the measure which most clearly symbolized for Jenkins the continuity between the Asquith and Attlee Governments – each in its generation having to overcome the same anti-democratic obstruction of hereditary Toryism. It seemed a natural subject for him to make good the absence of a readable popular history of 1911. The book was well-reviewed and very successful.

One reader who admired it was Mark Bonham Carter, now a director of Collins. It was he who suggested to Jenkins his next subject – a biography of the late Victorian Radical, friend and colleague of Joseph Chamberlain, brought down on the verge of high office by a sensational divorce scandal, Sir Charles Dilke. Jenkins was attracted by the suggestion, and the book, subtitled *A Victorian Tragedy*, was published by Collins in 1958. It is a curious combination of prurience and delicacy – prurience in that the bulk of the book is devoted to the divorce case, delicacy in that he treats it very circumspectly. (Dilke's was the famous 'three-in-a-bed scandal' which titillated the Victorians.) There was remarkably little politics: Dilke's rise is competently described, but his long, defiant and not unimportant career on the back benches after his fall is only perfunctorily sketched. One does not get the feeling that Jenkins liked Dilke much. On the central question of his guilt or innocence, his conclusion, after careful sifting of the evidence, is that Dilke was probably framed, but that his previous conduct left him vulnerable. *The Times*, stuffily, welcomed 'Mr Jenkins' dive into the mud', and was glad the subject had not fallen into more pornographic hands.[4] The *Literary Supplement*, on the other hand, was justified in commenting that Jenkins' 'pious diligence . . . recalls his earlier biography of Mr Attlee'.[5] *Dilke* is not Jenkins' best book.

It marked the beginning, however, of another of the closest friendships of Jenkins' life. He and Bonham Carter had overlapped but barely known each other at Balliol. Now between author and publisher there developed a working relationship which widened into the political arena when Bonham Carter was briefly returned to the House of Commons as Liberal MP for Torrington in 1958, and gave Jenkins the subject of his third and best biography. Bonham Carter was Asquith's grandson – the son of his daughter Violet who had married his secretary Maurice Bonham Carter. There had been no serious life of Asquith written since 1936. The gap was an obvious one for the author of *Mr Balfour's Poodle*, who already felt a special affinity with Asquith. The project won the approval of Lady Violet, and Jenkins began work after the disappointment of the 1959 General Election. He finished it, at a considerable rush, just in time for the General Election of 1964.

Jenkins' *Asquith* is always cited as the perfect matching of biographer to subject, and so it is. The qualities of the book stem from that evident sympathy. Asquith emerges from Jenkins' now elegantly fashioned prose as calm, rational, unhurried and superior. Jenkins is able to draw on his own experience of politics to present the complex issues of Asquith's career with understanding and rare lucidity. From the standpoint of the historian, however, the book's limitations derive from this same sympathy: the author is *too* close to his subject to give full weight to other views of him, too partisan to deal fairly with his opponents – whether the Tories during the House of Lords and Irish crises, or Lloyd George in 1916. Asquith is allowed to make errors of judgement, but his magisterial view of politics prevails over all. It is not Jenkins' style to question his basic assumptions. Nor is he interested in probing far into the private Asquith behind the imposing public face. In particular he treats the extraordinary relationship with Venetia Stanley with extreme reticence. Here, admittedly, he had trouble with Lady Violet, who persuaded him to omit a number of his intended excerpts from her father's letters. But when he was able to restore them for a second edition in 1978, they turned out to be remarkably few. As *Dilke* had demonstrated, Jenkins is not at ease with intimate portraiture. Even off duty, he is a politician to his fingertips, and his interest is political biography.

It is a revealing hobby, for it confirms his essentially non-intellectual view of politics and his lack of interest in political ideas and general theories. While the *purpose* of politics is the pursuit of progress (the more sensible and fair ordering of society), the attraction of the political life lies in the competition of individuals, within and between parties, for the highest office. There is no contradiction between private ambition and public service, for personal success lies through serving the public well. But the special appeal of politics over other forms of socially useful employment is the public rivalry for a place in history. No honest politician would deny this, certainly no successful one. Jenkins has been successful partly because he understands it so clearly, without apology or pretence. He has made political careers his special study. (Apart from *Attlee*, *Dilke* and *Asquith*, he wrote nine more short biographies for *The Times* in 1970–4, and he has also reviewed practically every biography of a major politician, British or American – he is particularly fond of comparisons between the two – for the past thirty years.) He is fascinated by the shape and structure of different careers, and loves drawing parallels and contrasts between, say, Balfour and Macmillan, or Bonar Law and Heath. Unquestionably the only rule he would lay down is that there are no rules: the strength he has derived from his reading of history is that he is exceptionally conscious of the importance of timing and the decisive role of chance in any political career. This lends him a sense of perspective when things appear to go badly; but also the nerve to gamble when the need of the moment demands it – as in 1981–2 at Warrington and Hillhead. With this outlook, Jenkins cannot help seeing his own career as a biography in the process of writing itself. This might be inhibiting – at times, notably in the early seventies, perhaps it has been; but more recently, since the idea of the SDP began to form in his mind around 1979, it is precisely the sense that now is his moment of historic opportunity that gives him resolution.

The too-simple identification of Jenkins with Asquith has done him a good deal of harm since 1964 – particularly in the Labour party, where it was felt by many to betray his true party leanings (the word 'Asquith' was once scrawled on his front pillar in Ladbroke Square, evidently as a word of abuse), but still today when it sums up for many people the rather comfortable and complacent image he often conveys. The paradox is that Jenkins himself has encouraged the identification. Since writing the book, he has become fascinated not merely by real resemblances but by minor coincidences. In his by-election victory at Hillhead in 1982 there was an obvious echo of Asquith's victory, returning similarly from the wilderness, at Paisley in 1920. But Jenkins was also delighted by the coincidence that the next day – appearing at the Scottish Liberal Conference in St Andrews and then doubling back to attend a West of Scotland SDP first anniversary dance at Paisley – chance took him to both Asquith's constituencies on the same day. Back in London, he held a lunch for his principal helpers at the Reform Club, in conscious imitation of Asquith, who had done the same thing after Paisley. There is no doubt that Jenkins does identify with Asquith, and has set himself deliberately to project that air of unruffled superiority to the more vulgar expedients of politics. He has succeeded all too well. But beneath the Balliol pose, Jenkins is not Asquithian at all. He is much more volatile and insecure, moody and mercurial. Personally, he is much more competitive, much more of a gambler than his image suggests. Politically, he is at once more genuinely radical and more constructive, an initiator of solutions himself, not merely the wise chairman. Possessing many of Asquith's statesmanlike qualities, he is also more of a politician. In a more ruthless world, he needs to be.

As well as his books, Jenkins wrote a lot of journalism in these years, in three different genres – political commentary, book reviewing and reporting on overseas visits. He had begun contributing to *Tribune* soon after he got into Parliament and wrote at the rate of about one article a month until 1951 – mainly fairly specialist economic pieces. From 1951 to 1956, however, he enjoyed a wonderful opportunity to practise the discipline of weekly journalism – with the benefit that very few people in Britain could read what he wrote – on an Indian paper, *The Current News Magazine*, owned and edited by D.F. Karaka. (Karaka was an Oxford-educated Indian politician – he had been President of the Union in 1934 – who had married Jenkins' cousin Connie, now known as Pita.) For the *Current*, as it was called, which claimed a circulation of 'under 1,000,000' and bore the banner 'The paper that's read in *clean* Indian homes', Jenkins wrote a weekly commentary on British politics and the wider social scene, not excluding such issues of burning interest to the Bombay middle class as the Boat Race, teddy boy fashion and Princess Margaret's romance with Peter Townsend. In 1953 he filed a highly individual report on the Coronation, opening with the bizarre spectacle of a crowd of peers in full robes and coronets assembling in Kensington High Street underground station for a special train to take them to the Abbey! In this column for Karaka, Jenkins was able to develop the skills of an accomplished journalist.

In 1957 he began writing for the *Spectator*, a connection which grew out of his increasingly cross-party friendships, which in turn were beginning to raise doubts about his true socialism on the Labour benches. The owner and editor of the *Spectator* at this time was Ian Gilmour (not yet Sir Ian, not yet in Parliament), whom Jenkins had got to know through J.J. ('Jakie') Astor, who was his 'pair' in the House of Commons. (He was particularly attracted to Gilmour's wife, the daughter of the 8th Duke of Buccleuch: when his critics allege that Jenkins has a snobbish fondness for titled Tory ladies, it is usually of Lady Caroline Gilmour that they are thinking.) For Gilmour, Jenkins actually wrote only four times in 1957–8; but during 1959, 1960 and 1961 he wrote a regular political commentary, seven or eight times a year, for Brian Inglis, who had taken over the editorship (while Gilmour remained proprietor). This was the great period of the *Spectator*, when Bernard Levin was making his name as the satirical political correspondent 'Taper'.

Jenkins was simultaneously the principal reviewer of political history, memoirs and biography for the *Spectator* – fourteen reviews in 1960 – while he was also reviewing occasionally for the *Telegraph*, the *Sunday Times* and other papers, and beginning to review regularly for the *Observer* – owned by the Astor family and edited by David Astor, who became another good friend at this time. The connection with the *Observer* has persisted to this day: Jenkins is still one of its most highly paid regular contributors, commanding several hundred pounds for a single review.

Thirdly, Jenkins developed a genre of political travelogue which is all his own. In his very first *Who's Who* entry, in 1949, he listed as his recreation 'foreign travel', but, curiously, removed it the following year. He did not pass up any opportunity to go abroad, however, and increasingly made good journalistic use of his visits. His technique was to take the political temperature of the country he was visiting, sometimes interviewing leading politicians and others, but at the same time to mix serious geo-political reflections with a traveller's first impressions. Thus after a tour of the Middle East in late 1958 (about which he also wrote in the *Spectator*) he gave the readers of the *Birmingham Mail* his impressions: Teheran he found 'a dull city . . . the streets have a non-descript air which I associate with the less attractive parts of Washington'; Amman 'reminded me more of Ebbw Vale than of a capital city'; Baghdad was 'a hot, sticky, ugly town . . . politically, however, it was the most exciting place which I visited'; in Beirut, Jenkins called on the leader of the Moslem rebels, who received him 'with three tommy guns rather ostentatiously on the wall, and then proceeded to give me his well-informed views about the Scarborough Conference of the Labour Party!'[6] He had first developed this style in the *Current*, for which he reported in 1953 a similar swing around the United States. One of his earliest experiments, written from Ljubljana in September 1951, began with a most elegantly arresting opening sentence: 'The season for the starting of European wars is drawing to a close, and the Yugoslavs, more than most peoples, heave a sigh of relief for every week that passes without a Russian move.'[7] He has always had the gift, without intrusive didacticism, of using his history effortlessly to illuminate the present.

All this was not only good journalism, but excellent background for a politician whose horizons were less and less bounded by the Treasury, but were expanding to take in the Foreign Office too. In particular, he was developing in the middle and late fifties the interest that was to become the major cause of his political life – the unity of Europe. Jenkins was one of the first British politicians of either party to shake off the wartime delusion of great power status and see where Britain's future really lay. In later years he came to regret that he had not seen it sooner: his most serious criticism of Bevin, and of Eden on the Tory side, was that they persisted for too long in believing that Britain's relationship to the rest of Europe should be, like that of the Americans, one of friendly assistance from the outside, rather than of partnership. ('A buttress, rather than a pillar.') Eden's failure to be represented at the 1955 Messina Conference at which the Six – France, Italy, West Germany and the Benelux countries – agreed the principle of the European Common Market, he regarded as Britain's greatest missed opportunity of the postwar period – the opportunity to help shape the EEC from its formation. At the time, Jenkins was nearer to seeing it than most. From about 1953, he started attending European conferences, at Wiesbaden and elsewhere. In 1956 he was a member of the UK delegation to the

Council of Europe and attracted attention with a notable speech in the
Consultative Assembly, 'much remarked upon in the lobbies afterwards', according to *The Times*.

> Illustrating his arguments with a quotation from Gladstone, he suggested
> that the common market was an affair of men just as much as of packages,
> and thought that the greatest drawback of not being associated with it
> would not be economic – although there certainly would be grave economic
> disadvantages – but political, for thus a new political division would be
> created in Europe.[8]

In all the arguments over the past twenty years about Britain's joining
the EEC, Jenkins has continued to hold that the political reasons for
membership are far more important than the economic. Nevertheless,
at this stage he still subscribed to the conventional British view that her
Commonwealth commitments made it impossible for Britain to join in
a full customs union with a common tariff against the outside world.
Once the Common Market had come into existence in 1957, however,
he quickly decided that Britain must find a way of joining her natural
partners. The Commonwealth was a nostalgic hangover from the im-
perial past which only led the country into such follies as the Suez débâcle
in 1956. The broad question of Britain finding her right level in the
world must override minor matters of tariffs.

> The chief danger for a country placed as we are [he wrote in 1959] is that of
> living rather sullenly in the past, of believing that the world has a duty to
> keep us in the station to which we are accustomed, and showing bitter
> resentment if it does not do so. This was the mood of Suez; and it is a mood
> absolutely guaranteed, not to recreate our past glories, but to reduce us to
> a level of influence and wealth far lower than that which we need occupy....
>   Our neighbours in Europe are roughly our economic and military equals.
> We would do better to live gracefully with them than to waste our substance
> by trying unsuccessfully to keep up with the power giants of the modern
> world.[9]

In July 1960, Jenkins resigned from Labour's front bench economic
team, to which Gaitskell had appointed him the year before, in order to
be able to speak freely on Europe – the first, but not the last time he
would put his European commitment before his career. By this time,
interest in Europe was increasing, but official attitudes in both parties
were still unformed. His first hope was to get Labour to take up the
running, as the forward-looking internationalist party which challenged
the 'complacent insularity' of the Tory Government. That October,
Michael Young of the Consumers' Association (of which Jennifer was

an active member: she succeeded Young as chairman in 1965) published a pamphlet calling for a new progressive party to campaign for EEC entry, world government and foreign aid abroad, plus consumerism at home, satirically entitled *The Chipped White Cups of Dover*. Jenkins took up this theme in the *Spectator*: 'An effective Labour party must be against retiring behind this rather squalid and insubstantial fortification, against the dangerous isolationism which is implicit both in unilateral-ism and in much of Mr Macmillan's foreign policy, and in favour of the steady merging of British sovereignty.'[10]

Again in the *Spectator*, he derided the idea that EFTA, the looser free trade grouping of second rank nations, could offer Britain, either eco-nomically or politically, a serious alternative to membership of the EEC:

No-one could believe that an arrangement which added only 35 million people to the British market could in itself be our answer to the economic challenge of the 160 million strong Common Market. No-one could believe that a trading arrangement with countries as peripheral as our new partners could in itself solve the problem of our political relations with Western Europe as a whole.[11]

It was the Government, however, not the Labour party, which first embraced this logic. In 1961 Macmillan sent Ted Heath to Brussels to open negotiations for British entry. This created a delicate problem for the handful of dedicated Labour Europeans. Jenkins was a founder member and deputy chairman, under Lord Gladwyn, of an all-party group, the Common Market Campaign, set up to prevent the question of entry becoming a party football: Peter Kirk represented the Tories and Mark Bonham Carter the Liberals, along with a number of other long-standing European enthusiasts and industrialists. Sensitive to the charge that they were supporting a Tory Government, however, the Labour Europeans found it prudent to set up their own Labour Com-mon Market Committee to campaign specifically within the party; Jenkins was chairman and Jack Diamond – while also Treasurer of the parent body – was Treasurer, charged with raising money that did *not* come from the City of London. At a press conference in September 1961, Jenkins claimed the support of eighty Labour MPs.[12]

Thus began Jenkins' long battle to prevent the Common Market being seen in the Labour party as a Tory ramp. Against the specifically socialist objection that it was a capitalist club, he argued – for instance in a speech to the 1961 party Conference – that there was nothing in the Treaty of Rome to stop a Labour Government nationalizing any in-dustry it liked. More broadly, he maintained passionately that membership of a united Europe was a progressive, outward-looking cause which Labour should instinctively support, and that the insular, backward-looking cause was 'unbecoming to an internationalist party' and 'unbecoming to a party which claims to stand for expansion and change and revitalization.'[13] The idea that the Commonwealth offered, either politically or economically, an alternative to the EEC – the alternative that struck the deepest chord in both parties – he considered utterly unreal. 'What use are we likely to be as the economic centre of the Commonwealth?', he asked in November 1961.

> As a source of development capital we shall be ineffective; as a supplier of imports we shall be uncompetitive; as a market we shall be stagnant; and as a base for sterling we shall be uncertain. Unless the other Commonwealth countries develop a quite new degree of economic altruism in their relations with the Mother Country, they will turn away from us far more certainly if we are out of Europe and weak than if we are in Europe and strong.[14]

The suggestion that Britain had a political responsibility to lead the Commonwealth he dismissed with particular scorn. At the level of rhetoric, it united the romantic escapists of left and right; but when Michael Foot and Lord Hinchinbrooke both talked of the Commonwealth, he pointed out, one was thinking of Mr Nkrumah and the other of Sir Roy Welensky. 'The new imperialism of believing that the emergent countries want to be led by us is only a few steps forward from the old imperialism of believing that they want to be dominated by us.' What they really wanted, Jenkins argued, was independence plus material aid. 'And they will respect us to the extent that we make a success of our affairs and are able to give that aid.'[15]

The overriding argument to which Jenkins always returned was that Britain must find her true level in the world. In December 1962 the former US Secretary of State, Dean Acheson, made his famous remark that Britain had 'lost an empire and not yet found a role', which aroused a furious outcry: Macmillan replied grandly that Acheson was making the same mistake as Louis XIV, Napoleon, Wilhelm II and Hitler. Jenkins thought the phrase exactly right, and Macmillan's response 'grotesque'.[16] He often thereafter quoted Acheson in support of his own case. But eighteen months earlier, in the *Spectator*, he had already made the same diagnosis in his own style:

> Few things could be less desirable than that this country should spend the next decades totally unable to solve its own problems, yet waiting pathetically and hopelessly to be asked to give a lead to everybody else. This would surely be a recipe not merely for British ineffectiveness, but for national

mental derangement. It illustrates the fact that whether or not we join the
EEC is now subsumed in a bigger question: whether we live in an atmosphere
of illusion or reality about our position in the world.[15]

Similarly, more picturesquely, in *Encounter*:

The choice which faces us ... involves more than our future influence in
NATO, and more than our future rate of economic growth.

Britain, at present, is suffering from a general ineffectiveness of performance and from a national mood which is half misplaced complacency and
half a growing lack of self-confidence. As a result we could easily go into
drab decline, turning in upon ourselves, blaming the world for our own
misfortunes, occasionally deceiving ourselves with dreams of a grandeur
which impresses nobody else, and behaving generally like a soured and
rejected elderly female relation who is living a provincial life in straitened
circumstances and disliking it very much indeed.

The adventure of going into Europe is from almost every point of view the
best prophylactic against this dismal development.[17]

This was the faith – an almost deliberately mystical and unquantifi-
able belief in the psychological benefits of the European 'adventure',
over and above the practical economic and political arguments – which
made Jenkins for the next decade and a half one of the most eloquent
advocates of British entry into Europe in any party, and the unchal-
lenged leader of the usually embattled Europeans in the Labour party.
From this commitment he derived a standing and an independence as
a politician which he had not previously possessed.

This new independence Jenkins also demonstrated by a willingness
to take up issues of his own on the domestic front, outside the mainstream
of political debate between the parties. In particular he became in 1958
the Parliamentary standard-bearer of a protracted but eventually successful campaign to reform the law on obscene publications. Obscenity
was pre-eminently an issue in which there were no votes; but since 1956
Jenkins had been a member of the Committee of Management of the
Society of Authors, which had become very concerned at the number of
prosecutions being brought against highly respectable publishers publishing perfectly serious books. The verdicts depended upon the widely
divergent interpretations placed by the different judges on the vague
and illiberal definition of obscenity laid down by Lord Chief Justice
Cockburn in 1868 – 'the tendency of the matter charged ... to deprave
and corrupt those whose minds are open to such immoral influences *and
into whose hands a publication of this sort may fall.*' Some were convicted and
some acquitted, according to no consistent principle. The law urgently
needed clarification, so that publishers should at least know where they

stood, and serious books not be treated as pornography; but the Home
Office consistently obstructed successive attempts by the Society to get it
changed. The replacement of Gwilym Lloyd George by 'Rab' Butler in
January 1957 raised hopes which were quickly disappointed. When in
November 1958 there was nothing in the Queen's Speech and no
sympathetic Member won a place in the ballot to introduce Private
Member's Bills, the Society determined that Jenkins should introduce
a Bill under the Ten Minute Rule.

The purpose of his Bill, as Jenkins summarized it in the *Spectator* was
that 'The common law misdemeanour of obscene libel disappears and
is replaced by a new statutory offence, of which the essence is the guilty
knowledge of the offender, who shall be judged by the likely dominant
effect of his work on those among whom it is *intended* to circulate' – not
the *possibility* of its corrupting anyone into whose hands it *might* fall.[18]
The work should be considered as a whole, and literary merit should be
admitted as a defence. There is not space to describe the stages of the
long parliamentary battle which was necessary to put this principle on
the Statute Book. Butler, though professing sympathy with the intentions of the Bill, was still wary of doing anything in a hurry and snared
the reformers' path with amendments calculated to defeat its purpose,
by widening several key definitions and making difficulties about expert
witnesses for the defence. Jenkins, with the support of, among others,
Kenneth Robinson and Chuter Ede (Labour), Mark Bonham Carter
(Liberal), and Hugh Fraser, Maurice Macmillan and Nigel Nicolson
(Conservative), fought skilfully to save as much as possible of his Bill,
compromising where necessary as the time available ran out; it carried
the Commons in April 1959, the Lords (considerably amended) in July,
and received the Royal Assent on 29 July. At a celebratory party at the
Savoy, and in the Society's magazine *The Author*, Jenkins received the
thanks of the literary world: 'The tactical skill exhibited throughout by
Mr Roy Jenkins MP may well assure that this long overdue Statute . . .
will go down to history as the Jenkins Act.'[19]

At Westminster, instead, the wits for a time nicknamed Jenkins
himself 'Obscenity Bill'. More seriously, however, it was recognized that
he had achieved a personal triumph from a brave and even quixotic
undertaking. The Obscene Publications Act, though it has not worked
out in practice quite as satisfactorily as its authors hoped – the police
were able to evade it by bringing charges under Section Three, before
a magistrate, rather than Section Two, which required a judge and jury
– was a major milestone in Jenkins' career, demonstrating to those who
were beginning to write him off as a literary *flâneur* that he possessed the

courage and the determination, the grasp of procedure and the capacity
for sheer hard work to put a Bill through Parliament. Harold Wilson
remembered this success in 1964, and the experience gained stood
Jenkins in good stead when he himself went to the Home Office in 1965.

His interest in the whole field of libertarian reform was now aroused,
and this became the second distinctive cause with which he tried, in the
late fifties and early sixties, to identify the Labour party. There were, of
course, particularly among his friends, enlightened liberals in the Tory
party; while there was a large body of older Labour members – probably
representing the majority of Labour voters – whose social attitudes were
conservative in the extreme. Nevertheless, as Jenkins argued in the
Spectator in August 1959, 'On the whole range of issues where much
progress remains to be made – hanging, Wolfenden [homosexuality and
prostitution], the licensing laws, betting reform, Sunday observance,
divorce, theatre censorship, police control, the abortion laws – there is
immensely more to be hoped for from a Labour Home Secretary than
from the most liberal Conservative Minister.'[20] At a time when no great
gulf of ideology seemed to divide the parties on the central issue of
economic management, this was the agenda which Jenkins wanted
Labour to put prominently in its window for the 1959 election; from
now on the timid obscurantism of successive Home Secretaries – Butler
being only the least bad – became a large part of his personal case
against the Conservative record since 1951.

In this emphasis – though not in his commitment to Europe – Jenkins
was in line with his leader. In December 1955, six months after the
General Election in which the Tories, presenting under Eden a fresher
face to the electorate, had increased their majority from 22 to 58, Attlee,
the great balancer, had retired and been succeeded by the more abrasive
Gaitskell. Gaitskell was initially unwilling to stand against Morrison,
but Jenkins was among his keenest supporters who urged him that the
party was ready for a younger man: if he too punctiliously declined,
another of his generation might stand in his place and win. In the event,
he won by a large majority on the first ballot, with 157 votes. Bevan
took no more than the left's usual 70-odd, while Morrison, who had
thought the inheritance rightfully his, was humiliatingly rebuffed with
only 40. Jenkins was jubilant at the result. Gaitskell, he wrote in one of
his last articles for *The Current*, 'has now emerged beyond all reasonable
doubt as the next Prime Minister of Great Britain.' He was not yet fifty,
and after such a victory could expect to be leader for the next twenty
years. 'During this period it can hardly be doubted that there will be

many years when he will enjoy the tenancy of 10 Downing Street.'[21] This was an uncharacteristically rash prediction. Even had Gaitskell lived to win the 1964 election, he would then have been the *third* Prime Minister after Eden. But of course it merely reflected Jenkins' confidence that the pendulum, having missed a beat in 1955, would swing Labour back into power in 1959 or 1960.

In that case he could certainly have expected a junior office. Between 1956 and 1959 Gaitskell went a long way towards healing the Bevanite rift and uniting the party behind his leadership. Bevan himself was reconciled and became Shadow Foreign Secretary, Wilson Shadow Chancellor and Crossman chairman of the election organization. At the same time, however, he aroused resentment in all parts of the party, left and right, by seeming to surround himself with an inner group of a few like-minded and congenial colleagues – Douglas Jay, Patrick Gordon Walker and Frank Soskice of his own generation, and Jenkins and Tony Crosland, his two younger protégés. This clique (as it appeared to outsiders) used to meet most Sunday evenings at one another's houses; they also formed the nucleus of the XYZ Club, a small dining circle originated by Gaitskell, Dalton and Jay before the war which actually continued as a focus of Gaitskellism even after Gaitskell's death. Gaitskell greatly resented criticism of his choice of friends: undoubtedly simple friendship was a large component of these Sunday meetings. In all that he has written about Gaitskell since his death, Jenkins has stressed 'the immensely high priority which he always gave to matters of personal relationship. He cared desperately about his friends, and the small change of social intercourse assumed an unusual importance in his life.'[22] ('Even if his political distinction did not exist', he wrote in 1955, 'there is no better guest at a party.')[21] It was inevitable, nevertheless, that the 'Hampstead set', as they were called (Gaitskell, Gordon Walker and Jay all lived there) should be suspected of exercising an undue influence over the leader; and the impression was by no means groundless. In May 1959, for instance, discussing pensions with Crossman, Gaitskell brushed aside Wilson's opinion: ' "Wilson isn't an economist", he said rather sharply.... "Talk to an economist like Jenkins or Crosland." '[23]

Jenkins actually believed that Gaitskell attached too much importance to pure economics, and anyway no longer regarded himself as primarily an economist. There is no doubt, however, that he was widely seen, for all his other activities, as Gaitskell's creature (as he had once been seen as Attlee's, only more so). A parliamentary commentary in the *New Statesman* by the left-winger J.P.W. Mallalieu in November

1957 clearly reflects this, at the same time giving a vivid picture of mannerisms which have not changed in twenty-five years, going on to encapsulate a characteristic Jenkins speech of the period:

> Jenkins is not everyone's favourite, for his public manner suggests arrogance. But he is reputed to be so close a confidant of Mr Hugh Gaitskell that only the keenest observer can detect where Jenkins' mouth ends and Gaitskell's ear begins. So when he speaks in the House, others grudgingly listen for the sound of things to come. On Tuesday, he spoke with his easy, controlled fluency, glancing occasionally at his notes more for pause and effect than from any need to refresh his memory. Only the movements of his hands seemed uncalculated. These hands twisted and writhed in front of him like snakes, and though from time to time he would thrust them deep into his pockets or plant them firmly on his hips beneath his wide open coat, back they would come in a few seconds to twist and writhe as before.
>
> But soon they did not matter, for Jenkins, his sallow face gently suffused with the concealed lighting of his smile, was blandly telling the House that it was well behind the times. It was all set to fight inflation. Wilson had polished his lance and Thorneycroft had all but got his stiff upper lip glued into position when, bless me, the enemy had sneaked off and an entirely new opponent had taken the field. World commodity prices were falling sharply. Other prices would fall, or at least steady, in their train; and in *their* train, if past history was any guide, would come recession. In other words, the menace against which we should be preparing was not inflation but deflation, beginning in the United States but spreading quickly to our own now unguarded shores. Jenkins also took a passing swipe at the notion, dogmatically held for a century and a half, that Britain benefits by maintaining sterling as an international currency....[24]

1958 was indeed a 'stop' year in the 'stop-go' cycle of the fifties; production stagnated, price rises slowed and unemployment rose (to a peak in January 1959 of over 600,000, before Macmillan and his new Chancellor, Heathcoat Amory, got it down in time for the General Election). Jenkins believed that this gave Labour the opportunity to come out strongly as the party of economic expansion. This was a difficult trick to pull off, at a time when living standards were rising steadily under the Conservatives. But it was politically essential, just because Labour was still damagingly associated in the public mind with rationing and restriction; and it was economically right, since wages had been rising ahead of production. Jenkins did not underestimate inflation (as Macmillan did, with serious long-term consequences). What he argued in 1958-9 was that only in an *expanding* economy could living standards rise *without* inflation. Growth was the key, backed by moderate wage settlements.

Growth was the essential motor of the Gaitskellite, or revisionist view of socialism, which had received its full theoretical development in Tony Crosland's *The Future of Socialism*, published in 1956. The revisionists' critical departure from traditional socialism was to throw out the Marxist assumption that what mattered was the *ownership* of industry – the assumption which equated socialism with nationalization. Crosland demonstrated instead that in a modern managerial economy, ownership had become irrelevant: the Government now had all the power it needed, by Keynesian methods, to control the economy without the need for further nationalization on the old monolithic model. In place of the state ownership of the means of production, distribution and exchange, the Gaitskellites enthroned as the new goal of socialism the ideal of equality, to be achieved by the redistribution of wealth (towards which end more flexible forms of public ownership might serve as one means) and the abolition of inherited privilege. In practical terms, the prerequisite of this programme was running the economy in such a way as to create wealth, so as to be able to distribute its benefits more widely among the people. Hence sustained growth became the Holy Grail which Labour blamed the Conservatives for failing to find in 1959, and which they themselves came to power in 1964 confidently pledged to produce.

There was in Gaitskell's political philosophy, Jenkins wrote in 1971, 'a strong strand of unselfish hedonism.... He wanted to make people happier.'[25] The same hedonistic note runs through *The Future of Socialism* ('a greater emphasis on private life, on freedom and dissent, on culture, beauty, leisure, and even frivolity'),[26] and runs through Jenkins' philosophy too. Some puritanical socialists (Stafford Cripps, Tony Benn) practise personal austerity and think it good for others; the Gaitskellites, on the contrary, enjoyed their pleasures, and wished to allow the population at large to share them. 'We must be a party of a rapidly rising standard of living', Jenkins proclaimed at the Labour party Conference in 1958. 'I am very suspicious of those people, sometimes on the left, often themselves with a standard of living well above average, who claim to see the corrupting effect of more motor cars or more washing machines or other material benefits.'[27]

The benefits of sustained growth, the confidence that Labour could produce it, and the belief that growth, almost by itself, could be relied upon to promote equality – these are the themes of a short book which Jenkins was invited by Penguin to write for the 1959 General Election, *The Labour Case*. (Lord Hailsham and Roger Fulford put the case for the Conservatives and Liberals.) Aimed at the floating voter, and expressing an avowedly personal view, it makes no mention of the alarmingly penal methods of enforcing equality which Jenkins had favoured six or seven years before. His former zeal to confiscate private fortunes has dwindled to capital gains tax; while equality of educational opportunity is now to be achieved simply by raising standards in the public sector. (The proscription of private education, which was to become an issue in the early days of the SDP in 1981, Jenkins had already, by 1959, rejected as an intolerable interference with personal freedom: his own children were at private schools.*) There is a chapter on Crossman's National Superannuation Scheme ('A Great Social Initiative'), followed by another ('Will It Cost Too Much?') calculating, on the expectation of $17\frac{1}{2}$ per cent growth over five years, that it could not only be paid for but would even leave room over for tax cuts! *The Labour Case* represents a high water mark of revisionist optimism. The emphasis is not on economics at all, but on the new freedom that will come with affluence. The final chapter ('Is Britain Civilized?') lists all the Home Office reforms that Jenkins had previously advocated in the *Spectator*, calls for greater public spending on the arts and sports facilities, and ends – consciously echoing Crosland – with a heady vision of the permissive sixties:

> Let us be on the side of those who want people to be free to live their own lives, to make their own mistakes, and to decide in an adult way and provided they do not infringe the rights of others, the code by which they wish to live; and on the side of experiment and brightness, of better buildings and better food, of better music (jazz as well as Bach) and better books, of fuller lives and greater freedom. In the long run these things will be more important than even the most perfect of economic policies.[28]

It must be stressed that *The Labour Case* was written specifically to persuade the floating voter that Labour was no longer the party of nationalization, high taxation and austerity: it claims only 'to set down why one person, holding rather moderate views' – Jenkins' own description of himself – 'believes it to be of overwhelming importance that the General Election should result in a Labour Government.'[29] It is intended to be reassuring. Even so, one wonders how many other members of the Labour party could have written a book which so entirely eschews anything that a political scientist would recognize as socialism. In a widely-quoted interview in 1980, Jenkins remarked that he 'had not used the word socialism for years'; he might have added that when he did use it, even as far back as 1959, he had interpreted it extremely vaguely.

* So, it may be remembered, were Tony Wedgwood Benn's.

The principal object of a socialist party should be to enlarge the freedom of everyone to live their own lives fully. This fullness cannot be achieved without a good standard of living and a real equality of opportunity for everyone (neither of which has ever been approached without considerable state intervention); but it is just as important that people's lives should be their own as that they should be full.[30]

'Of course', he wrote in an earlier passage, 'the Labour Party does not stand only for economic expansion and a touch of realism about Britain's world position.' (That 'only' must have raised some eyebrows.) 'Since its earliest days it has been infused by a desire to promote a more just as well as a more prosperous society.' (Again, the word order is unusual.)

It is a socialist party, and it looks forward to a society in which class barriers will disappear, in which rewards will be equated with service, and in which everyone, successful and unsuccessful, will have the opportunity for a full and satisfying life....

At the same time it is a practical party. It is quite as much concerned with immediate reforms as with ultimate purposes. These reforms must be in the right direction. Any radical party must specify this, for without a sense of moving towards a goal, the idealism which is essential to the momentum of a left-wing party could not be generated. But the Labour Party does not ask its supporters to buy tickets for the whole journey. It is always difficult to see how the course of politics will develop. The solution of one set of problems invariably uncovers new ones, the nature of which often cannot be seen in advance....

Living as we do under a party system, in which at least two of the parties have firm bases of support, alternating governments will no doubt continue to be the pattern of British politics....[31]

In this revealing passage is the core of Jenkins' political philosophy – or rather, lack of one. Labour is a socialist party, yes, but that means little more than a desire to give people better lives, with no commitment to any particular method of going about it, no prescribed blueprint for a particular economic structure of society. What is more important is that Labour should be a *practical* party, pragmatically remedying whatever ills need remedying and can be remedied at a given moment, before the Conservatives in the nature of things come back for another turn. The visionaries have their part to play; but utopian ideals of the long-term future must not be allowed to get in the way of another instalment of short-term progress. 'The Labour Party does not ask its supporters to buy tickets for the whole journey.' Jenkins positively shrinks from anything that could be called an ideology. He is not merely non-doctrinaire, he is anti-doctrinaire – a political agnostic who believes in salvation by works, not faith. (There is just one important exception to their scepticism – Europe, into which he poured an emotional commitment for which he found no outlet in domestic politics.) It was this lack of faith in the kingdom of heaven on earth which made him increasingly uncomfortable in the party of his birth; but he has the same approach in 1983, with the SDP. Others may intellectualize what social democracy is; Jenkins will not be drawn. The answer is as vague, and as unimportant, as what socialism was in 1959. The SDP exists to do what needs doing, to solve the problems of the moment by the application of enlightened common sense, to make people happier. This anti-intellectualism, in an extremely clever man, has puzzled the commentators and political analysts: but no-one has ever been able to accuse him of woolly-mindedness in action. It is in some ways a handicap to an opposition leader, who needs to be able to fire enthusiasm for goals that may not be entirely realistic. But it has been a positive strength to Jenkins as a man of government, and is part of what equips him to be an exceptional Prime Minister.

FOUR

Gaitskell's Fight for the Labour Party, 1959–1964

At the General Election held in October 1959 Labour suffered a third consecutive swing to the Conservatives, and the Government increased its majority again from fifty to one hundred. Jenkins' majority in Stechford – 12,000 in 1950, 10,000 in 1951, 6,700 in 1955 – fell below 3,000. 'The Conservative Party', he wrote in the *Spectator*, 'now looks more firmly established in the favour of the British electorate than any previous political faction since the Great Reform Bill.'[1] He was not surprised: privately he had been predicting for the past year that Labour could not compete with Macmillan's 'Never-had-it-so-good' mood of insular materialism. But this third defeat set many people, inside and outside the party, wondering if Labour could ever win again. Within hours of the result the unity that had prevailed before the election was shattered. *Tribune* put the blame on revisionism and called for a return to true socialism. At a famous meeting at Gaitskell's house on the Sunday morning, the leading Gaitskellites came to the opposite conclusion: Labour had lost because it seemed an old-fashioned party, still associated with doctrines of nationalization and class war which made no appeal to the new, increasingly affluent, electorate. Contrary to the allegations of the left, the Sunday meeting concerted no plan for a Gaitskellite offensive; but Jenkins and Douglas Jay nevertheless took the lead in launching one. Together they appeared on *Panorama* the next evening. A week later Jay published an article in *Forward* proposing that the party should drop further nationalization from its programme, eschew class rhetoric, and even change the party's name to 'Labour and Reform' or 'Labour and Radical'. 'We are in danger', he wrote, 'of fighting under the label of a class which no longer exists.'[2] At the beginning of November, Jenkins gave a lecture to the Fabian Society suggesting that without a radical change of image, Labour might do even worse next time:

> All the indications are that it was the younger voters, living on the newer housing estates, who provided much of the swing against the Labour Party. Next time they will be fortified by another five-year crop of young voters and by more people moving into better housing conditions.

Like Jay, he thought that Labour needed to break away from its exclusive association with the working class:

> It would be a tragedy if the Labour Party, which has been a pioneer of a classless society, were not to adapt itself to the break-up of some class solidarities and class loyalties which is now taking place.

And he too urged that Labour should recognize the electoral unpopularity of nationalization:

> I think we should examine whether we cannot achieve our great aims of social justice and a reasonable planning of the nation's resources without creating much more in the way of public monopoly.... We must kill the misplaced view that the Labour Party is a dogmatic nationalising party, existing primarily to pop more and more industries into the bag.[3]

Bravely putting this argument to the Parliamentary party on 21 October, however, Jenkins and Christopher Mayhew received short shrift. 'Most of the party were deeply shocked', wrote Crossman, 'by what they felt was a betrayal by Gaitskell's closest friends.... We reached the end of the week with the Hampstead poodles in complete rout.'[4] Gaitskell himself had so far said nothing publicly to encourage this independent kite-flying. But it was his idea, sprung on the party at the Conference in November, formally to adopt the changes Jenkins and Jay had advocated by amending Clause IV of the party constitution so as to qualify the stark commitment to nationalize 'the means of production, distribution and exchange'. Neither Jay nor Jenkins had proposed this. Tony Crosland advised specifically against tampering with a hollow but hallowed symbol of the party's socialist identity; Jenkins was away in the United States at the time, but returned highly sceptical of the 'philosopher's stone' which Gaitskell had seized upon in his absence.[5]

Nevertheless both he and Crosland loyally defended their leader's ill-advised initiative, insisting that all he was trying to do was to leave the party less open to misrepresentation by its opponents. In particular, Jenkins rejected as 'a complete fallacy' the claim that modifying Clause IV would 'take the stuffing out of politics' and reduce Labour to 'a sort

of junior Conservative party'. It was precisely the impression that
Labour's first priority was wholesale nationalization that blunted the
party's cutting edge on the really important issues between the parties.
In the *Spectator* he gave a personal list of these, placing public ownership
very unenthusiastically near the bottom:

> The great issues of today and tomorrow are those
> 1 of Britain accepting her new place in the world;
> 2 of colonial freedom;
> 3 of whether, as we grow richer, this new wealth is used exclusively for
>   individual selfishness or for the growth of necessary community services
>   and whether, in consequence, we follow or escape the American precedent
>   of great private affluence surrounding rotting public services;
> 4 of whether we reverse the present anarchy in the use of land sufficiently
>   quickly to prevent the permanent destruction of the amenity of life in this
>   overcrowded island;
> 5 of the right of the individual to live his private life free from the intolerant
>   prejudices of others or the arrogant interference of the State and the
>   police;
> 6 of whether we can expose and destroy the abuses and inefficiencies of
>   contemporary private industry without offering only the sterile alternative
>   of an indefinite extension of public monopoly;
> 7 of whether, as existing class barriers break up, they are replaced by a new
>   and nasty materialist snobbery or by a fresher and more co-operative
>   approach.[6]

It is a good, if unspecific, Radical agenda; but only in the broadest sense
of the word a socialist one.

For this very reason, Gaitskell's attack on Clause IV was doomed to
failure. Labour was self-consciously a *socialist* party, and socialism was
understood by most party members to involve at least a theoretical
commitment to a socialized economy, even if in practice the party had
very little intention of nationalizing anything else – except re-nation-
alizing steel – in its immediate programme. Gaitskell was being too
logical for a party that lives by myth. The 1959 Conference – not just
the left, but the great sentimental majority of the party – would not
stand for what Wilson cleverly compared to taking Genesis out of the
Bible. 'It is perhaps always a mistake to raise matters of dogma in a
Left-wing party', Jenkins reflected in the *Spectator* as the Gaitskellites
licked their wounds, adding characteristically, 'They are probably best
left to be made irrelevant by the development of practical policies.'[7]

Nevertheless, writing four years later, when Gaitskell was dead, he
thought not only that they had been right to confront the party with the

need for change (as other socialist parties on the continent, notably the West German SPD, had been changing their Constitutions in the light of new conditions) but that Gaitskell had actually achieved a posthumous victory.

> Without doubt, he and those of us who were close to him made serious tactical mistakes in 1959. We overestimated the rationality of political movements. Equally without doubt, however, the battle which then began, and continued, in different phases, for two years, had to be fought. . . .
>
> No-one looking at the programme, outlook and assumptions of the Labour Party today could doubt that Gaitskell, in a long-term sense, had won his battle. The party is incomparably closer to what he wanted than to what his opponents wanted. It would not go the whole way at his bidding. But it would not have gone at all had he not taken the risk of pointing the way.[8]

That was written in 1963, for the first anniversary of Gaitskell's death. By 1973, when Jenkins wrote a second appreciation, the victory had turned sour: the fundamentalist tide was flowing back, stronger than ever, and taking over the party. Now Jenkins still believed that Gaitskell's *strategy* after 1959 'was as good as it was courageous. But his tactics (enthusiastically supported by me) had been appalling.' He now thought the concentration on Clause IV 'clearly a mistake. . . . It was the wrong war, in the wrong place, fought at best to an unsatisfactory draw.'[9] All that Gaitskell had done was to draw attention to Clause IV, making it harder to ignore and storing up trouble for the future.

The second, and more protracted phase of Gaitskell's two-year battle with the party was over unilateral disarmament. Since the middle fifties, CND had been winning converts among the constituency parties – these were the great years of the Aldermaston marches – and in 1960 it won enough support at trade union conferences to carry a unilateralist motion against the platform at the Scarborough Conference. Overwhelming though the implications of the issue were – nothing less than the best way of preventing nuclear war – the dispute inside the Labour party was essentially the same as over Clause IV. While Gaitskell and the whole party leadership – including, to the horror of the left, Bevan (who died in July 1960) – genuinely believed that the independent British deterrent was a vital part of NATO's nuclear umbrella, they also believed that it was essential to Britain's independence and prestige as a world power; and the corollary of this was that it was essential to Labour's credibility as a responsible alternative Government that the party be not committed to giving it up.

The merits of the technical arguments aside, the battle, as Gaitskell

saw it, was about whether Labour was a party of power or of protest. A
unilateralist party, he believed, would never win the confidence of the
electorate that it was fit to govern: hence his famous pledge at Scarborough, when defeat was certain, to 'fight and fight and fight again to
save the party we love'. There was another aspect of credibility, too,
however, which particularly exercised Jenkins. This was that the party
leader and the majority of the Parliamentary party could not be seen
by the public to be changing their view on an important question of
policy at the dictation of the party Conference (and effectively at the
dictation of a single union leader, Frank Cousins of the TGWU, whose
huge block vote was enough to swing the Conference either way). At a
press conference in his constituency, Jenkins pointed out that there was
hardly a man who was likely to be in a future Labour Cabinet who was
not committed against unilateral disarmament. 'For the conference to
force such a policy upon these men could hardly fail to destroy the
Labour Party as we know it today.' Either they would have to stand up
and say things they did not believe, or they would have to resign and
leave the party virtually leaderless.

> The plain fact is that the vote at Scarborough will have very little effect on
> the defence policy of Britain and the West. It will certainly not rid the world
> of H-Bombs or the threat of war, but what it might easily do is so damage
> the Labour Party as to destroy the hope of a Labour Government for a
> generation.[10]

He was pleased that the Birmingham Labour party had reversed its
position even before the conference, and predicted in the *Daily Telegraph*
that 'The chances of next year's conference reversing this year's decision
are very high.' He thought that if the PLP stuck to its position, it had
only 'a short-term holding operation' to conduct until a temporary 'gust
of opinion' at Scarborough blew itself out.[11]

Events proved him right; the 1960 vote was reversed at Blackpool in
1961. Meanwhile what depressed him about the unilateralist controversy was again the party's tendency to opposition-mindedness. Labour,
he wrote, must 'recover its good sense, its nerve and *its will to win*.'[11]
To demonstrate that will, the serious politicians in the party – those
who really wanted the responsibility of power, not just the luxury of
protest – must be ready to stand up to the left. He now formed the view
that the party could never achieve unity by compromise. 'The Left has
no interest in compromise. Its main desire is to remain the Left and,
whatever it is offered, it will respond to it by asking for more.'[7] To his
clear mind, even an outright split was preferable to a phoney compro-

mise as proposed by Tony Wedgwood Benn (who had suggested that the Conference might pass *both* motions!) or Harold Wilson (who in November stood for the leadership against Gaitskell's 'divisive' style). Already Jenkins had the measure of Wilson's idea of leadership:

> It is peculiarly difficult to see how Mr Wilson, were he by chance to achieve success, would view his new position. He is clearly not a unilateralist.... Does he therefore wish the conference next year to change its decision or would he wish indefinitely to advocate in the House of Commons a cause which was not his own? And if he wishes to achieve a change, how can this be done except by the argument which Mr Wilson regards as so disruptive of party unity?
>
> To pretend that compromise is always possible and that policy statements can mean both everything and nothing is a certain recipe for the continued erosion of the Labour vote.[11]

The leader's task, Jenkins wrote, was to restore unity between the party and its supporters in the country, the potential Labour voters whom the Conference despised. In November 1960 he issued a warning which anticipated with remarkable clarity the struggle for the soul of the party which was to break out in earnest after 1970:

> Unless the Labour Party is determined to abdicate its role as a mass party and become nothing more than a narrow sectarian society, its paramount task is to represent the whole of the Leftward-thinking half of the country – and to offer the prospect of attracting enough marginal support to give that half some share of power. This view was cogently expressed in the recently-published manifesto of the 'Victory for Sanity' group.[7]

This was Jenkins' public endorsement of what was shortly to become the Campaign for Democratic Socialism, a right-wing ginger group set up in June 1960 to mobilize support in the constituencies and the trade unions for Gaitskell's leadership and against the unilateralist and funda-mentalist left. It was a deliberately extra-Parliamentary campaign, formed partly to counteract the impression that Gaitskell's only sup-porters were his Hampstead intellectual friends: Jay, Gordon Walker, Jenkins and Crosland were all in fact present at the foundation, but their names were kept out of the publicity. The moving spirits were Frank Pickstock, an Oxford City alderman, and a number of younger men, former candidates not yet in Parliament though in most cases very soon to be: Bill Rodgers (Secretary of the Fabian Society since 1953); Dick Taverne; Brian Walden; and Denis Howell (who had been an MP in 1955-9). Other supporters later well known in Labour politics in-cluded Shirley Williams, Bryan Magee, Merlyn Rees and Ivor Richard;

also Philip Williams, who became Gaitskell's official biographer. It was Pickstock, Philip Williams and Tony Crosland who wrote most of the manifesto, of which 20,000 copies were circulated in October 1960: it sought to reassert 'the views of the great mass of Labour supporters against those of doctrinaire pressure groups', and to strengthen what it called the 'central tradition' of the party – 'a non-doctrinal, practical, humanitarian socialism – a creed of conscience and reform rather than of class hatred.'[12] As a grass-roots movement of the moderate right, CDS was a very great success: it was largely responsible for securing the reversal of the 1960 unilateralist vote in 1961, and played a big part in bringing the party through this turbulent period and reasonably united into the 1964 election. Its mistake, in retrospect, was to disband in October 1964 when it thought its purpose had been achieved. Historically, both in respect of the ideas it propagated and in the identity of so many of its leading members, the CDS is a clear precursor of the SDP. From it stems the powerful reputation of Bill Rodgers as the strong man and organizer of the Labour right for the next twenty years. The least well known to the general public of the 'Gang of Four', Rodgers was in party terms the key figure in the foundation of the SDP, who personally brought over from Labour more dissident MPs, certainly than Shirley Williams or David Owen, possibly even than Jenkins. In so far as the Gaitskellites kept together after Gaitskell's death, and in so far as they gradually evolved into Jenkinsites, Rodgers was the whip who kept them together. Jenkins himself played relatively little active part in the CDS – much less than Crosland: organization is not his *forte*, and he was very taken up with *Asquith*. But it expressed precisely his view of the Labour party, and he gave it his full support.

Despite the success of the CDS in turning back the tide for the moment, Jenkins was very much aware of the presence within the party of an 'irreconcileable' element – evident especially at the Conference – which was 'far more interested in the destruction of Mr Gaitskell than in the return of a Labour Government.' In 1961, at Blackpool, he was appalled at the ignorant applause for 'farragos of half-baked Marxist nonsense' and the undiscriminating rapture which greeted a very bad speech by Cousins. (If Gaitskell made a speech a quarter as bad, he wrote, his most loyal supporters would not clap it.) Characteristically he ascribed the delegates' lack of interest in subjects that did not bear on the internal party struggle to being too long without the discipline of power:

> The party is now suffering from ten years of passing too many programmes without any of them being carried into effect. What it now needs above all

is not more policy proposals but the ability to carry through some of those it already has. It would then begin to be more interested in constructive solutions.[13]

Even in 1962, however, he was not confident of Labour's chances of winning next time, and was even becoming disillusioned with politics altogether. Despite Gaitskell's high personal standing after Blackpool, despite the Government's increasingly unsure handling of the economy and the unpopularity of Selwyn Lloyd's 'pay pause', Labour had no lead in the opinion polls: it was the Liberals who were gaining support. (In March they won their sensational by-election victory at Orpington.)

> The recovery from the sudden fever of unilateralism has been quick and fairly complete, but the disappearance of the disease did not take with it the underlying and independent debility which was there before Scarborough and is still present today. As a result, the decline in the Government's support reflects itself in almost everything other than an increase in those who say they will vote Labour. . . . This is the central gloom of the present political situation.

The Government seemed to enjoy an immunity from the electoral consequences of failure. 'Few things could be worse for the whole tone of British politics.'[14]

Jenkins believed that the Government itself was lowering the tone of politics. (Deep in *Asquith*, he was continually drawing parallels and contrasts with the earlier period.) He shared Gaitskell's distaste, bordering on contempt, for Macmillan's style of government, which he thought tricky and meretricious. ('The besetting sin of Mr Macmillan and his colleagues', he had written in 1959, 'is a degree of intellectual dishonesty which has not been seen in British politics for a long time past.')[15] He believed that the Prime Minister deliberately surrounded himself with second-rate colleagues to enhance his own stature. ('The result is that we have a weak Chancellor of the Exchequer [Selwyn Lloyd], a foolish Foreign Secretary [Home], and a general Cabinet intellectual level which is such that it seems perfectly natural to have Dr Charles Hill in charge of all land use planning, of housing and of local government reform.')[14] If Labour did not offer a convincing alternative, however, there was no chance of any third force being able to form a Government. With the Liberals doing so well, there was the usual press talk of a Lib-Lab realignment, with which Jenkins' name was invariably linked. Twenty years before the SDP-Liberal alliance, he was not ill-disposed to the possibility; even in public he dismissed it merely as impracticable and premature, not as wrong in principle.

'Every practical politician', he wrote in the *Spectator*, 'knows that all talk of a realignment of forces on the Left is now quite out of the question, at least until after the next election.'[14] But two years earlier, in 1960, he had written in the American magazine *Foreign Affairs* an aside which expressed – almost to the point of self-parody – the real doubt he felt at this period about the Liberals as serious political allies of the Labour right, drawing attention to 'the split between the agreeable, civilized radicalism of Mr Grimond and his immediate colleagues on the one hand and the outlook of large numbers (perhaps the majority) of Liberal voters on the other. Many of these are more "Poujadist" than radical, and vote Liberal merely to express a general discontent.'[16]

Jenkins was not blind, in 1962, to the possibility that Labour might split if it lost again in 1964. But in the meantime the urgent priority of politics was that the Conservative Government should be defeated – and only a revived Labour party could hope to defeat it. To generate the necessary enthusiasm, however, he still believed passionately that Labour must project itself as a modern, forward-looking and adventurous party: in other words, a European party, both in the sense of adapting its view of socialism in line with the social democratic parties of the continent, and by firmly resisting the temptation to oppose, for opposition's sake, the Government's application to join the Common Market.

> Such a move would greatly strengthen the fears of those who think the Labour Party is now more at home defending a conservative position than mounting a radical attack. This will be particularly so if the nostalgic Commonwealth approach is allowed to gain momentum within the party. . . . The plain truth is that in any tight political or economic sense the Commonwealth is inevitably a declining interest. And the Labour Party already has enough declining causes to support without gratuitously adding another one to the list.[14]

Labour must beware, Jenkins told the 1962 party Conference in Brighton, of being 'more pro-Commonwealth than the Commonwealth itself. Let us fight hard for legitimate Commonwealth interests . . . but do not let us be left in occupation of a position which most Commonwealth leaders have themselves evacuated.'[17]

Jenkins made a point of speaking at Conference – unlike Tony Crosland who entirely neglected it. In seven years between 1956 and 1962 he missed only once, in 1959, when he was in America; and he always spoke combatively in the most controversial debate. The idea that he was a Hampstead socialist, writing elegantly in the *Spectator* and whispering heresy in the leader's ear, but afraid to face the party with his right-wing views is nonsense; though he had not yet the standing to hope to be elected to the NEC, he knew the importance of being heard at Conference and, like Gaitskell in the early fifties, did not shirk the ordeal of arguing an unpopular position once a year. In 1960 he made a fighting defence of Gaitskell's attempt to amend Clause IV ('We exist to change society. We are not likely to be very successful if we are horrified at any suggestion of changing ourselves');[18] and in 1961 and again in 1962 he made powerful pleas for Labour to take a positive attitude towards Europe, stressing that the other socialist parties of the Community wanted Britain in: 'Let us go in to help them, to work with them, to achieve something for ourselves but also to contribute something to the common pool. Let us go in with hope and confidence, and not with constant backward-looking, nagging suspicion.'[17]

By the time he made this speech, however, his hope of swinging the party round to his view had suffered a shattering blow. Earlier in the debate, Gaitskell had appalled most of his friends by coming out decisively against entry. For months he had held to a broadly neutral line, neither pro-Europe nor definitely anti-, waiting for the outcome of Heath's negotiations before making up his mind. A majority of the Shadow Cabinet – including Harold Wilson, James Callaghan, Denis Healey, Michael Stewart and Patrick Gordon Walker – was inclined to be against: only George Brown and John Strachey were clearly in favour. In the spring, the pro-Europeans believed that Gaitskell was beginning to tip their way; but a critical hardening of his mind against Europe occurred as a result of a disastrous meeting which Jenkins arranged for him with Jean Monnet, the 'father' of the European idea. Gaitskell subjected Monnet to a searchingly detailed interrogation about the nuts and bolts of tariffs; he found Monnet's replies evasive, and when Monnet finally told him that he must have faith, he replied that he did not believe in faith, but in reason.[19] To Jenkins' mind, however, Gaitskell's own position was at least equally emotional, based on an outdated sense of obligation to the Commonwealth and exactly that exaggeration of Britain's importance that he most deplored. (Gaitskell's argument in favour of entry, when he was arguing that way, was that Britain should go in to *lead* Europe, rather than that she should go into partnership with her equals, as Jenkins had always urged.) His speech at the Brighton Conference in 1962 was unashamedly emotional, invoking 'a thousand years of history' and the memory of Gallipoli and Vimy Ridge against Britain tying herself too closely to the continent. The younger Gaitskellites and the activists of the CDS, Europeans practically to a man or woman, who in every other respect revered Gaitskell's leadership, were stunned: Bill Rodgers and some others actually kept their seats and refused to clap. (The left, meanwhile, was for once delighted: Dora Gaitskell whispered to Charles Pannell, 'Charlie, all the wrong people are cheering.')[20] By coming out against the Common Market, Gaitskell paradoxically did more to re-unite the party, after the traumas of the past three years, than anything else he could have done. But he provoked a temporary crisis in his relations with both Jenkins and Crosland.

'I ... had the opportunity', Jenkins wrote in 1964, '(although it was a small consolation at the time) to see his political qualities and defects through, as it were, the other end of the telescope.'

> I inevitably felt a little more sympathy with those who had differed from him in the past! Courage could be interpreted as inflexibility and an aggressive respect for rationality as a tendency to equate little points and big ones. Yet, by and large, he appeared just as impressive as a temporary opponent as he had so long done as an ally and leader. ...
>
> Nor did this difference make close personal relations with him impossible. At first I thought it would, but that was under the shock of a sudden break in a long habit of agreement. But then he made it clear that he was still faithful to his old rule of the primacy of private relations. For the last few weeks of his active life we were back on terms of the closest friendship.[21]

Had Gaitskell lived, their disagreement over Europe would have very soon receded: for on 14 January 1963 President de Gaulle abruptly vetoed the Conservative Government's application for entry. With that, the European issue went off the boil for several years: it would no more have mattered whether the prospective members of a Gaitskell Cabinet in 1964 were pro- or anti-EEC than it did in the early years of the Wilson Government. Nevertheless, de Gaulle's veto was another bitter disappointment to those, like Jenkins, who had staked their careers on Britain going in; it added a further twist to his growing disenchantment with full-time politics.

Worse was to follow; for on 18 January Gaitskell died of a rare and incurable virus infection. The seriousness of his condition had only been realized a few days before, and the shock of his death was very sudden. For Jenkins, who was on a lecture tour in America at the time, it was a terrible blow. With Gaitskell's death, he wrote ten years later, 'a light went out of British politics which has never since returned.'[22] It was not only his friend he mourned, nor his own political prospects, though these at the time seemed intimately bound up with Gaitskell's. More than this, he mourned the loss of the only leader he thought could save the Labour party and make of it the sort of party he wanted it to be, and thought it should be. Although over the next seven years his own career prospered beyond all expectation without Gaitskell's patronage, the party developed in just the wrong direction, so that by the next time there was a vacancy for the leadership in 1976, when he was in a position to contest it, it was no longer the sort of party that he wanted, or could realistically aspire, to lead.

Gaitskell, Jenkins wrote, 'had an over-riding public purpose, which was to lead both his party and his country towards the rational, responsible and philosophically coherent social democracy in which he passionately believed.'[23] Jenkins has the same ambition for the SDP. Writing about Gaitskell, Jenkins clearly reveals his own attitude to leadership. What he admired most about Gaitskell was his unflinching honesty, his refusal to lower his personal standards for political advantage, his refusal to play politics. 'He would not stoop to conquer. He did not stoop. He almost conquered.'

> He left a great legacy: a Labour Party poised for victory; a tradition of welcoming, not evading the most difficult issues; and a memory which shows that honest speech and a warm heart are no obstacles to success in politics.[24]

The last sentence, in this 1973 version, is greatly toned down from the equivalent sentence in Jenkins' earlier appreciation, published in a memorial volume by several hands edited by Bill Rodgers in 1964. That ended uncompromisingly: 'a memory which is a standing contradiction to those who wish to believe that only men with cold hearts and twisted tongues can succeed in politics.'[25]

At whom could this thrust have been aimed but Harold Wilson, who had succeeded to the leadership after a contest with George Brown and Jim Callaghan? Wilson was the left's candidate, for reasons dating back to 1951, although since then he had assiduously cultivated the middle ground; Brown, deputy-leader since 1960, was the candidate of the trade union right, Callaghan an alternative right-winger for those who thought Brown, though greatly gifted, temperamentally too unstable to be trusted with the leadership. Tony Crosland was among those who backed Callaghan – an investment which paid him dividends in years to come. Jenkins stuck to Brown, who was at least strongly in favour of the Common Market. Dick Crossman, a Wilson supporter, took Jenkins and Jennifer to lunch at the Athenaeum the day before the second ballot. He found them both 'completely knocked out by Gaitskell's death. It makes a huge gap in their personal lives, bigger even than the gap in Crosland's.'

> Jenkins had only got back from America on the Sunday before the first
> ballot, too late to play any part in the Brown campaign. Nevertheless Roy
> was as implacable as ever and I spent most of lunch trying to make him say
> what makes him support a thug like Brown against a man of Wilson's
> quality. Jenkins found it surprisingly difficult. First he tried to call Harold
> intellectually dishonest, but he really couldn't pretend that Douglas Jay or
> Patrick Gordon Walker show greater intellectual integrity. All Roy could
> say was that it was worse in Harold's case because he was more gifted....
> Finally Roy said, 'The fact is that Harold is a person no one can like, a
> person without friends'. 'So much the better for him as leader', I replied.
> 'You admired Attlee. That loneliness was Attlee's quality'. Roy was indig-
> nant at the comparison and both of us finished lunch genuinely baffled as to
> what it was that caused the revulsion in each of us that the other didn't
> share.[26]

Differences of personal taste and style apart, it was really Wilson's
intellectual trickiness that Jenkins abhorred – something Attlee could
never have been accused of. It might have been thought that Wilson,
now presenting himself as the modern, go-ahead young technocrat
with little ideological baggage, would make a strong appeal to the
leaderless Gaitskellites; indeed the margin of his eventual victory (by
144 votes to 103 over Brown) showed that he did win support from right
as well as left, and in government he proved pragmatic to a fault. But it
was his propensity to act like a revisionist while keeping his old associates
happy by still talking socialism that exasperated Jenkins: this was precisely the opposite of the integrity he admired in Gaitskell. (It was
characteristic that Wilson admired Macmillan for just the qualities –
the capacity to operate behind a smokescreen, like a conjuror – which
Gaitskell had despised.) At the time of his stand against Gaitskell's
'confrontational' leadership in 1960, Jenkins had elaborated in the
Spectator a satirical comparison between Wilson and the judge in the
Lady Chatterley trial:

> One imagines that had he been in Mr Griffith-Jones' place, he would have
> told the jury that while he personally was strongly in favour of the book he
> thought it very important that he should act as the best possible spokesman
> of those who were not, and that, with good will, there should be no difficulty
> in reaching a compromise between publication and suppression.[7]

That was not Jenkins' idea of leadership. Wilson's highest purpose was
to keep the Labour party together: his claim to respect is that he
succeeded for as long as he was leader. It may well be argued that the

Gaitskell-Jenkins approach would have caused a split earlier. But the next fifteen years were to show that, in the long run, compromise could not save the Labour party.

On the day after Gaitskell's death, Bill Rodgers cabled to Jenkins in America: 'You are our leader now.' This was a farsighted expression of loyalty, but premature. Gaitskell left no immediate heir. The right had no alternative but to stay with Brown, and hope for the best from Wilson. Neither Jay nor Gordon Walker had the personality to inspire anyone, while Crosland and Jenkins were too young: of the two of them, it was to Crosland, as the author of *The Future of Socialism*, that most of the younger MPs and candidates on the right of the party looked, rather than to Jenkins, the author of *Dilke* and *Mr Balfour's Poodle*. Jointly they were appointed in Gaitskell's will his literary executors; it was Jenkins, however, whom Dora Gaitskell invited to write her husband's life. He agreed, but had to give up the project after the 1966 election, when it was clear that he would have no time for several years. This was probably a fortunate escape, enabling him to emerge from Gaitskell's shadow. In the meantime, however, he withdrew further from full-time politics. He was working hard on *Asquith*, and the year before he had become Director of Financial Operations for the John Lewis Partnership, of which he was already a Director.* (John Lewis, the retail store, is a firm admirably in line with Jenkins' political principles, a highly-successful experiment in co-operative ownership and profit-sharing.) Then in the summer of 1963 he was offered the editorship of *The Economist*.

He was tempted, even though it would have meant giving up his seat in the House of Commons. 'It was very much touch and go that summer', he told Kenneth Harris in 1967, 'whether I stayed in politics or not.' In September he had a talk with Wilson, told him of the *Economist* offer and asked him quite directly whether he could expect the level of office, if Labour won the election, for which it would be worth turning the *Economist* down. They discussed the sort of job he would like: Jenkins emphasized that though he had started out as an economist, his interests were now much wider – he would be attracted by defence, for instance, and some home departments, particularly transport; practically anything, in fact, except social services. Wilson obviously could not promise anything, but he gave some assurance that Jenkins could expect a job commensurate with his position in the party – in other words, he would

---

* This was his only business connection, though he was also a Governor of the British Film Institute, 1955–58, as well as a member of the Management Committee of the Society of Authors, 1956–60, and on the Executive of the Fabian Society from 1949 to 1961.

operate no vendetta against the right. This was enough. Jenkins declined the *Economist* offer. By 1971 he had persuaded himself that he was
never seriously attracted. 'I couldn't really see myself doing it. Politics
is my life. I've never wanted to do anything else. I knew that when it
came to the point, I couldn't and wouldn't quit. And I didn't.'[28] Still,
however, up to the election, 'politics sat extremely loosely on my
shoulders'.[27]

In the Shadow Cabinet elections in November, he nevertheless did
pretty well. He and Crosland – still twinned – came respectively seventh
and sixth among those not elected; but of the twelve elected, only Denis
Healey was under fifty – the average age was fifty-seven. Their somewhat lax attendance at the Commons did not prevent them being seen,
with Healey and the even younger Tony Wedgwood Benn, as the
leaders of their generation. Before his death, Gaitskell had spoken
indiscreetly of his intention to promote both Jenkins and Crosland
straight into the Cabinet. Wilson was not likely to do that: still less
would either he or Jenkins have guessed that within fifteen months of
Labour coming to power, Jenkins would be Home Secretary, and two
years later Chancellor of the Exchequer. But he was reasonably assured
of a worthwhile second-ranking office. And Labour seemed certain to
win at last. Macmillan, his image already punctured by the Profumo
and other scandals, had been forced by ill health to resign the Tory
leadership: Lord Home had 'emerged' in questionable circumstances to
succeed him. By contrast, Wilson – invoking 'the white heat of the
technological revolution' – had no difficulty in looking the forward-
looking Prime Minister needed to get Britain going again after 'thirteen
wasted years'. In the spring of 1964 Labour was ten points clear in the
polls; the Liberals had fallen back. But Home held on, as he was entitled
to do, until the autumn; and the lead dwindled.

It later became a commonplace of Labour polemic to claim that the
Chancellor, Reginald Maudling, deliberately stoked up a short-lived
boom for electioneering reasons, piling up the huge balance of payments
deficit which confronted Labour in October. The precedent was much
in Jenkins' mind in somewhat similar circumstances in 1970. With
hindsight, it is clear that Maudling should have taken more measures
to damp down demand; but at the time Labour's economic spokesmen,
Callaghan and Wilson, only criticized him for not expanding more.
(Jenkins was marginally more cautious, recognizing that Maudling had
a problem in controlling the boom without extinguishing it.)[29] By
September, when Home finally called the election for October 15,
Labour leaders had woken up to the scale of the deficit that would face

whichever party won, and were loud in allegations that the Tories were trying to steal another election on a false prospectus. In Birmingham on 30 September, Jenkins added his voice to this chorus, asserting in picturesque language that the Government was preparing a severe package of import controls to be imposed in November or December:

> Only Mr Maudling has to protest that everything is all right. He sits heavily but apprehensively on top of the Treasury like a chairman of an anti-volcanic society meeting on the top of Vesuvius and hoping he can get the vote of thanks over before the gurgles underneath him turn into another eruption.[30]

Labour it was that faced this unenviable inheritance when the smoke had cleared – by an overall plurality of only 200,000 votes and a precarious majority of just five seats. In Stechford, Jenkins raised his personal majority to 5,388, nearly double its low point in 1959, but still less than half what it had been in 1950. All that mattered on the morning of victory, however, was that Labour was back in office: the party was saved by a whisker from a fourth defeat that might well have been mortal. It now had its chance, after all, to prove itself what Wilson claimed it was, 'the natural party of government'. And Jenkins had the chance to prove himself, beyond his rivals, a formidable man of government.

FIVE

Aviation and the Home Office, 1964–1967

When Harold Wilson came to form his Government, it was no surprise that there was no room in the Cabinet for the younger men in the Labour party. After thirteen years in opposition he was practically obliged to find places for all those – like Fred Lee, Tom Fraser, Frank Soskice and Arthur Bottomley – who had experience of junior office in 1945–51 (apart from himself, only Patrick Gordon Walker, Lord Longford and Arthur Jenkins' old colleague Jim Griffiths – now brought back sentimentally by Wilson as Secretary for Wales – had served in Cabinet under Attlee); he also needed to reward a lot of loyal old soldiers who had sat on the Opposition front bench for years and could not – by a notably soft-hearted Prime Minister – be denied. Wilson, at forty-eight, was himself his Government's youthful face: the average age of his Cabinet was nearly fifty-seven, distinctly higher than Home's, which contained eight men under fifty. Denis Healey, appointed Minister of Defence, was the only member younger than the Prime Minister, and he had reserved his place as a member of the Shadow Cabinet since 1959. In a Cabinet dedicated to the fine old Labour principle of Buggins' Turn, there was no room for Roy Jenkins, for Tony Crosland, for Tony Wedgwood Benn or indeed for anyone born after the First World War.

Jenkins was, however, included in the first batch of non-Cabinet Ministers appointed on Sunday 18 October, along with Peggy Herbison (Pensions), Kenneth Robinson (Health), Charles Pannell (Public Building and Works), Elwyn Jones (Attorney-General), Dingle Foot (Solicitor-General) and Hugh Foot (created Lord Caradon and sent to the United Nations). The average age of these six was fifty-seven; Jenkins, named as Minister of Aviation, was forty-three and it was his appointment which attracted the headlines. 'Youngest Minister Gets

Tough Air Job' ran the front page banner of the *Daily Mirror*.[1]

The press had earmarked Aviation for Fred Lee (who got Power) or John Cronin (who got nothing), who had been Labour's spokesman in opposition. They had marked Jenkins down for the number two job at the Department of Economic Affairs, under George Brown. In fact Tony Crosland went to the DEA. One might imagine that for the party's ambitious young economists the DEA, which was supposed to be the powerhouse of Labour's new style of economic management, would be the place to be, even as number two. This was not how Crosland saw it. Bill Rodgers and his wife were having dinner at Ladbroke Square the evening Jenkins' appointment was announced. Jenkins came off the telephone very pleased, with a message that Rodgers should go at once to the DEA, where he was to be number three. When he got there, he found Crosland furiously jealous that Jenkins had got his own department.

In the political pecking order, having your own Ministry – any Ministry – is better than being number two in any other department. In the first direct test of what was from now on to be a growing rivalry, Jenkins had been marginally preferred to his slightly older friend. Over the next five years the accumulation of such slights, as Wilson continued to pick Jenkins for critical advancement just ahead of Crosland, proved more than their old relationship could bear.

Aviation was regarded as a challenging job, and Jenkins as a good appointment. Wilson's choice showed that he recognized in his future Chancellor both an effective and clear-sighted problem-solver, who could be placed straight away at the head of a complex department; and a man of widening international interests, beyond economics – one respect in which he scored over Crosland. He had already foreshadowed in their conversation of October 1963 that he had in mind for Jenkins a job on the foreign affairs/defence side of the Government. Since then he may well have been influenced by a pair of long investigative articles that Jenkins had written for the *Observer* on the problems of BOAC and the British aircraft industry generally, published under the headline 'How Not To Run A Public Corporation' in July 1964.[2] Though he had not been an Opposition spokesman, Jenkins came to Aviation not wholly unprepared.

He was specifically charged with two tasks. First, he was to undertake, in consultation with Denis Healey at the Ministry of Defence, a thorough review of the prospects and the proper size of the aircraft industry, on the lines of President Kennedy's 'Project Horizon', which had greatly impressed Wilson. Second, he was to preside over the winding up of his

Ministry as a separate department, its functions to be divided between the Ministry of Defence and the new Ministry of Technology. This was not in fact achieved during Jenkins' term, nor in his successor's, but the department was eventually wound up in 1967 by John Stonehouse – who in 1964 was Jenkins' Parliamentary Secretary.

The problem Jenkins confronted, broadly stated, was whether Britain could afford to maintain an independent aircraft industry at all. Exports of British aircraft were in steep decline: without export sales to recoup the soaring expense of development, the cost to the British taxpayer of buying British planes was becoming intolerably high. But if BOAC, on the civil side, and the Ministry of Defence, on the military, bought foreign (i.e. American) planes, that spelled decline for the British industry and redundancy for all the technological brains and the skilled workforce that it employed.

Jenkins' response was the classic one, inevitably, of setting up an enquiry, headed by Lord Plowden, to examine the state of the industry and the alternative options and report in a year's time. In the meantime several specific problems pressed for an immediate answer – whether to cancel or go ahead with particular expensive projects inherited from the Conservatives.

The first was *Concorde* (then still spelled by the British *Concord*). Labour did not come into office predisposed against *Concord*: rather the reverse – in 1962, at the time of the signature by the Conservative Government of the treaty with the French to build a supersonic airliner, John Cronin had chosen not to divide the House against it. But the Treasury had always been hostile: and in the very first few days after Labour came in to face a balance of payments deficit of £800m, it put up to the Cabinet a 'Brown Paper' proposing the usual range of emergency expenditure cuts, in which was included a 'review' of the *Concord* project, the estimated cost of which to each country had already jumped in two years from £85m to £140m. At the very first Cabinet meeting on 20 October, both the top economic Ministers, James Callaghan (Chancellor of the Exchequer) and George Brown (DEA), and the Minister of Defence, Denis Healey, were in favour of outright cancellation.

Jenkins suffered immediately the disadvantage of being outside the Cabinet: his Permanent Secretary, Sir Richard Way, only heard on the Whitehall grapevine what was afoot. He ran his Minister to earth in the bar at Brooks's, and there followed a hectic weekend trying to alert the Ambassador in Paris (who was out of town on a shooting trip) to warn the French Government of the British desire for a review before they read it in the newspapers. In the succeeding weeks, Jenkins and Sir

Richard flew several times to Paris for talks (allowing the new Minister an early opportunity to get his picture in the papers waving purposefully at airports). The Department was actually more anxious about retaining French goodwill for other projects than about fighting in the last ditch for *Concord*. Jenkins himself, as he revealed in his maiden speech to the House of Commons as Minister on 5 November, was by no means disposed to fight for the plane.

He emphasized at the outset that the only decision taken was that the project should be reviewed. But the burden of his speech was a powerful recital of all the factors tending in favour of cancellation. Quite apart from the balance of payments situation, he argued that the moment was ripe for a review, since the resources committed so far were still relatively small, but were about to take off. Moreover, as the cost spiralled, the likelihood of being able to sell the plane diminished, so that there was the prospect of even BOAC and *Air France* having to be subsidized to fly it. The sonic bang was proving worse than anticipated, which might impose operating restrictions, making the operating economics still worse. Even from the point of view of technological research, there might well be greater benefits from a multiplicity of less glamorous projects than from one or two 'prestige' ones. There was no overwhelming demand for supersonic travel. Finally, from the international point of view, there was no threat to co-operation with France in abandoning *Concord*: there were plenty of other fields for collaboration. Jenkins specifically denied that in supporting a review he in any way qualified his commitment to Europe, and was particularly at pains to stress that the issue would not be decided over his head. 'As long as I am Minister of Aviation there is no question of my not being fully responsible for any decision touching that Ministry.' He was able to quote the conclusion of his second *Observer* article, published on 19 July, 'before any thought of taking office in this capacity had entered my head.' 'The *Concord*', he had written, 'may be a better project than the VC10. But it needs much harder economic analysis than that ever received. And it needs it quickly.'[2]

'We must not', he concluded, 'automatically assume that everything which is new, everything which is advanced, everything which sounds exciting, is necessarily the best way to deploy our scarce resources.' It was part of his function to act as sponsor to the British aircraft industry, but only a part. 'My job is to look at the industry not only from the industry's point of view but from the nation's point of view as well, and that, as far as I can, I propose to do.'[3]

To the Cabinet's Economic Development Committee on 16 November Jenkins offered a range of alternatives to outright cancellation, including trying to bring the Americans in on a tripartite project.[4] But in his talks with the French he found them resolutely unsympathetic to British doubts. On 20 January he had to announce that the review was complete, and that *Concord* was to go ahead. Although the British Government still retained 'some doubts about the economic and financial aspects of the project', they had been impressed by French confidence and were resolved to stand by the treaty.[5] The truth was that the Cabinet could find no way to renege on it: the agreement negotiated by the Conservatives had omitted to include a break clause. Legal opinion, called for by the Foreign Secretary, Patrick Gordon Walker, suggested that France would be entitled to £1,000m in compensation if Britain unilaterally cancelled; and to this argument, that it would be more expensive to cancel than to go on, Brown and Callaghan were obliged to bow, though Healey still argued that the French would not insist on payment. Despite Jenkins' proud assertion, it was in Cabinet that the decision to go ahead was taken.[6]

The second expensive plane which the Labour Government was determined to review was the nuclear strike bomber, the TSR-2, designed as a replacement for the old Canberra and being built by Hawker Siddeley in Coventry. There were actually three British-built military aircraft under threat in the November 1964 defence review. The HS 681 was a short take-off transport plane, a replacement for the Argosy, and the P 1154 was a supersonic vertical take-off fighter, intended to replace the Sea Vixen and the Hunter. But it was on the TSR-2 that controversy centred. The decision raised in acute form the question of whether the RAF should fly British planes, at greater expense if necessary, to support the survival of the independent British aircraft industry, or go for American planes which, being built for a bigger market, could be bought more cheaply. The Ministry of Defence, under Denis Healey, was moving towards scrapping all three British planes and buying instead the F 111A (in the case of the TSR-2), Hercules transport planes (in place of the HS 681) and Phantoms, plus more British Buccaneers (in place of the P 1154).

In the House of Commons on 9 February 1965, Jenkins defended the scrapping of the HS 681 and the P 1154, but still held out some hope for the TSR-2. At the Cabinet the day before, however (non-Cabinet Ministers may be called to attend Cabinet when items affecting their departments are under discussion), he had recommended scrapping that too, even though Hawker Siddeley had made an 'almost embarrassingly good' new offer on costs and delivery time.[7] In the House he made a

wider review of the whole future of the aircraft industry, which con-
sumed 25 per cent of the Government's research and development
spending to produce models which were then unsaleable and now made
up only $2\frac{1}{2}$ per cent of British exports. (The death knell had sounded for
the TSR-2 when the Australian Government decided in 1963 to buy the
F I I IA instead.) The lesson from the TSR-2 – whether it eventually went
ahead or not – was that the aircraft industry must never again tie up all
its resources in one or two commercially uncertain projects. The future
must lie (here Jenkins could restore his European credentials) in international co-operation.

> Whatever decisions we have taken in the past weeks, and whatever decisions
> we may take in the next few months, we are at the end of the road as far as
> exclusive British manufacture of complicated weapons systems for an exclu-
> sive British market is concerned. We can afford to make the products only
> if others will buy them. The corollary is that we must be prepared to buy
> some of the products of others. An all-British industry equipping an RAF
> flying all-British planes is out, whether we like it or not.

The Government's purpose was simultaneously to give the RAF the
planes it needed, while easing pressure on the Budget; to offer the
aircraft industry a secure future, while redeploying some valuable manpower; and to give a big push towards closer collaboration between the
Western allies.[8]

'A masterly speech', *The Times* enthused. 'In less than 45 minutes Mr
Jenkins took the aircraft industry and shook it inside out.' Still the
Cabinet had to take the decision on TSR-2. Healey's proposal to make
a straight substitution of the F I I IA ran into strong opposition from the
defenders of the British industry, led by Crossman (a Coventry MP), and
backed by marching aircraft workers. But the Chancellor was adamant,
particularly after the failure to cancel *Concord*, that TSR-2 could not be
kept going at a cost of £4m a month: he needed the £35m that he would
save in 1965-6 by cancellation. The compromise agreed on 31 March
was to cancel the British plane, but to take up only an option on the
American.[9] Jenkins' contribution to this fudged result was to hold out
some hope that the gap might yet be able to be filled at least partly by
British aircraft. In the event, however, a year later, it was the F I I IA
which was bought, as the Ministry of Defence had clearly intended all
along.

In the Commons, the Tories moved a censure motion, which gave
Jenkins, replying for the Government, the opportunity for his first
triumph at the dispatch box – significant as the first of many over the

next five years in which he won a reputation as the Government's star Parliamentary performer. If his speech in February had been impressively reasoned, this was in quite a different vein. After only six months in office, the Government was already in trouble. It had lost a by-election at Leyton, reducing its precarious majority from five to three; the economic situation was gloomy; and the party was becoming rapidly demoralized.

The Times on 14 April had some better news:

> As if to prove that they can still win in the place where it matters, the Government pulled off a huge victory in the House of Commons last night, defeating the Opposition censure motion on the cancellation of the TSR-2 by a clear 26 votes.
>
> The end came after a thunderous tub-thumping display by Mr Roy Jenkins, Minister of Aviation, which set the Commons alight after what had been – by censure debate standards – a rather dull day.
>
> What Mr Jenkins had to say hardly mattered, even if the House had been able to hear more than a fraction of it. In fact it was largely a repetition of what Mr Healey had said earlier, but Mr Jenkins' style was so belligerent that he could have spoken Swahili and still provoked a riot.[10]

What he actually said was that the TSR-2 was a good plane, which had to die because it cost too much and could not be exported – not so much a prize project as 'a prize albatross'. If the Tories thought that this was a successful project, he shuddered to think what their failures might look like! He skilfully refused, when pressed by Angus Maude and Christopher Soames, to put a price on the F 111A; and vigorously denied that the cancellation damaged the British aircraft industry; on the contrary, he asserted, the decision released its resources for the more fruitful field of Anglo-European co-operation.[10]

The third main decision to occupy Jenkins during his fourteen months as Minister of Aviation was the very one he had considered in his *Observer* articles in the summer of 1964: what to do about BOAC? The problem was the same one in civil guise – whether the airline should fly the flag or buy the cheapest in an effort to make a profit. In 1963 Jenkins' Conservative predecessor, Julian Amery, had appointed a new chairman, Sir Ian Guthrie, with instructions to make a profit. Guthrie's response had been to cancel BOAC's order for thirty British Super VC10s, in favour of American Boeing 320s. In the *Observer*, Jenkins had argued that this was unacceptable: though BOAC should in principle fly the cheapest plane available, the corporation was too far committed to Vickers for its VC10s to pull out of the order now. The Government should make good the financial disadvantage to BOAC in this instance, and write off its £80m past loss, but with the instruction that it should operate as economically as possible in the future.[2] In office a few months later, he had the opportunity to put his prescriptions into practice, and very largely did so, dissolving BOAC's marriage with Cunard and re-shaping its relations with the Government; with the difference that the amount of the Corporation's debt actually written off was £110m.[11]

The speech in which Jenkins announced this, on 22 November 1965, was notable for a hint that if the Government was going to put a great deal of investment into the British Aircraft Corporation's development of a new subsonic airliner, it might simultaneously consider the nationalization of the industry. The proposal that it should at least buy a stake in both BAC and Hawker Siddeley was one of the recommendations of the Plowden Committee, which published its report in December 1965. Its other recommendations were very much on the lines Jenkins had been laying down – notably an emphasis on collaboration with Europe, and concentration on projects whose costs were not disproportionate to their market;[12] it was fitting that Jenkins' last business before leaving the Ministry of Aviation was to visit Germany for talks about the unglamorous and relatively inexpensive European airbus project. The implementation of Plowden, however, he left to another Minister, Fred Mulley; he himself was translated three days before Christmas 1965 to higher spheres.

Despite the handicap of being outside the Cabinet, Jenkins made an immediate mark as Minister of Aviation. As early as December 1964, Crossman noted in his diary those Ministers who were obviously enjoying their jobs and were better men for the responsibility they wielded – Wilson and Brown (but not Callaghan, out of his depth at the Treasury); Crossman himself; Jenkins and Crosland.[13] Four months later he was assessing the relative political weight of different Ministers. Besides the big three, he asked, 'Who else counts?'

> I suppose the Minister of Defence could count. But it is my impression that at the present the only man who has come out on the defence side with a will and a mind of his own is Roy Jenkins at Aviation. I have said that non-Cabinet Ministers don't matter, and certainly they don't elsewhere. But Roy Jenkins is an example of a non-Cabinet Minister who has steadily raised his status.[14]

The previous January he had had the chance to convert that raised status into Cabinet rank; but with remarkable self-confidence he had turned it down. The vacancy arose as a result of the embarrassing defeat of Patrick Gordon Walker in the Leyton by-election. Defeated at Smethwick in October, after a dirty campaign which reversed the national swing to Labour, Gordon Walker had been appointed to the Foreign Office anyway, while he found another seat. Leyton was vacated for him – the previous MP took a peerage – only for the electorate to show what it thought of these arrangements by rejecting him. Clearly he could not carry on after such a double rebuff; so, only three months into office, Wilson was obliged to find a new Foreign Secretary.

One possibility, urged by Crossman, would have been to appoint Denis Healey – a foreign affairs specialist – and move Jenkins to fill Healey's place at the Ministry of Defence. Wilson, however, preferred to move Michael Stewart from the Department of Education – a grey, all-purpose figure who would allow him effectively to run his own foreign policy; he then offered the education job to Jenkins.*

There seems to have been no doubt in his mind that if a Cabinet vacancy arose, Jenkins ('by far the outstanding success among Ministers outside the Cabinet', he wrote later in his record of the Labour Government) had established an undeniable claim to it, even though he knew from the 1963 talk that Jenkins had little interest in the social services. Jenkins, however, confirmed that he would rather wait for the position he really wanted, the Home Office, where Frank Soskice, in poor health, was proving a broken reed. 'A brave decision', Wilson wrote: 'few politicians would refuse their first chance of joining the Cabinet.'[16] It was nevertheless a decision highly characteristic of Roy Jenkins, displaying a mixture of cool nerve and calculation.

After bandying about the names of Reg Prentice, Fred Willey and Tony Greenwood, Wilson next offered Education to Tony Crosland, who accepted it. Somewhat tactlessly, Jenkins rather devalued Crosland's promotion by letting it be known that he had had first refusal: the second time in three months that the younger man had been shown to have the edge in the Prime Minister's favour. Crossman was impressed, and thought that Jenkins might be in line, not for the Home Office, but for the DEA 'if George Brown falls'.[14]

In the meantime, Crossman was right to think that Jenkins enjoyed simply being in office, inside the Cabinet or out. Aviation, he told the *Observer* in February, was a job which suited him very well: most major areas of policy-making impinged on it – economic and industrial policy, defence policy, relations with the French and Americans – 'it's not an isolated department.' In the same interview he gave a revealing glimpse

---

* Wilson actually told Cecil King, that he nearly promoted Jenkins straight into the Foreign Office.[15]

of his attitude to work, comparing his new life quite surprisingly with his old.

> In a sense I work very hard as a Minister, but in another sense I don't think I work as hard as I used to: I only regard writing as real work. The most difficult thing is sitting down at a desk with a blank sheet of paper.... As a Minister you hardly write anything. You have something in draft form: you can rewrite it if you want to; or approve it; or say "Do you mind redrafting it?" ... There's a momentum in a Minister's work.... Even if you're not on best form, you have a certain number of people to see and drafts to approve, and so you get through the morning's work because the morning's work doesn't have to be created by oneself.

He went on to give a characteristically precise timetable of his working day:

> I wouldn't say that in the last few months in office I've been excessively overworked. I arrive at about 10 in the morning and work through till about 1.15 fairly solidly: meetings, work on papers and so on. I then go out and lunch with somebody; I don't always talk business then by any means. I have an hour and a half for lunch. If there's not something arranged I go to the House of Commons or Brooks's Club.
>
> In the afternoon my hours are a quarter-to-three to a quarter-to-eight. Apart from this I do perhaps an average of an hour working on papers outside the office. I do half-an-hour every day in the car; that's one of the advantages of having a chauffeur-driven car, which I've never had before in my life. I can get through a lot of papers between Ladbroke Square and my office.

Notice the refusal to take work home in the evening.

As a Minister, Jenkins found that he worried less than he used to.

> I don't mean that I don't think terribly carefully about what I should do. But I'm much less a prey to destructive worry – thinking about things one cannot alter – than I used to be....
>
> There have been moments of high tension, certainly.... Certainly I have thought, "God, it matters terribly how I do that in the next half hour". And occasionally there's an absolutely sickening feeling that one's going to do it badly. But I draw a great distinction between worry about the future and worry about the past. Worry about the future is sometimes good: worry about the past is almost always debilitating.[17]

In 1965 Jenkins had little need to worry about the future. After the thirteen long years of frustrating opposition, he was on his way: he was in office, he was a success, and his ability would now surely carry him very near the top. He could at last be confident that, whatever happened, he would enjoy a significant career, to rank beside the others on his shelves.

'Mr Jenkins, with his languid throw-away manner', the *Observer* interviewer concluded, 'could be an easy man to underrate.'[17]

Few Home Secretaries have ever wanted that office more ardently than did Roy Jenkins in December 1965, or have come to it better prepared. Though an old and in theory a senior department – one of the three 'great offices of state' – it has as often as not in this century been occupied by grey men of the second or third rank (or of the first rank, on the way down). The Home Secretary has no concern with economic policy, which is where the power in modern government lies: his responsibilities cover a wide range of somewhat miscellaneous administrative functions, ordinarily routine but with an unusual potential for blowing up in his face. It is a department of regulation and control – the application of its rules inevitably throws up a lot of hard cases; while there is no subject on which the British press more stridently vents its fury when things go wrong – a policeman is killed, a prisoner escapes – than on that complex web of insoluble social problems known collectively as 'law and order'. For these reasons the Home Office has more often been a graveyard of reputations than a seedbed: in the previous sixty years the only Home Secretary to have gone on to the Prime Ministership was Winston Churchill – and it took him thirty years.

It was just because it had been for so long a backwater of timid illiberalism, however, that Jenkins saw in the Home Office an opening for a clear-sighted reformer to make his mark. During the long years of Conservative rule he had made Home Office matters – or, more accurately, those areas of its responsibility to which the Home Office preferred to turn a blind eye – one of his special concerns; he had derided the obscurantism of successive Tory Home Secretaries, and been unimpressed by the one, Rab Butler, from 1957 to 1962, who had been expected to bring to the job both a more open mind and the authority of a senior Minister. He had had the experience, in 1958, of putting on the Statute Book by his own efforts as a backbencher, obstructed by the department all the way, one important extension of personal freedom: more than any other department he was likely to be offered, he was eager – despite its disadvantages and dangers – to have the resources of the Home Office under his command to promote further progress in the same direction.

It was for this prospect that he had been prepared to turn down the

Department of Education eleven months before; and for once Wilson was happy to give one of his colleagues his head in the job he coveted. After a year in office, teetering along on its tiny majority, the morale of the Government was low: looking for an opportunity to go back to the country for a more secure mandate, Labour actually slipped in August nine points behind the Conservatives in the opinion polls. (Home had just been replaced as Tory leader by Edward Heath.) Frank Soskice's ill-health offered the Prime Minister the chance to remedy one of the dullest of his original appointments, to bring into the Cabinet the junior Minister who had made the most outstanding mark, and by doing so to restore the already tarnished image of his administration as an engine of modernization and social change. The trick worked for both of them. Over the next two years Jenkins made the personal success he had hoped for, achieving a number of overdue and irreversible reforms which transformed the social climate of the country; while through the deepening economic gloom the Home Office shone as the one redeeming beacon in a record of depressing failure. Despite the successful appeal to the country, skilfully brought off in March 1966, the swollen Labour benches had little to cheer except the reforming energy and the debating triumphs of the new Home Secretary.

Jenkins' two years at the Home Office are a classic example of the right man being in the right job at the right time. An aura of myth now surrounds his tenure, which still excites controversy. Coinciding with Beatlemania, the miniskirt and 'Swinging London', but also with the Rolling Stones, the drug scene and the first Vietnam demonstrations, the period 1966-7 is now seen for good or ill as a turning point in the social history of the country – either a halcyon time of personal liberation or the onset of national decadence. While Jenkins himself still speaks with pride of the 'civilized society' he helped to inaugurate, Margaret Thatcher and Mary Whitehouse portray him as the criminal who loosed the demon of permissiveness in the land. Of course Jenkins only reflected, did not create, the new moral climate which twenty years of peace and growing affluence suddenly produced in the middle sixties: it was not he (nor even the Labour Party) who abolished National Service in 1960; it was the Tories who gave the country the Profumo scandal in 1962. But he was far more in tune with his times than most Home Secretaries; he was openly on the side of the sixties revolution, not against it and, if a 45-year-old politician could hardly be its patron saint, he can justly be seen as its benevolent sponsor. To an extent, obviously, he was lucky in his timing – there was a shopping list of libertarian reforms on the agenda, for which the national mood (and

the parliamentary majority) was now right. At the same time he had
worked for his luck: he had campaigned for ten years for the abolition
of hanging, the legalization of homosexuality, the relaxation of licensing and Sunday Observance laws, the ending of theatre censorship. He
had turned down earlier promotion in order to get the chance to
advance these causes. He was not able to deliver the whole list, but he
carried homosexuality and abortion law reform and the abolition of
theatre censorship. (Hanging had already been suspended for a trial
period a few months before he took office.)

There is an argument that Jenkins showed a lack of political courage
by promoting the homosexuality and abortion reforms under cover of
backbenchers' initiatives, instead of boldly proposing them himself as
Government Bills. This is nonsense. There is a long tradition that such
legislation, on which MPs vote according to conscience, should be seen
to be the product of the House of Commons, not of the Government of
the day. Although an unsympathetic Government can always block
such legislation; although indeed an actively sympathetic Government
is required to grant it enough parliamentary time; and although in these
cases the majorities clearly came from the Labour majority in the
House, there was every advantage (not just political advantage to the
Government, but benefit to the authority of the legislation) in carrying
it without making the Government formally responsible. Opposition to
both Bills was strong and emotive, and the Government would have
damaged itself with sections of its own supporters had it become too
closely identified with either. Political effectiveness must be judged by
results. Not in the least disguising his personal support for them, Jenkins
played an essential part in getting them on the Statute Book, without
compromising the Government. Those who had campaigned for both
reforms gave him credit for a very shrewd and skilful operation.

Jenkins' strategy required finding private members to take up each
of the causes in question. When he became Home Secretary, abortion
and Sunday Observance Bills had already been introduced in the House
of Lords, by Lords Silkin and Willis respectively, but they still needed
sponsors in the Commons. A Sexual Offences Bill had already gone
through the Lords, piloted by Lord Arran, and had a sponsor ready in
the Commons in the person of Humphry Berkeley (then a Conservative
MP, later a member of the Labour party and now of the SDP). In
February 1966 Berkeley's Bill was given a Second Reading in the
Commons; but the next month the General Election supervened. The
Bill fell, and Berkeley lost his seat. So when Parliament reassembled all
three Bills had to be started again, and all needed Commons sponsors.

Of the three, Jenkins was most concerned to secure the legalization of homosexuality. When the 28-year-old Liberal, David Steel, drew third place in the ballot for private members' Bills, and came to seek the Home Secretary's advice on which of countless worthy causes he should use his good fortune to promote, Jenkins urged him to take up Arran's Sexual Offences Bill. In the event Steel chose abortion reform instead, but this was almost equally acceptable to Jenkins. The Welsh-Jewish Labour member for Pontypool, Leo Abse – a Freudian maverick with a special interest in sexual matters – took up the homosexuality Bill. From then on Jenkins gave every help and encouragement to the sponsors of both measures. He afforded them the full resources of the Home Office in drafting and technical assistance; and he persuaded the Cabinet, the Leader of the House (Richard Crossman) and the Chief Whip (John Silkin) to give them the necessary allocation of Government time to defeat their opponents' filibusters and see them through. Despite a massive majority of 223-29 on Second Reading in July 1966, Steel's Medical Termination of Pregnancy Bill needed two all-night sittings on the Report Stage in June/July 1967 before it was carried (by a much smaller majority of 167-83). In the earlier debate, Jenkins gave his reasons for supporting easier abortion. In the first place, the existing law was 'uncertain, harsh and archaic'. In the second case, it was constantly flouted by those who could afford the expensive services of illegal abortionists: present practice was 'very much a question of one law for the rich and one for the poor'. A law which left many otherwise law-abiding citizens on the wrong side of it was a bad law, which could undermine the authority of the whole fabric of law if it were not amended.[18] When the Bill finally carried, Jenkins paid generous tribute to David Steel, 'a young man with a marginal constituency and without a massive party machine behind him', praising his 'exceptional courage' in piloting the bitterly opposed measure safely through all its stages.[19] A seed of respect and mutual admiration was sown in these months between the young Opposition backbencher and the Home Secretary which was to bear fruit a dozen years later, when the young backbencher was leader of the Liberal party and the former Home Secretary was alienated from Labour and consigned apparently to the political scrapheap.

Abse's Sexual Offences Bill passed the Commons in July 1967 by 99 votes to 14, legalizing homosexual practices between consenting adults in private. Again, Jenkins made clear his personal support for the Bill at every stage of its passage, and at its conclusion congratulated Abse on an important and civilizing measure. Abse for his part has paid tribute to Jenkins' vital role in ensuring that it went through.[20]

No member took up the Home Secretary's offer of drafting facilities for a Sunday Observance Bill; but the two measures carried represented a substantial, and sufficiently controversial achievement for one year. The Tories had enough fun already with the gibe that the only people to benefit from three years of Labour Government were buggers and abortionists, without throwing in sabbath-breakers as well. Jenkins had one more liberalizing measure up his sleeve, however, before he left the Home Office: he was determined to abolish the Lord Chamberlain's anachronistic power of censorship of the live theatre. This he was prepared to introduce himself as a Government Bill. But he had battles, first with Crossman, who could not find him time in the legislative programme in 1967; more seriously with the Palace (frightened at the possibility of impersonation of the Queen), supported by the Prime Minister (frightened by a threatened stage version of *Mrs Wilson's Diary* from *Private Eye*).[21] By insisting to the point of threatening resignation, however, Jenkins got his way: though he had to leave it to his successor to put the Bill through, the British theatre was able to celebrate its freedom in 1968 most appropriately with the 'hippie' musical *Hair*, hymning 'the dawning of the Age of Aquarius'. (Soon afterwards came the promised production of *Mrs Wilson's Diary*.)

A more important (though perhaps less visibly effective) liberalizing measure which Jenkins had to leave to his successor at the Home Office was the 1968 Race Relations Act. From the moment he became Home Secretary he was at pains, in frequent speeches to immigrant organizations and other bodies, to identify himself with the improvement of race relations, asserting the need for more coloured policemen and coloured magistrates, and hinting that the 1965 Act might have to be strengthened in respect of discrimination in housing and employment, as a second generation grew up which was not prepared to tolerate what their parents had accepted. Characteristically, Jenkins was concerned for Britain's liberal image in the world. Defining integration 'not as a flattening process of assimilation but as equal opportunity, accompanied by cultural diversity, in an atmosphere of mutual tolerance', he declared in May 1966 that Britain must approach much closer than so far to this ideal 'if we are to maintain any sort of world reputation for civilized living and social cohesion.' He took a strongly positive view of the contribution that Commonwealth immigrants, like previous waves of immigrants from the Norman Conquest to the refugees of the thirties, could make in overcoming 'our natural island lethargy'. Looking ahead, he was optimistic, seeing no comparison with American racial troubles;

the coloured population was no more than 2 per cent, there was no institutionalized colour bar and no settled habit of hostility on either side. The challenge to the country's absorptive power, he asserted not entirely convincingly, was less than many it had surmounted in the past; but he warned that failure now would store up greatly increased problems for the future.[22]

During 1967 Jenkins decided, in consultation with the Race Relations Board, of which he had appointed his friend Mark Bonham Carter the first chairman, that the 1965 Act did indeed need strengthening. A new Bill was largely prepared before Jenkins left the Home Office, giving the Board additional powers to discourage discrimination in housing, employment and the provision of services, but it was left, somewhat incongruously, to James Callaghan to put it through the House of Commons.

Callaghan also inherited the problem of the Kenyan Asians. In this episode, Jenkins was unquestionably lucky. The dilemma of what to do about a possible 200,000 Asians being driven out of Kenya and entitled, by the possession of British passports granted in 1963, to come to Britain was a cruel one for a Labour Government, and particularly for a self-consciously liberal Home Secretary. In October 1967 the Cabinet's Home Affairs Committee decided that Jenkins must prepare legislation in case it became necessary to stem the flood.[23] By the time the Cabinet decided that it *was* necessary, however, the following summer, Jenkins was safely in the Treasury, and it fell to Callaghan, with no liberal reputation to lose, to incur the odium of 'racist' legislation to deny black British passport holders their right of entry. Though he indulged his freedom to express in Cabinet his dislike of Callaghan's measure,[24] there can be little doubt that Jenkins would have had to introduce very similar legislation had he still been Home Secretary. What he wrote in 1973 about Gaitskell's opposition to all controls on Commonwealth immigration in 1962 applies to himself in 1968: 'It was a position to which it is now difficult to believe that he [Gaitskell] could possibly have held. As a practical democrat he would have had to move. But he would have suffered great anguish in the process.'[25]

The impression that Jenkins was a 'lucky' Home Secretary rests on the circumstance that there was an agenda of liberal reforms for which the nation was ready, just waiting for the right Minister to come along and put them through. Although he deserves more credit than this allows, it clearly contains an element of truth. In other respects, however, 1966 was a very difficult moment for an avowed libertarian to come into office. The Home Secretary's primary responsibility is for law and order. Jenkins took office in the middle of an unprecedented crime wave. Hanging had just been abolished, five months before, and though murder was actually the one crime whose incidence was *not* rising, there was a strident backlash linking the rising figures to the loss of the supreme deterrent. In August, three policemen were shot dead in London, and the outcry knew no bounds. A 'soft' Home Secretary who had been a prominent supporter of abolition was an easy target. In addition Jenkins announced in October a posthumous free pardon for Timothy Evans, hanged in 1950 for a murder he almost certainly did not commit; and the previous month he personally quashed, on medical grounds, a sentence of birching on a prisoner in Maidstone jail. At the London Police Federation conference on 20 October he was roundly booed on all three counts, and half his audience walked out.[26] Two days later an embarrassing rash of prison escapes climaxed when the Soviet spy, George Blake, walked out of Wormwood Scrubs. The Home Office was suddenly a dangerous place for a liberal Home Secretary. The way Jenkins rode out these storms, the coolness he displayed under pressure and the firmness with which he stuck to and explained his line was even more impressive than the skill he showed in the more congenial parts of his job.

He was at pains from the moment he took office to reject the syllogism that being 'libertarian' on questions of personal liberty made him 'soft' on crime. It was a political necessity for him to be seen to make the combatting of the soaring crime rate his top priority, and he did not shirk it. At the same time he produced a typically elegant formulation to deny any contradiction between the two sides of his policy.

> Let us be as tough as we can be, though not blindly tough, in the war against crime. But do not let us for a moment confuse toughness with a policy of preserving archaic laws, designed not to protect society but to enforce, for no clear social purpose, the prejudices or tastes or lack of tastes of one group of people before another. We certainly do not strengthen the police in their battle against real crime if we make or keep as crimes, actions or behaviour which great bodies of civilised, law-abiding opinion do not regard as anything of the sort.[27]

Strengthening the police was Jenkins' first answer to 'real crime'; strengthening the courts his second. He firmly rejected the cry of the hanging and flogging lobby that the answer lay in harsher penalties and longer sentences, but insisted that the real deterrent was the certainty of detection and conviction. The first involved the more efficient use of police manpower. Efficiency and modernization became the Home

Secretary's watchwords. In May 1966 he announced a sweeping programme of reorganization reducing the number of autonomous police
forces in the country from 117 to less than 50 in seven years. This was a
rate of amalgamation not popular with the seventy chief constables who
would lose their jobs, and a good deal faster than his advisers thought
he could get away with; but having made up his mind on anything, it
is Jenkins' way to press on with implementation as quickly as possible.
'This took real courage and determination', Sir Robert Mark paid
tribute ten years later, 'but proved so obviously right that Jenkins was
quickly accorded ... the enhanced respect of police and public alike.'[28]
To the policeman on the beat he offered a technological revolution,
accelerating the provision of two-way radios so that they should no
longer be isolated units but could be sent immediately where they were
needed. It was under Jenkins' influence, too, that policemen began to
be taken off the beat. He paid a well-publicized visit to the United States
to study American policing methods, and came back greatly impressed
with saturation policing by radio-car as he had seen it in Chicago. This
is one reform of the Jenkins era against which – following Brixton and
other troubles – there has been a sharp reaction in recent years.

Jenkins' principal reform on the conviction side, however, has stuck
– even though it was much more controversial at the time. In 1967 he
broke with centuries of history by introducing majority verdicts in jury
trials, to combat mounting evidence that sophisticated criminals were
evading conviction by the bribery of a single juror. This was very much
his personal initiative, as *The Times* noted:

> One or two judges have lately been heard arguing for the reform, but Mr
> Jenkins has still been very bold in Home Office terms – he has moved quickly
> to his decision without going through the old timid ministerial routine of
> waiting for a recommendation from a high-powered committee. The de-
> cision is taken: all that remains is a study of safeguards so that a jury verdict
> shall not be mere headcounting.[29]

The idea of tampering with such a sacred tenet of English justice
aroused a good deal of emotional opposition in all parts of the House of
Commons; but the Shadow Home Secretary, Quintin Hogg, was in
favour of the change and his legal eloquence helped to see it comfortably
approved on Report Stage by 180 votes to 102. This was not only the
boldest but probably the best thing that Jenkins accomplished directly as
Home Secretary. There has never been any serious call to reverse it.
With the safeguard that a majority verdict (of not less than 10-2) can
only be accepted after a sustained attempt to reach unanimity, a nasty

abuse was – if not entirely ended – at least made much more difficult. The majority option has strengthened the jury system, not weakened it.

Majority verdicts were only the most controversial clause in Jenkins' major legislative achievement at the Home Office, the 1967 Criminal Justice Act – a somewhat miscellaneous ragbag of measures covering in one way or another practically the whole field of crime and punishment. On the prevention side, it required the licensing of shotguns (reversing Soskice's 1965 Firearms Act). Trial procedure was simplified by the streamlining of committal proceedings, while in addition to majority verdicts, convicted criminals sentenced to more than six months were debarred from jury service and 'sprung alibis' – alibis produced in court without notice – were outlawed. There was much here to restore the Home Secretary's standing with the police; by the time he left office he had won their confidence to a remarkable degree. The other half of the Act, however, consisted of measures to reduce pressure on the prisons: the introduction of suspended sentences; increased use of fines; easier bail; earlier parole; and alternative methods of treating drunks. These were not calculated to appease the punitive lobby.

The problem of the prisons threw the dilemma of a liberal Home Secretary into the sharpest relief. They were desperately overcrowded. In two years since 1964 the prison population had jumped from 29,000 to nearly 36,000 (in 1938 the same buildings had held only 11,000). The buildings themselves were old, crumbling, insanitary and quite unsuited to the modern idea that the purpose of prison is not so much punishment as rehabilitation. They were built, as Jenkins had continually to explain, on the principle of 'cell security', with the prisoners locked in their cells most of the day. Rehabilitation required, on the contrary, a relatively open regime with the prisoners allowed considerable freedom within the perimeter of the prison ('perimeter security'). Overcrowding militated against rehabilitation; on the other hand attempts to run an open regime in overcrowded buildings made it much too easy to escape. Escapes had been running at a high level for some years before 1966: contrary to the impression fostered by the press, they did not suddenly increase when Labour came into office. Nevertheless cartoons and other comment fed a growing feeling that the Home Secretary did not need a Criminal Justice Bill to empty the prisons: they were emptying themselves quite rapidly enough already.

When George Blake, the Soviet spy sentenced in 1962 to forty-two years, escaped from Wormwood Scrubs on 22 October, the Tories had a field day in the House of Commons: with their backbenchers baying them on, Heath and Hogg pressed the Home Secretary furiously for an enquiry. Jenkins announced that he had invited Lord Mountbatten to head an enquiry into the whole question of prison security; but he hesitated over whether the terms of reference would specifically include the Blake episode, for the punctilious reason that he was not seeing Mountbatten until the evening and wished to settle them with him before he told the House. His statement came over as woefully inadequate. 'He committed the sin', *The Times* wrote later, 'of momentarily behaving like a civil servant', when he should have been a politician.[29] If so, he was politician enough a week later when the Tories tabled a censure motion on him.

> To deafening applause [the *Daily Mirror* reported on November 1] Home Secretary Roy Jenkins turned the tables last night on Tory leaders who attacked his handling of the George Blake case.
>
> For 45-year-old Mr Jenkins it was a Commons victory unequalled by a Minister since Labour returned to power two years ago. . . .[30]

'It was difficult to recall [the *Daily Telegraph*] such a loud and long ovation at the end of any debate.'[31] 'With devastating contempt and a flow of invective rarely heard in the House of Commons these days' [*The Times*],[32] Jenkins swept aside the censure motion and scattered his critics. Again it could be said that he was lucky; the Tories offered themselves for the slaughter with a singularly ill-judged motion. But no-one could have taken more comprehensive advantage of the opportunity offered. He demolished the suggestion by Hogg and Enoch Powell that Henry Brooke had placed special curbs on Blake which Labour had relaxed. Lord Butler had incautiously said that Blake should never have been in Wormwood Scrubs: suavely Jenkins pointed out that it was Butler himself in 1962 who had sent him there!

> But the one simple point that won the day for Mr Jenkins, beyond his slaughter of Mr Sandys for doubting the loyalty of the police force, and above his merciless scorn of Mr Heath, lay in the Mountbatten enquiry itself. He had been asked by the Opposition to put a specific instruction on the Blake escape into the terms of reference, and this he had done. He had been asked for a speedy enquiry, and this one would be completed by the end of the year. What more did they want?
>
> What they wanted, it was very plain, was a strong helping of sweet revenge for the events of last Monday. They wanted the head of Mr Jenkins on a pikestaff, and that of Mr Wilson as well. In the event they got neither, and nor did they deserve to.
>
> Not for the first time, Mr Heath and his advisers will have to get back to the drawing board.[32]

Nothing puts a Government's supporters in better heart than this sort of routing of the Opposition. 'The demolition job was so total', Crossman noted, 'that when the vote came many of the Tories just weren't there. It was a tremendous reversal achieved by sheer debating skill. . . . It did a lot to change the atmosphere.'[33] From now on the Home Secretary was established as an unquestioned high flier to be treated with respect by colleagues and opponents alike. Many of the younger right-wingers in the Labour party – people like David Marquand and Bob Maclennan – who had entered the House of Commons for the first time in 1966 and fifteen years later were to join the SDP, recall this speech as the moment of revelation when they began to look to Jenkins as their leader.

In the longer run, it must be said, Jenkins did not solve the problems of the prisons. Mountbatten's report, recommending greater use of electronic alarm equipment and the segregation of the most dangerous prisoners in a new prison on the Isle of Wight, seemed to those concerned with the radical reform of prison conditions an irrelevant disappointment and a missed opportunity. The Criminal Justice Act did a little, but not nearly enough, to reduce for a few months the relentlessly increasing pressure on the system; the prison population continued to grow, so that by the time Jenkins became Home Secretary for the second time in 1974 it was over 40,000. In 1966–7, it is fair to say, he made a beginning; he grasped what was then a fairly new problem, and introduced some minor innovations to deal with it, before he was translated to other spheres. It is in 1974–6 that he can be criticized for not doing more.[34]

Jenkins' success in 1966 in turning to his own advantage a row which might have sunk another Home Secretary is an example of his exceptional political skill. In these two years as a whole he achieved a remarkable balancing act by managing to appear always liberal, but *toughly* liberal. He had another parliamentary success in November 1967 when the Tories tried a second time to censure him for his action over the summer in closing down an approved school where there had been allegations of serious cruelty. He 'coolly and capably' (Crossman) defended his action, refused a further enquiry and again wiped the floor with Hogg.[35] His decisiveness, having made up his mind, was formidably impressive. A trivial but characteristic example, which greatly impressed the Department, occurred early in his term, in February 1966. A teenage girl was taken into care by a local authority for truancy, when all that had happened was a silly argument between her mother, who insisted that she should wipe her school cutlery before she used it, and the headmistress who forbade her to wipe it. The mother had kept the

girl away from school. The press got hold of the story and blew it into
a front page scandal. Jenkins acted quickly – even before Wilson could
get on the phone to tell him to act – demanding that the Department
find some power under which he could order the girl's release; they
succeeded, with some difficulty, and she was freed the same day. The
Home Secretary basked in the role of St George, who had saved the
wronged girl from the bureaucratic dragon.[36]

Jenkins received excellent press coverage for almost everything he did
– for the reason that he had his personal public relations officer. John
Harris had been Hugh Gaitskell's personal assistant in the early sixties.
After Gaitskell's death he became Director of Publicity at Transport
House during the 1964 election, then personal assistant to Patrick
Gordon Walker at the Foreign Office. He stayed at the Foreign Office
after Gordon Walker's defeat to serve Michael Stewart, but he was
above all a Gaitskellite, and when Jenkins became Home Secretary he
moved to the Home Office. From then right up to the present, in office
and out, except when Jenkins was in Brussels, he has stayed at Jenkins'
side, as press officer, *confidant* and campaign manager: his *alter ego*, his
evil genius or his minder – opinions of Harris vary, but his constant
presence is almost always seen as vaguely sinister. Even Jenkins' friends
often find it exasperating to have Harris zealously guarding all access to
his master. In fact his positive influence with Jenkins is not great.
Jenkins uses him as a congenial sounding-board, someone with whom
he can relax, who shares his sense of humour (and has even come to
share many of his mannerisms), rather than as a true adviser. Harris
more often reflects the way Jenkins' mind is already moving than tries
to change it. He is more Sancho Panza than Svengali.

In the mid-sixties he was assiduous and extraordinarily skilful in
promoting Jenkins in the press as Labour's one successful Minister in a
general picture of incompetence and economic failure. His activity was
not unnaturally resented by Jenkins' senior colleagues, who were beginning to look nervously over their shoulders at this ambitious young man
too clearly on the make. Their jealousy – in the Prime Minister's case
verging almost on paranoia – is very plain in Crossman's diary. Wilson
was frankly delighted in 1966 when the Blake escape caught Jenkins
momentarily off balance. 'That will do our Home Secretary a great
deal of good', he told Crossman, when Jenkins phoned him 'in a great
stew' with the news. 'He was getting too complacent and he needs
taking down a peg.'[37] Jenkins' triumphant rebound from this reverse,
however, rather moved him up another peg. The following April, Wilson
was furious when Jenkins – with John Harris's help – stole his thunder

by being seen to take command of the Torrey Canyon tanker disaster (off Wilson's own Scilly Isles). 'The moment he took over on that Sunday afternoon', the Prime Minister complained, 'he tried to give the impression that he found everything in a shemozzle and that no decisions were taken until he, the decisive Roy Jenkins, took command. . . . He's rigged the whole Sunday press as well.'[38] Wilson preferred his 1964 reputation as a one-man band.

In June 1967, Crossman was recording that Harris had 'poisoned Roy's relations with Harold',[39] and had a talk with Tony Crosland to see if Crosland, as his oldest friend, could warn Jenkins of the harm his henchman's activities were doing him. But Crosland told him that he and Jenkins hardly saw one another now. He too was irritated, according to his wife, that 'one can't open a newspaper without reading what a paragon he is.'[40] He told Crossman that he thought Jenkins was 'behaving in a very funny and remote and ambitious way.' Crossman, who had not realized how far the rivalries of office had driven the former Gaitskellites apart, drew the conclusion that Jenkins was 'running his drive for power completely on his own.'[41]

As Leader of the House of Commons, responsible for the Government's legislative timetable, Crossman was repeatedly put out by the Home Secretary's insistence that he must have parliamentary time for his urgent Bills ahead of other Ministers in the queue – in the 1966–7 session, on top of the Criminal Justice Bill, he wanted a Gaming Bill, a Dangerous Drugs Bill and time for Steel's Abortion Bill ('Roy . . . has been throwing his weight about a bit');[42] in the 1967–8 session, on top of the Race Relations Bill, the abolition of theatre censorship ('Roy Jenkins is getting more imperious every day').[43]

The press, particularly the *Daily Mirror* (overreaching itself under Cecil King), was running Jenkins strongly to succeed Callaghan as Chancellor, even tipping him to displace Wilson as Prime Minister. This was not a situation Wilson could tolerate: by July, Crossman was expecting 'a great confrontation between Harold and the man he detests and whose influence he really hates in Cabinet.'[44] The next month Wilson carried out a characteristic reshuffle of the economic departments, taking charge of the DEA himself with Peter Shore promoted to the Cabinet as his deputy, and replacing Douglas Jay with Tony Crosland at the Board of Trade. 'Now', he equally characteristically congratulated himself, 'I've got seven potential Chancellors, and I've knocked out the situation where Jenkins was the only alternative to Callaghan. You know . . . this is one of the most successful political operations that's ever been conducted.'[45]

Meanwhile the central plank of the Government's economic policy was inexorably collapsing. From the first day after the election victory of October 1964 the Prime Minister, with Callaghan and Brown in agreement, had determined that despite the £400m deficit, despite heavy and continued pressure in the money markets ('the gnomes of Zurich'), the value of the pound should be preserved. The decision was taken for political reasons (Labour had devalued in 1949, and Wilson did not want the party to be seen as the devaluation party), and for patriotic reasons (the parity of the pound became the symbol of Britain's credit in the world). It was taken, and held to with stubborn resolution, in defiance of most of the Government's economic advisers, who saw the attempt to maintain the value of sterling as a futile distraction of resources from the Government's real purposes, and doomed to failure in the long run anyway. There was a political case for not devaluing straight away in 1964, when the Government's very existence was precarious. By 1966, when the Government had secured a majority of a hundred, there was none. There was now mounting pressure within the Cabinet that what Wilson had declared 'the unmentionable' must be not merely discussed but accepted and got over with as quickly as possible, if the Government were ever to be free from recurrent financial crises requiring repeated doses of painful deflation to reassure the bankers. Jenkins, though not departmentally concerned with economic policy, was among the leaders of this revolt, which combined the 'intellectuals' of right and left – himself and Crosland, Crossman and Barbara Castle – against the Prime Minister, his beleaguered Chancellor and the Cabinet loyalists like Michael Stewart. George Brown was converted to the devaluation camp. A simple economic judgement was complicated by two factors. First, it was in Wilson's nature to see the devaluation movement as a front for a plot against himself, and hence to identify his own position with the maintenance of his policy; secondly, he was able to exploit the suspicion that the real purpose of devaluation was to pave the way for a new approach to the Common Market. Jenkins, built up by the press as the heir apparent and also the party's leading pro-Marketeer, was the principal villain in both plots.

Wilson was in fact moving cautiously towards making an approach to Europe; the addition of Crosland and Jenkins and Tony Benn (then a pro-Marketeer) to the Cabinet in 1965-6, the removal of Douglas Jay and the addition of George Thomson in 1967, were changing the balance of the Government. But he wanted to make the running at his own speed, taking the party with him, and in the meantime suspicion of the EEC was a good bogey with which to coax Barbara Castle and other anti-Marketeers back into line on the devaluation issue. When the 'plot' came to a head in July, Wilson bought off Brown with the Foreign Office and the other malcontents with the promise of an economic strategy committee – on which, in the event, only Crossman was included. The Prime Minister remained 'profoundly suspicious' of his Home Secretary, and determined to keep him at arm's length.[46]

Jenkins, for his part, while enjoying his own work at the Home Office and naturally pleased with his rapidly growing reputation, was becoming distinctly disillusioned with Wilson – if he had ever had any illusions to lose. 'Heavens', Crossman exclaimed to him after a Cabinet meeting in December 1966, 'I wish we could have been given a clearer vision of his [Wilson's] long term policy in Rhodesia.' 'I'd give anything for evidence that we have a long-term plan for any part of this Government's policy, thank you very much, Dick', Jenkins replied.[47] But he gave the strong impression of a man biding his time. 'Roy keeps himself to himself with extreme care. . . . He speaks very little but when he does it's always terse and to the point, as though he had kept a lot in reserve.'[48]

In May 1967 he broke cover for the first time with an implicit criticism of Wilson's leadership. Labour had just done disastrously in the local elections, losing control of the GLC and many other authorities all round the country. Speaking to the London Labour party, Jenkins made the usual defence of the unpopular but necessary measures taken by the Government and held out the hope of a 'modest increase' in living standards in the coming year. But such an improvement would not touch the core of the problem:

> The core of the problem is to give the party and the nation a clear sense of direction: a lifting of the sights, a view at once sharp and far-reaching, of where we want to get to by the end of this Parliament, an exposition of the purposes, a good deal more elevated than merely keeping the Tories out, for which this Government exists.[49]

The elevated purposes which Jenkins still hoped the Government could achieve were, as set out in this key speech, three. First, the raised horizon of which he spoke was Europe; the Government was by now committed to making a second application to join the EEC, and there was real hope that de Gaulle was ready to lift his 1963 veto.

Second, though he did not say how, Labour must restore its commitment to economic growth. Redistributive taxation was not enough, and might actually be counter-productive, both economically and electorally. In a significant passage he suggested that Labour's constituency had now moved beyond the old working class to embrace the new classless meritocracy (as he had been urging since 1959). 'The Labour Party, as the 1966 election showed conclusively, is a party with an appeal to all income and occupational groups.' The Government had *both* to look after its traditional supporters *and* to retain its new support. 'The only way in which we can marry our demand for protection for the lower paid and higher social expenditure with a buoyant standard of living for our most productive citizens is by a rapid rate of growth for the remainder of this Parliament.' This was widely taken as a clear condemnation of Callaghan's wasted Chancellorship, and an announcement of his own credentials for the job.

Jenkins' third purpose was his own particular contribution as Home Secretary: 'We exist as a party, not only to make a more comfortable society for all its members, but also to make a more civilized, more free and less hidebound society.' Referring to the abortion and homosexuality Bills then going through Parliament, he risked a definition: 'To enlarge the area of human choice, socially, politically and economically, not just for a few but for the whole community is very much what democratic socialism is about.' In 1967 'democratic socialism' and 'social democracy' were still interchangeable terms.[49]

On 18 November 1967 the Government was finally forced to devalue the pound. In spite of all Wilson's and Callaghan's talk of an upturn, the trade figures remained obstinately bad. The Six-Day War in the Middle East, the Arab oil embargo and the closing of the Suez Canal increased the pressure, assisted by a dock strike. The pound could only be supported by heavy drawing on reserves, at a rate which could not continue. After three years' unavailing struggle, the Treasury, the Chancellor and even the Prime Minister were obliged to admit defeat. The Cabinet was told two days before the country: sterling was devalued by 17 per cent from a parity of $2.80 to $2.40. Wilson went on television to reassure the nation that 'the pound in the pocket' had not been devalued: defiantly he tried to present the collapse of his central policy as a great opportunity, a chance for a fresh start. Callaghan, more honestly, recognized it as a defeat which made it impossible for him to remain Chancellor, and insisted on resigning.

So the second job in the Government, for which Wilson claimed to have seven candidates, was vacant. The story of how he came to appoint the one whom, a few weeks before, he had been most determined to keep out, is a tangled one. Tony Crosland was confident that he, as a trained economist and, since August, President of the Board of Trade, was the natural choice. Crossman thought at the beginning of November that Crosland was 'booked for the Treasury'.[50] Most of the press thought Denis Healey a more likely alternative. Jenkins got the job, however, for the same reason that he was the favourite in the first place – that he was the best man. He was enough of an economist to carry conviction; he had impressed both the House of Commons and the country by his strength and clarity of mind, his decisiveness, his political agility and his effectiveness in debate. He would bring both sound judgement to the making of policy and political skill to its presentation. Whatever their intellectual qualifications, no other candidate was so good at the dispatch box: Crosland conveyed an air of slightly supercilious dilettantism, while Healey's manner was too often arrogantly overbearing. 'As a parliamentary performer, as a sheer debater', Alan Watkins wrote in the *New Statesman*, 'Mr Jenkins is in a class apart from the rest of either front bench.... He not only looks superior: he is superior.'[51] When it came to the crisis of his Government, Wilson needed the best man available, even if he were a rival; he could console himself that he was at least involving Jenkins irrevocably with the Government's fate, as he had not been involved hitherto. If he was tempted to go for Crosland or Healey, Crossman and Silkin as Leader of the House and Chief Whip helped to convince him that Jenkins was the man to 'give us the lift we need.'[52] There was another factor which is sometimes thought to have been decisive: Wilson wanted the minimum reshuffle of the Government, and there was a chance that Callaghan would agree to take the Home Office. Ironically, it was Tony Crosland who persuaded him that he should not retire to the back benches but remain in the Government; if he did so the Home Office was the obvious job, and a straight swap was the Prime Minister's most convenient expedient. So, it is said, Crosland talked himself out of the Treasury. In reality, though the straight swap was undoubtedly convenient, it was not the decisive factor. Twice already since 1964 Wilson had chosen Jenkins ahead of Crosland, for Aviation and for Education. In 1967 Jenkins was the man he needed. Nobody except Crosland himself thought that Wilson had made anything but the obvious choice.

SIX

Chancellor of the Exchequer, 1967–1970

When Jenkins and John Harris crossed the bridge that connects the old Home Office building to the Treasury, Harris later recalled, it was like going into France in 1940. In the aftermath of the devaluation it had fought for so long to avoid, the Treasury was a defeated and demoralized department. No other Chancellor in modern times has entered on his heritage in such grim conditions. Having been purposely kept off the key economic committees by the Prime Minister for the past three years, Jenkins had to start from scratch picking up the pieces of a failed policy. He had, however, three advantages. First, he himself was generally thought to be a good appointment, both competent and tough. ('Roy's the Boy' [*The Economist*];[1] 'Jenkins the Cash has the makings of a first-class Chancellor' [*Daily Mirror*].[2] Second, he was known to have been one of those who had argued for devaluation very much earlier, at least as far back as July 1966. Thus he came in with the authority of one who bore no responsibility for the inglorious manner in which devaluation had ultimately been brought about, but personally vindicated by the débâcle. Third, he took office when the critical decision had been taken and Callaghan thrown to the wolves in expiation of it: he had a clean slate to write on, the responsibility but also the opportunity to make a success of the new, post-devaluation economic strategy. In spite of everything, therefore, it can be maintained that Jenkins was, once again, lucky.

'Thanks to the new situation created by devaluation', declared the *Financial Times*, 'the Treasury becomes for the first time a job worth having by an ambitious politician. With luck, firmness and patience he might even find himself presiding over the long-delayed British economic miracle.'[3] Jenkins' May speech to the London Labour Conference was widely recalled to evidence the approach he would bring to running the economy. 'Mr Jenkins is an expansionist who believes in prosperity' (*The Economist*).[1] 'He is an expansionist, first and foremost, recognizing that faster economic growth is the only respectable objective of economic policy, and that Labour's record in this over the past three years is abysmal' (*The Spectator*).[4] The welcome the new Chancellor received from Fleet Street was remarkably uniform, if not always calculated to allay the suspicions of the Labour left. 'His combination of economic understanding, parliamentary skill and political judgement', *The Times* believed, 'makes him the most promising appointment to the Exchequer since Hugh Gaitskell in 1950.'[5] 'If the purity of his Socialism is highly suspect to some of his more militant colleagues', reflected the *Economist*, 'it does no harm to his standing in the City.'[1] Several papers foresaw the possibility of trouble between Jenkins and the party. The *Financial Times* noted with approval that he had grasped the disincentive effect of high taxation and had called for 'a competitive and thrusting business climate', but went on perceptively: 'The speed with which he can move will be limited, not merely by financial stringencies, but by the fact that the Benches behind him consist not of the radical alliance which he might like to see, but of the British Labour Party, warts and all.'[3] For the *Sunday Times*, 'One question overshadows every other. Will the Labour Party let the Chancellor do what must be done?'[6]

There was a good deal of comment on the personal tensions that were known to lie behind Jenkins' appointment. 'It had been widely supposed', noted *The Times*, 'that Mr Wilson would shrink from this further rapid promotion of Mr Jenkins, who is so evidently *papabile*.'[7] Robert Carvel in the *Evening Standard* – making one of the earliest journalistic references to the new Chancellor's taste for wine – predicted that relations between numbers 10 and 11 Downing Street might not be easy: 'Good claret and good HP sauce do not always go together', but he reckoned that 'Mr Wilson, however reluctantly, seems to have made an inspired choice.'[8] The *Economist* warned that the Government could not afford to give way to jealousy: 'The whole Cabinet must realize that Mr Jenkins is Labour's last ace; if he fails his successor is not Mr Crosland or Mr Healey, but Mr Macleod.'[1] Loftily, the *Financial Times* advised him to ignore these pressures: 'He will do well to remember that the best path to political success in his present post is to behave as unpolitically as possible, and to leave the next election to look after itself.'[3] This advice Jenkins followed.

He made a slightly false start, by assuring a worried meeting of the PLP that there were no conditions attached to Callaghan's Letter of Intent to the IMF, then having to admit to the House of Commons that there were after all certain 'realities' which the Government had to accept if the pound was to get the international support it needed until its new value stabilized.[9] This was not uncharacteristic, recalling his initial hesitancy over the Blake escape, before he had fully marshalled his case. Jenkins is always something of a slow starter. He likes to feel his way into a job, to think out his position clearly. At the Treasury, he was thrown in at the deep end on the immediate morrow of a crisis, with no previous opportunity to familiarize himself in detail with the situation. It is not surprising that he should have floundered briefly before he found his feet.

He had the great advantage, however, that the basic economic situation was clear, and the task that faced him generally agreed. The economic arguments that still rage about the 1964-70 Government overwhelmingly concern 1964-7 - whether and when the Government should have devalued. The consensus is now almost universal that they should have done - in 1966 if it was not politically possible in 1964. The overvalued pound was causing huge balance of payments deficits, putting pressure on the currency which the Government had to keep borrowing to relieve. The Wilson/Callaghan strategy of trying to restore the balance of payments by deflation alone, without devaluation, was doomed. Confidence is a question of belief, and their optimism was too often falsified by bad trade figures to be believed. Pressure on sterling was continuous, exacerbated by every crisis which might affect the monthly results - the 1966 seamen's strike, the Middle East war in 1967. Without devaluation, the Government's whole effort and most of its resources had to go into propping up the pound at an unrealistic level.[10]

Devaluation had to come. But it was not by itself the answer to the balance of payments problem. Wilson in his optimistic broadcast gave the impression, and much of the PLP at first imagined, that devaluation was the simple, magic alternative to the deflation of the past two years, and that the squeeze on public and private spending could now be relaxed, allowing the Government to get on with doing all the socially desirable things a Labour Government exists to do. Jenkins had very quickly to disillusion them. The task of the new Chancellor after devaluation was to *use* the competitive advantage that devaluation gave to build up the balance of payments, so as to make sterling *secure* at its new value. There was then, and is now, no serious argument about this. What Jenkins had to do was to encourage a massive switch of resources from consumer spending into exports - a requirement rendered the more massive because devaluation had been so long delayed; the accumulated deficit, and thus the accumulated debt to be repaid, was more enormous than it need have been if the ultimate inevitability of devaluation had been accepted sooner. There could be no early easing of the pressure on either public spending or the domestic consumer.

Jenkins came to the Treasury with the reputation of being an expansionist, and an ardent desire to live up to it by getting the economy growing again as quickly as possible. But any policy for growth depended as absolute prerequisites on a balance of payments surplus and a stable pound. Any premature relaxation of controls on the domestic economy would have immediately sucked in more imports, undermined the balance of payments and put renewed pressure on the pound, bringing the dismal cycle back to square one. To achieve the necessary surplus would take, Jenkins told the House of Commons in a grim speech, 'two years' hard slog', with no weakening and no short cuts.'[11] Deflation was thus still the order of the day, to the dismay of the left who complained bitterly that a Labour Government was not elected to carry out what they considered Tory measures. The difference was that with devaluation, it was deflation with some prospect of ultimate success. The Government was no longer trying to defy the facts of life: for the first time it had a rational strategy – if it could stick to it.

Jenkins did stick to it, and in the end the balance of payments did move into surplus. During 1967–70, while private consumption increased by only 5.4 per cent and public consumption by only 1 per cent, exports (including re-exports) rose by 27 per cent, outstripping a 17 per cent rise in imports. By 1970, the 1967 deficit on current account of £294m had been turned into a surplus of £731m – in real terms the biggest since 1950 – which rose again in 1971 to a resounding £1,090m. But 'two years' hard slog' was what it took to get the figures right. During 1968, the position actually deteriorated, before devaluation had time to take effect. It needed a year for the reduced price of exports to result in an increase in sales sufficient to offset the immediate deterioration of the terms of trade; on top of this, there was an unexpected increase in the volume of *imports*, due to stocks having been run abnormally low in 1967. The turn-around was agonizingly slow in coming, and in the meantime there were still frequent alarms, further runs on the pound and the recurrent spectre of a second devaluation. It required, in fact, five separate packages of deflationary measures, between November 1967 and April 1969 before the figures began unmistakably to turn in August 1969.

Jenkins is open to the criticism – indeed, he has admitted it – that he was slow, when he first took over the Treasury, to take strong enough action to restrain consumption. Part of the blame belongs to Wilson and Callaghan, whose immediate post-devaluation package of credit restrictions and spending cuts was quite inadequate: Wilson was still over-optimistic, while Callaghan, on the point of resignation simply refused to carry the odium of any more bad news. The two-month delay before Wilson announced another heavy round of expenditure cuts in January was perhaps inevitable, given that there had been no preparation of the ground before devaluation: this was the biggest cost-cutting exercise of its kind introduced up to that date, and it was bound to take time to assemble. But Jenkins was at fault in postponing the third bite at the deflationary cherry – curbs on private spending – until March 1968. Instead of bringing in an immediate holding budget, he merely issued stern warnings of what the Budget proper would contain – an elementary psychological error which predictably set off a 'beat-the-budget' spending spree, pushing imports up to a record level and the deficit to £70m in February alone. 'In retrospect', he admitted in 1971, 'I think it would have been better to deal with personal consumption in late January or early February, rather than in mid-March.' The official reasoning was that he could not take too much out of the economy before exports had increased sufficiently to take up the slack; he also did not want to have to rely entirely on crude increases in the duty on the most obvious targets – but subtler measures needed time to prepare. Jenkins was inclined to feel later that he had been poorly advised by the department at a time when he had not yet the mastery of it to be able to impose his own instinct. From the successful vantage of 1971 it did not matter. 'We lost a few months in early 1968, but the effect was not decisive. The turnaround in the balance of payments may have been delayed by a few months, but not by more.'[12] In the desperate atmosphere of the time, however, when success was anything but assured, two lost months were a serious matter.

Politically, it was the expenditure cuts announced in January 1968 which marked the acceptance by the Government of a new strategy, following devaluation. Though announced by Wilson, for reasons of personal jealousy ('With this build-up of Roy', he told Crossman, 'I can't possibly afford not to make the Statement myself'),[13] they represented a major victory for Jenkins, the moment when he stamped his authority on the central direction of Government policy for the next three years. The January package cut £700m from projected spending for 1968–9, with further cumulative savings in later years. It took an unprecedented eight Cabinet meetings in two weeks, totalling thirty-two hours of discussion, to get it agreed; but agreed it was, with no significant concessions and only one unimportant resignation; and those thirty-two hours were the making of Jenkins' Chancellorship. At the beginning, just after Christmas 1967, Crossman was writing in his diary that Jenkins 'doesn't yet exert any authority or have any real weight against the men who face him on the other side of the table – Callaghan, Brown and Healey.'[14] By the end, on January 15, he had become 'the dominating force in Cabinet'.[15] In between, Crossman vividly describes how Jenkins achieved that dominance.

First he forced the Cabinet to accept that all the tears and travail of the Callaghan years had been wasted effort; in reply to Crosland arguing that cuts of only £400m would be enough, he demonstrated that the deficit in the last months of 1967 was as bad as in 1964. 'We were not merely back to square one but back to square zero. . . . For those of us who know about the autumn behaviour of Harold and Jim, this was a deadly rehearsal of the facts.'[16] Of course, the cuts in domestic spending – particularly the reimposition of prescription charges (the very principle on which Wilson had resigned with Bevan in 1951) and the postponement of the raising of the school leaving age to sixteen (which Lord Longford made a reason for resignation now) – were no more agreeable to him than to any other member of the Government. Nevertheless he insisted that the slaughter of some sacred cows was an essential element of the whole exercise: '£40m saved on prescription charges', he told Crossman, 'is worth £140m elsewhere, because of the impression it makes on the bankers.'[17] The overseas cuts were a different matter. Despite the anxious representations of the United States, Australia, Singapore and the Gulf States, Britain made the historic decision to give up the attempt to remain a world power. All British forces were to be withdrawn from East of Suez (except Hong Kong) by the end of 1971, with large reductions in military manpower overall and cancellation of the order for the F-111. This was something Jenkins had positively wanted for years, that Britain should stop overstraining her resources to maintain a military role that was beyond her and adjust instead to being a European power fulfilling a role in the defence of the West commensurate with her reduced circumstances. For three years Wilson, with those other old-fashioned patriots Callaghan and Brown, had fought to avert this, as he had fought against devaluation: Britain's world role and the $2.80 parity were the twin symbols of a national greatness he sought to sustain as stoutly as any Tory, even though the one played a large part in undermining the other. It was a particular satisfaction for Jenkins to be able to bring about this historic withdrawal within weeks of becoming Chancellor. At Cabinet on 12 January he demolished George Brown's Foreign Office case for staying on. 'Just because there can't be genuine savings in the next two years on defence', Crossman summed up his argument, 'there has to be a major change of foreign and defence policy from that of the last three years. He said it in a way which destroyed the credibility not only of George but of all the other people who have been running the Great Britain policy since 1964. It was the challenge to the authority of the old Government that he managed to bring out.'[16]

'After lunch came Healey's last-ditch effort to save the F-111', Crossman's account continued. 'When he'd finished the PM asked him four questions very unsuccessfully, since he was scored off by Denis in a fairly rude and devastating way.'

> But when Roy began his interrogation things went very differently. He did far better than the Prime Minister in fencing with Denis, undermining him first on the economic side and above all on the political side, showing the essential need to match the cut in commitment by a cut in hardware, and challenging him as to what hardware should be cut, challenging him on Polaris as well. Denis was no match for Roy.[16]

The majority that Healey thought he had assembled for saving the F-111 melted away. By sheer effectiveness in Cabinet, Jenkins not only established his own authority but converted the Government – under pressure of economic necessity – to a reversal of policy which he had been advocating for the past ten years.

His position was strengthened by the fact that the Prime Minister was effectively in his power. Wilson's personal prestige had been severely dented by devaluation: having appointed a new broom at the Treasury, he had no choice but to co-operate with him – his own position would not survive the loss of a second Chancellor. Despite a complete absence of personal rapport, therefore – there was no social contact at all between the Wilson and Jenkins families during the three years that they were neighbours in Downing Street – they established a reasonable working relationship, though it had its ups and downs. Crossman, balanced fairly equally between them – personally loyal to Wilson for old times' sake, but generally with Jenkins on policy – is a good barometer. In March 1968, shortly before the Budget, Crossman – ever anxious to promote an inner Cabinet with himself a member of it – reckoned: 'At present we've got a Harold/Roy dyarchy – two extremely uncommunicative, suspicious men who are working together tolerably well, who know the Budget secrets and are keeping them to themselves.'[18] But in April Jenkins was exasperated by Wilson's habitual deviousness and lack of candour;[19] while in May, Wilson was once again 'obsessed by his

suspicions of Roy Jenkins and John Harris',[20] when Jenkins pointedly
declined to dissociate himself from an article by Cecil King in the *Mirror*
calling for an end to Wilson's leadership. In June he was 'furious' at a
speech Jenkins had made at Birmingham, 'convinced that Roy is com-
peting for the radical vote'. ('That speech . . . was deliberately intended
to put me in my place. I must show that I am stronger than him.'[21] A
week later the Prime Minister and his Chancellor were reconciled, after
what Wilson described as 'a wonderful talk';[22] and by September Wilson
was congratulating himself that he had picked the best man to succeed
Callaghan.[23] These alternating moods of co-operation and mistrust
continued throughout the life of the Government; the situation remained that Jenkins held the whip hand, and Wilson knew it.

Jenkins demonstrated his veto over the Prime Minister's economic
appointments in April 1968, when George Brown resigned from the
Government in a fit of temper and Wilson took the chance to complete
the restructuring of the administration begun in November. Michael
Stewart went back to the Foreign Office, and Wilson proposed to send
Barbara Castle to the DEA. But Jenkins would not have it. He had seen
what 'creative tension' between the Treasury and the DEA had done for
Callaghan's standing as Chancellor, and he was determined that he was
going to run the Government's economic policy himself or not at all.
Mrs Castle, though consoled with the empty title of First Secretary, had
to be content with an enlarged Ministry of Labour, renamed the Department of Employment and Productivity. The DEA maintained a
ghostly existence for another eighteen months under Peter Shore, before
it was discreetly buried. Quietly but firmly, Jenkins had preserved the
traditional prerogative of his office and his own position as the second
man in the Government. The 'Mark II' Wilson Cabinet was often said
to be led by the troika of Wilson, Jenkins and Castle (in place of Wilson,
Callaghan and Brown). But there was never any doubt that Jenkins
held more power than Mrs Castle.

Jenkins' first Budget, introduced on March 19, was a personal
triumph, despite its swingeing contents. It was brought in against the
background of a major crisis in the international money market. The
devaluation of sterling had been followed by massive speculation against
the dollar and a panic rush to buy gold. Britain was losing hundreds of
millions of pounds a day from her reserves, and the pound faced a
second devaluation which would have brought down the Government.
On 15 March, the sale of gold had to be suspended while the Central
Banks hastily agreed standby credits of $4000 to relieve the pressure.
The week before, Jenkins had already given the Cabinet a view of the

situation 'so terrifying that it was not recorded in Cabinet minutes....
This was the big stick', Crossman recorded, 'with which he ... beat
Cabinet into accepting a tremendous budget.'[24] To cut personal spending in line with public spending, he took another £923m out of the
economy in new taxation – an unprecedented figure. The targets were
for the most part traditional and indirect: drink, cigarettes, petrol, car
tax, a general increase in purchase tax, a much higher tax on betting
and gambling, and Selective Employment Tax up 50 per cent. The
innovation, however – more accurately a variation of the special levy
which Stafford Cripps had introduced in Jenkins' first Parliament, in
1948 – was a direct levy on personal incomes over £3,000 a year, on top
of income tax and surtax, beginning at 2/- in the £ between £3,000 and
£4,000, rising to 9/-.in the £ over £8,000. 'One of the harshest pieces of
personal taxation ever introduced by a Chancellor', the *Annual Register*
called it.[25] This was Jenkins harking back to the Roy Jenkins who had
written *Fair Shares for the Rich* in 1951, though this once-off levy –
expected to raise £100m – fell a long way short of the abolition of
private fortunes he had then favoured. The Budget as a whole impressed
the Cabinet and enthused the demoralized Labour benches in the
House of Commons. 'Above all', wrote Crossman, 'it was genuinely
based on socialist principle, fair in the fullest sense by really helping
people at the bottom of the scale and really taxing the wealthy. It was
a tremendous performance and for once deserved the backbenchers
rising behind him and waving their order papers.'[26]

It got a good press too, led by Peter Jay in *The Times*:

> Roy Jenkins has risen fully and magnificently to the occasion. Yesterday's
> Budget was really everything that was economically needed. It should give
> devaluation a virtually certain guarantee of success....
>
>   Britain has now beyond any shadow of doubt done everything required to
> correct the fundamental weakness of the economy and the balance of pay-
> ments.[27]

But Jay was rejoicing too soon. Jenkins could bask only briefly in his
March success. Through 1968 the trade figures remained depressing.
At the end of April, Crossman found the Chancellor 'a very worried
man.... "We aren't making much headway", he said, "and the money
which should have been sucked back to London still isn't coming in." '[28]
Imports were still rising faster than exports. The August figures were
'disastrous', and contingency plans were drawn up for import quotas.[29]
September and October were better, but November brought another
crisis: when the Germans refused to revalue the mark and the French
were thought to be about to devalue the franc, the pound once again

came under pressure. Jenkins had to fly back from a 'traumatic'[30] meeting of Finance Ministers in Bonn to introduce another (the fourth) package of emergency measures, squeezing a further £250m from personal consumption by taxation (petrol, cigarettes, spirits again, plus 10 per cent on all rates of purchase tax) and hire purchase restrictions, and controlling imports by an ingenious new device requiring traders to deposit 50 per cent of their value before customs would release them. This was the lowest point of Jenkins' Chancellorship, the darkest hour of what he later called 'a long dark Arctic night'.[31] A year after devaluation, there still seemed to have been nothing gained by all the sacrifices. The need for yet further measures deeply disillusioned Labour's own battered supporters, who abstained in large numbers in the key divisions, and seriously damaged national confidence even in the 'Mark II' Government. The polls showed Labour twenty points or more behind the Tories. At the beginning of December there was a wave of rumours that Wilson or Jenkins or both had resigned, even that the Queen had abdicated! Wilson, at his best with his back to the wall, brushed aside calls for a coalition and the Government soldiered on, still walking a tightrope from one month's figures to the next. In January 1969 the deficit fell to £10m, but in February it was back to £64m. In April, in his second Budget, Jenkins had to take another £200m out of purchasing power, though he managed it this time by less directly painful means, mainly Corporation Tax and SET.

This fifth deflationary bite, however, was the last. During the summer of 1969 the figures began to come right, as exports at last took off. Appropriately enough, Jenkins had just opened an Export Services Exhibition at Earl's Court, on 9 September, when the August results reached him from the Treasury, showing a surplus of £40m. Having finally turned, the tide was soon flowing strongly, and the surplus for the last five months of 1969 easily outweighed the deficit in the first seven. December alone chalked up a surplus of £350m. Jenkins had staked everything on getting a strong balance of payments. It had taken far longer than he or anyone expected. For eighteen months he had lived a nightmare. But he had kept his nerve; and now, on what he called 'the central economic front' of his Chancellorship, he had won. Having set himself a clear and limited target, he had characteristically achieved it.

Jenkins' interest in problem-solving combines with his knowledge of British history to give him an unusual fascination with the machinery of Government. He takes a great pride in having, as Home Secretary and

Roy Jenkins aged two, Christmas 1922.

Arthur Jenkins in 1935, the year he entered Parliament.

Roy and Jennifer Jenkins, with their parents, after their wedding at the Savoy Chapel in January 1945. Hattie Jenkins is on Jennifer's left, with Sir Parker Morris.

Dr Benes, the exiled President of Czechoslovakia, speaks at the Oxford Union in March 1940. As Secretary, Roy Jenkins is seated in front of the President, Madron Seligman. Behind Benes can be seen Tony Crosland (left) and Edward Heath.

Jenkins addressing dockers in Oxford Union style at the Central Southwark by-election, April 1948.

Hugh Gaitskell speaking against unilateral disarmament at the Labour Party Conference, 1960: 'Fight and fight and fight again . . .'

Jenkins speaking in favour of joining the Common Market at the Labour Party Conference, 1962: 'Let us go in with hope and confidence . . .'

Jenkins with Clement Attlee, 1959.

The Chancellor of the Exchequer with his advisers at a meeting of the OECD in Paris in 1969: from left to right, Sir Douglas Allen (Permanent Private Secretary), John Harris and David Dowler.

The Chancellor of the Exchequer at his desk in the Treasury.

Jenkins at East Hendred in 1969 with Jennifer and their two younger children, Cynthia (then 17) and Edward (14).

Jenkins playing tennis at East Hendred in 1976.

The Opposition Front Bench after the 1970 General Election: from left to right, Barbara Castle, Denis Healey, Harold Wilson, Roy Jenkins, James Callaghan.

Jenkins with Jeremy Thorpe and Edward Heath during the EEC Referendum campaign in May 1975.

The President of the EEC Commission with US President Jimmy Carter in 1978.

The 'Gang of Four' – Bill Rodgers, Shirley Williams, Roy Jenkins and David Owen – with some of the 80,000 letters received after the setting up of the Council for Social Democracy in February 1981.

A tale of two by-elections: Jenkins has a quiet word in a working men's club in Warrington, July 1981 (left), and steps out to meet the electors of Hillhead, March 1982.

David Owen applauds Jenkins' closing speech to the SDP's first annual Conference in October 1981.

as Chancellor, held two of the three great offices of State below the
Prime Ministership itself – a pride not unrelated to the knowledge that
Asquith had held the same two offices, in the same order, on his way to
Downing Street. After the 1970 election, from the perspective of opposition, he wrote for the *Observer* and the *Sunday Times* two thoughtful
inside views of what it was like being Chancellor, comparing it – in a
way that it would occur to no other contemporary politician to attempt
– with the experience of being Home Secretary.

He contrasted the intellectual self-confidence and creative informality
of the Treasury (where Christian names were used) with the much
greater defensiveness and formality of the Home Office (where everyone
was referred to strictly by surname). More seriously, he compared the
way decisions have to be taken in each department. The climate of the
Home Office 'is one of tropical storms that blow up with speed and
violence out of a blue sky, dominate the political landscape for a short
time, and then disappear as suddenly as they arrived.' (He cited the
Maidstone birching case and the escape from Dartmoor of Frank Mitch-
ell, the 'mad axeman'.) Meanwhile there is a heavy permanent work-
load of administration and legislation. 'The climate of the Treasury, on
the other hand, during most of my time there, was that of a long dark
arctic winter, only slowly melting into a tentative spring. Changes,
whether pleasant or unpleasant, could usually be foreseen at least a few
weeks ahead, and were part of a general ebb and flow of events rather
than some sudden unexpected occurrence.'

> The special burdensomeness of the Chancellor's job ... arises out of three
> special factors: the endemic nature of Treasury crisis; the size of the stakes if
> things go wrong; and the amount of time which has to be devoted to dealing
> with one's colleagues. Abstract these factors, in other words postulate a calm
> situation with the economy going well and the rest of the Government on
> holiday, and the Chancellor's job would be peculiarly light, unless it were
> the period of run-up to the Budget. It would be difficult to find more than
> a couple of hours' work a day....[32]

Jenkins goes on to say that of course these conditions could never
prevail for long in the Treasury. 'Even if no other crisis intervened,
other Ministers would return from holiday' – at which point the Chancellor is fully engaged in every aspect of Government policy: 'He has to
attend all major ministerial meetings, and nearly always be either
protagonist or antagonist.'[32] But the question of the hours Jenkins
worked as Chancellor has become something of an issue, fostered by
Harold Wilson, who has become fond of telling interviewers that Jenkins

always 'knocked off at seven o'clock'. Jenkins himself, in the *Observer*, thought that he worked 'somewhat shorter hours than my immediate predecessor [Callaghan] but considerably longer ones than my predecessor but one [Maudling].'

> The hours were testing but not killing. It was only after I had been there for five months that I first had a day completely free from Treasury work. Subsequently I avoided such continuous over-application. Even so, I habitually worked on boxes of official papers or wrote speeches for at least six hours of each of the two weekend days, and from Monday to Friday I did something like a 12-hour day. But I very rarely worked after midnight, and still more rarely did I start, even in bed, before 7.30 a.m.[30]

It is true that Jenkins makes a point of keeping a definite portion of his time free of work – not merely for social indulgence but for essential relaxation, to keep himself sane and retain his sense of perspective. He believes strongly that tired and harassed men do not make good decisions, and that those who let their job take them over merely make work for themselves. Of Stafford Cripps' habit of doing four hours' solid paperwork before breakfast every day he asked in 1972, 'What on earth did he do? It is not necessary, particularly for a man of quick mind and weak body, to steal this additional four hours from sleep or leisure for the administration of the Treasury.'[33]

Jenkins' body is not weak – his health has always been excellent – and his mind is very quick. What those who criticize his hours overlook is his exceptional power of working rapidly, economically and decisively. In this respect he does closely resemble Asquith, who prided himself, in a phrase that could equally apply to Jenkins, on possessing 'energy under the guise of lethargy'.[34] Jenkins has the same ability to get through in an hour work that would take most men two or three hours: not only does this leave *time* for relaxation, but after such concentrated effort, he *needs* it. Even in the leisure hours which his power of concentration allows him, however, Jenkins could not possibly be called lazy; he is easily bored, is competitive in everything that he does, and he has a horror of wasting time which he likes to measure out precisely. Reviewing the second volume of Crossman's diary in 1976, he found little to quarrel with except the suggestion that he lacked 'industriousness' – a quality which he thought, characteristically, Crossman confused with 'freneticism'.[35]

Another thing he denied was that his country cottage was 'ramshackle'. In 1966, when he became Home Secretary, he and Jennifer had bought what is actually a very neat whitewashed vicarage at East

Hendred, south of Oxford (five miles from Asquith's country home at Sutton Courtney). Here there was room for a tennis court, more private than the one in Ladbroke Square; there was also a lawn which they gave over to croquet, a game whose tactical subtlety makes a deep appeal to Jenkins and at which he has become devilishly good. The children were now growing up: in 1967 Charles was eighteen, Cynthia sixteen and Edward thirteen.* They went to private schools, though when there was some bad publicity about Labour Cabinet Ministers taking advantage for their own children of schools the party was pledged to abolish, Charles left Winchester 'at his own request' to go for his last terms to Holland Park Comprehensive. One reason for sending them to boarding schools was that both parents were working. Jennifer was now Chairman of the Consumers' Association and also a Central London magistrate (though she had to give this up while her husband was Home Secretary). When he became Chancellor, they valued East Hendred more than ever. They moved reluctantly into number 11 Downing Street, but Jennifer in particular found it 'gloomy and inconvenient' as a family home, and 'absolutely hated' living there.[36] She collected prints and portraits of former Chancellors to try to restore some sense of history to the house, which had been hideously hacked about inside. But even with his distinguished predecessors looking down at him, Jenkins did not like living on top of his job.

Any idea that Jenkins, because of his insistence on keeping some time to himself, was not – metaphorically speaking – 'on top of his department' is amply disproved by his record as the most effective Chancellor of recent years. It contains an element of truth, in so far as he did not try personally to master every aspect of the department. But it is one of his greatest strengths as a Minister, not a weakness, that he concentrates upon priorities and is able to keep the broad view always in his mind without cluttering it with inessential detail. If Crossman, as Secretary of State for Social Services, thought him, as he often did, ill-briefed on the intricacies of pensions, that was because pensions are, to the Treasury, relatively marginal. More than most Ministers, Jenkins is good at delegating to his juniors. He was successful in accomplishing his major task precisely because he left the minor ones to others.

In his *Observer* article in 1971, he described the special pressure of a Minister's work – as usual, by elegant analogy. He first compared the business of writing with walking up a mountain: the writer works at his

* Today (1983) Charles works for the Economist Intelligence Unit, Cynthia at a Law Centre in Birmingham, and Edward is at the Bar. Cynthia has recently given birth to Jenkins', first grandchild.

own pace, generating his own momentum, and pausing for breath when he needs to. 'There are no onlookers to mock his periods of ineffective immobility.'

> Ministerial work, on the other hand, is much more like skiing down a slalom course. The momentum is all on one's side, provided it can be controlled. There is little difficulty about generating the will to proceed. There is rapid and relentless movement from one event to another. . . .
>
> This pattern has the advantage that each event comes up with such rapidity that there is very little danger of falling through hesitation or over-anxiety. They have to be taken as they come, at the run; and a lot of things are better done this way. . . . The disadvantages . . . are first, that if one falls it is very uncomfortable. The speed ensures that. So does the crowd of spectators which lines the piste. . . . Second, and more important, there is the difficulty of preserving perspective and direction. This is one reason why it is desirable to have fairly frequent pauses for reflection between the runs, to keep in touch with a wide variety of people who are interested in much more than the technique, and to have some advisers who will inconveniently ask 'why' and not merely provide answers to the question 'how'.[30]

Even so, it is a marked feature of Jenkins' style that he likes to work through a few close and trusted advisers, to an extent that in 1964–70 it caused some muttering in Whitehall. Not only did he take John Harris with him from the Home Office to the Treasury as his ever-present personal assistant; he also managed to carry with him into both these departments his private secretary from the Department of Aviation, David Dowler, with whom he formed an exceptionally close relationship, most unusual between a Minister and a career civil servant. Dowler, then in his late thirties, had already been picked out as one of the high fliers of his generation – 'an administrator of remarkable vigour, skill and decisiveness', according to *The Times*,[37] but in addition erudite, witty and caustic; he became much more than a private secretary to Jenkins, rather another personal adviser, almost as much a loyal partisan as Harris. Between the two of them – and Dick Taverne, whom he also persuaded Wilson to allow to follow him from the Home Office, where he was Under-Secretary, to the Treasury, where he was first Minister of State and then Financial Secretary – there was some ground for his colleagues' feeling that Jenkins surrounded himself in his successive offices with the same comfortably protective little clique. Nor did the departments themselves altogether like his way of working. Jenkins dislikes big meetings, and preferred to deal only with the two or three absolutely necessary people – with the result that some quite senior civil servants barely saw him at all. Once, Sir Douglas Allen himself, the

Permanent Secretary at the Treasury, found that the only way he could get a real talk with the Chancellor was by booking the seat next to him on a flight to Washington. His reputation in Whitehall is thus ambivalent: while those who had the experience of working closely with him generally admired him very greatly, others found him remote. He had favourites, and that was not popular.

David Dowler died, of a blood infection, in January 1970, soon after transferring, for career reasons, back to the Home Office. Jenkins' obituary tribute, published in *The Times*, picked out, among other qualities, the sense of priorities which made Dowler especially congenial to himself:

> He had one of the best and most alert critical minds that I have ever encountered. He could of course always spot the weak point in an argument when he was looking for it. But that is not a unique gift. What was almost unique was that he hardly ever failed to register the weak point even when he was not consciously looking for it, when our attention was engaged on something quite different and when the issue might quite easily have been decided without concern or consideration. Yet he was never in danger of regarding criticism as an end in itself. He knew instinctively what was important and what was not: he was always looking for a solution and not an impasse.[38]

To Dowler must belong a considerable part of Jenkins' success in his three offices between 1965 and 1969.

If the Treasury did not take Jenkins' style altogether to its heart, he nevertheless left his mark on the department in a number of ways, aside from policy. He failed, admittedly, to persuade his senior officials to follow his example in adopting more sensible hours of work: they prided themselves on 'working far into every evening as a matter of course', and Jenkins could not stop them.[39] But he had some success in breaking down the department's obsessive secrecy. His decision, in his first Budget, to publish a summary of the forecast on which it was based was one step forward; another was his decision the following year to publish an annual projection of Government spending for 3-5 years ahead. Jenkins also went further than any of his predecessors in taking his colleagues into his confidence in advance of the Budget, by holding a series of bilateral talks with individual Ministers. Skilfully handled, this served the good political purpose of neutralizing opposition; but of course it was also risky, since it gave more opportunity for opposition to develop than when the Chancellor's proposals were sprung on the Cabinet in the traditional way at the last moment.

Jenkins made a number of structural changes within the Treasury to give higher priority to the study of future taxation policy and fiscal strategy in general. More important was his success in starting to wind up the sterling area. This was very much his personal initiative. For at least ten years past, he had been urging that the continuing status of the pound as a world currency was another post-imperial burden which Britain had no longer the economic strength to keep up, but which contributed significantly to the pound's weakness. The responsibility of being a reserve currency was not something Britain could pull out of overnight; but in 1968 he negotiated the Basle agreement whereby some fifty other countries helped to share the burden of carrying the world's sterling balances, thus easing some of the pressure of Britain's balance of payments problems on the pound. (Jenkins was firmly against Enoch Powell's melodramatic free market solution of simply allowing the pound to float – 'I think I see the Tiber foaming with much chaos', he told the Labour Party Conference at Blackpool, a few months after Powell's notorious immigration speech.)[40]

Jenkins was also unusual among modern Chancellors – Maudling was another exception in this respect – in that he wrote much of his own Budget speeches: further proof that he was very much the master in his department. His Budgets were for this reason greatly admired as – both technically and structurally – exceptionally well-crafted and polished productions. 'A masterly minor performance again', Crossman wrote after he had unveiled his 1969 speech to the Cabinet, 'each item beautifully prepared by Roy and beautifully rehearsed.'[41] It is a rare ability to be able to fashion detailed economic proposals into an elegant form. But it was not simply literary skill. Beneath the polished surface lay a hard intellectual commitment to ensuring that the fundamental argument was sound, as Jenkins himself illustrated in his tribute to David Dowler:

> Before the last budget there was a passage in the economic analysis which, through successive drafts, we could not get right. It was not the policy nor the appropriate phrases but the structure of the argument which would not fall into place. One evening David announced that he would come into the office at five next morning and making use of four uninterrupted hours try to get the points in their correct logical sequence. He did precisely that. Thereafter we had no trouble with the structure of the argument.[38]

This sort of perfectionism extended to Jenkins' delivery in the House. 'He had obviously prepared and rehearsed the speech', Crossman commented again in 1969, 'because he had said it would last for two hours and twenty minutes and in fact it lasted exactly two hours and twenty-three. A man can only know that if he has read it aloud beforehand. He dealt with Nabarro with perfect skill,* and that too was something he had obviously practised in front of a mirror and got absolutely right.'[42] The capacity for taking infinite pains for big occasions goes to the heart of Jenkins' political style. It is partly the historian in him that takes performance on the floor of the House of Commons so seriously; he believes that historically that is where the political battle is won and lost.

> Parliamentary speaking ... is, under the British system, of vital importance to a Minister. If he cannot defend his policies with at least a modicum of *élan*, he is under a very grave handicap. ... There is not a single Prime Minister of the century ... who has not achieved a dominance of some sort over the Commons, and has not used this as a method of imprinting his personality upon the country. ... Nor can civil servants, even the most dedicated and talented, construct speeches that are either effectively polemical or carry a worthwhile personal imprint. This is one task that a Minister, if he regards the occasion as important enough, must do for himself.[30]

This belief was the reason why Jenkins – at Aviation over the TSR-2 cancellation, at the Home Office over George Blake and the Court Lees approved school, and at the Treasury in his Budget speeches and on other set piece occasions – always came to the House meticulously prepared and repeatedly wiped the floor with his opponents. This was despite the fact that he 'hates' making big speeches. Before his first Budget speech Crossman, sitting next to him, felt him 'trembling like a leaf'.[26] But, as with all great performers, the nerves are essential to the performance. Anyone who watches Jenkins closely can see that, beneath the urbane manner, he is very highly-strung: before any speech, during any interview, he crosses and uncrosses his legs, wrings his hands, examines his fingernails, plays with a pen. His familiar hand gestures while speaking are a semi-controlled release of the tension that is within him. But he thrives on the danger of speech-making, particularly in the electric atmosphere of the House of Commons on a big occasion, with the opposition massed in front of him and supporters cheering him on from behind. As Chancellor, even though until the last few months in a desperately beleaguered Government, he never failed to give them something to cheer, as Crossman always vividly recorded. In May 1968 he 'demolished' Iain Macleod at the end of a guillotine debate on the Finance Bill;[43] in November he 'pulverised' Macleod again in the Queen's Speech debate.[44] He 'had a great triumph with his speech on

---

* Sir Gerald Nabarro had alleged that the Chancellor intended to increase car tax (and claimed the credit when he did not).

the Letter of Intent approved by the IMF' in June 1969;[45] and in
November he 'trounced' Anthony Barber 'to smithereens' when Barber
accused the Government of rigging the export figures.[46] Even Harold
Wilson devoted a page of his memoir of the Labour Government to
what he called 'as neat a job of parliamentary annihilation as had been
witnessed for years.... Roy Jenkins tore [Barber] apart, calmly and
clinically.... Mr Barber had barely recovered a year later when he
himself became Chancellor.'[47]

Jenkins' authority in the House led naturally to his being seen as a
rival for Wilson's job and his predestined heir – despite the fact that he
had never had any base of support in the party outside Parliament and,
as Chancellor, was continually having to ask for sacrifices that affronted
its deepest convictions of what a Labour Government was for. His
reputation was entirely as an indispensable man of government, but his
party credentials remained, to many party members, suspect. For his
own part, Jenkins' view of the party was as ambivalent as the party's
view of him: some of his friends date the beginning of his final disenchantment to this period. He was greatly encouraged by the loyal
support he always received from his own constituency party in Stechford; but he was often depressed by the refusal of the most vocal sections
of the wider party to see the economic necessity, as a condition of any
further socialist advance, of what he was trying to do. His response was
the same as Gaitskell's. He would not pander to the party's self-deceiv-
ing prejudices with sentimental bromides and the distracting search for
scapegoats that were the mark of Wilson's leadership: he was determined at every opportunity to confront it with reality. At the moment
of deepest gloom, at the 1968 Party Conference at Blackpool, when the
delegates threw out the Government's prices and incomes policy by a
majority of 5-1, he faced them with courage and skill:

> I do say to you, therefore, that it is not some malevolent quirk of international
> bankers which makes a balance of payments surplus necessary for this
> country, it is the hard facts of life....
>   If you want to have less to do with bankers, if you want fewer IMF visits
> here, the answer is straightforward: help us to get out of debt. [Applause] It
> is no good urging independence and denying us the policies to that end.[40]

The Labour party respected Jenkins, but it could not love him. He
still, even as a prospective leader, refused to adopt its millenarian
rhetoric or modify his social life to suit its expectations. His image did
not worry him, he told Anne Scott-James in an unapologetic interview
in 1968, 'because the old cloth cap idea is dead.' 'The hairshirt attitude

doesn't make one a better or more honest politician', he told her. 'It's important to see as many people outside politics as possible.... As for Smoothiechops [*Private Eye*'s nickname for him], it's not the name I would choose for myself but it doesn't wound me deeply.' Anne Scott-James concluded that Jenkins' skin seemed of just the right thickness: 'The word I'd use is well-adjusted.' Her article was headlined 'Roy Jenkins: Is he too good to be *true*?'[48]

This swelling chorus of newspaper admiration was personally gratifying, but politically dangerous. It fed, for one thing, a streak of vanity in him, tending to exaggerate a native pomposity of manner. (Anne Scott-James did a second interview with him in 1970, noting that he was now more 'solemn and formidable' than in 1968: he was now the second man in the Government – 'And he looks it'.)[31] More seriously, the more the press praised him, the more he became the hero of the cultivated, liberal middle class, the more the Labour party distrusted him and the less it was prepared to have him foisted on it as a future leader. So long as Labour was the Government and he was Chancellor of the Exchequer he held a position of great authority, with every prospect, despite the gut feeling of the party, of succeeding to the premiership if anything had happened to Wilson. In the Parliamentary party he had a growing body of devoted supporters: younger men of the 1966 intake like David Marquand, John Mackintosh, Brian Walden and David Owen – all somewhat in Jenkins' image, right-wing 'intellectuals' – looked to him as their leader. They had entered the House, if anything, as Croslandites, having read *The Future of Socialism*; but Jenkins' faster advancement and superior performance had made them Jenkinsites. They were for the most part undisguisedly anti-Wilson, who in return was equally suspicious of them, seeing in them the old CDS re-formed around a new leader. (Only to Owen of this talented group did he give a job.) To these declared Jenkinsites could be added a large number of members of the solid centre-right who admired his competence – so long as the party was in office. As soon as it was back in opposition, however, and other, more political issues replaced the balance of payments and the pound, this wider support ebbed away to candidates more in tune with Labour's rediscovered proletarianism. The 'cloth cap idea' was *not* dead.

Crossman asked himself several times in these years whether 'this elegant, patrician, easy-going, tennis-playing, aloof, detached dilettante' could ever be a Labour leader.[49] His answers varied, but he never changed his view of Jenkins as aloof and somehow detached from a Government in which he was number two. In July 1969, for instance, discussing who was 'in' and who outside the inner circle: 'Roy is perfectly in but he is not psychologically and personally in with us. He still remains aloof, the Chancellor in No. 11, biding his time, calculating, with his own friends, his own society.'[50] Crossman had a strong sense that Jenkins (with John Harris his 'evil genius')[51] was looking beyond the success of the present Government, looking to his own career. 'Roy may want to have a record of upright Chancellorship for his survival', he wrote in October 1968. 'He will still be a young man in the next Government or the next Government but one. For all I know there may be a break-up of the two-party system.'[52] This was shrewd, up to a point. It is certainly true that Jenkins felt semi-detached from the Labour party, wholly detached from Harold Wilson except in so far as they were forced to work together, and as conscious as any other member of the Cabinet that the Government was not going to go down in history as a great reforming administration. In the circumstances, there was nothing for him to do but to plough his own furrow as straight as he could; there cannot but be an element of self-interest in any politician wanting to do his own job as well as possible, but Jenkins believed, rightly, that his particular job of getting the balance of payments right was of supreme importance for the country, besides being the one unquestionable achievement on which the Government was likely to be able to go back to the electorate for a renewed mandate in 1970. To this extent Crossman was right. But 'easy-going', 'dilettante', 'detached' in the sense of being emotionally uninvolved in the crises and the daily dramas of political life – Jenkins was none of these things, as Crossman's own record occasionally shows. In November 1969 Crossman caught him out at Cabinet over employers' National Insurance contributions. 'He had started off tense and querulous and it suddenly occurred to me how feminine, petulant, unwise and hysterical he is. . . . Roy was once more plunging about like a delicate, highly-bred horse, angry, indignant and frustrated by this Social Services Secretary and his staff. . . . On both occasions he'd humiliated himself utterly, first before his political colleagues and then before his own staff and mine. He is enormously sensitive and must feel this desperately.'[53] This was a truer insight behind Jenkins' mask of effortless superiority. It is only kept in place by an effort, and when it slips, it can slip badly. The real Roy Jenkins, of whose existence the general public has very little inkling, is passionate, emotional, highly volatile and surprisingly insecure – temperamentally a gambler investing more nervous energy than is always wise on every roll of the political dice. If racial stereotypes have any validity, Ian Trethowan's already quoted observation about Jenkins' tennis is very accurate: 'The Englishman in him may just be playing for a little gentle exercise. The Celt ... wants to win.'⁵ So, in politics, the aloof Englishman may have been taking the long view, 'sitting in an ivory tower with John Harris and David Dowler, cut off from the rest of the world, planning Roy's political future',⁵¹ as Crossman believed; but the Celt had a much more simple, primitive desire to win the battle for the balance of payments, and felt desperately tense until he had done so. The real Roy Jenkins is much more 'Celtic' in this sense than he looks or sounds.

The failure of Jenkins' Chancellorship was his failure to control incomes. This was a vital part of the post-devaluation strategy of shifting resources out of domestic consumption into exports; but it was the part which most directly affronted the trade unions, challenging the very reason for their existence. For a year or so after 1964, cajoled by George Brown in the first enthusiasm of a Labour Government, they had gone along with a voluntary policy reasonably well; but in the July measures of 1966, the Government had imposed a six-month wages and salaries freeze, followed by a further period of 'severe restraint'. By the time Jenkins went to the Treasury in November 1967 the unions' good will was exhausted; yet it was more than ever essential to keep incomes under control, if the bankers were to be kept happy. Jenkins' 1968 Budget was therefore predicated on a statutory $3\frac{1}{2}$ per cent ceiling on increases in wages, salaries and dividends, except where justified by increased productivity, to last at least eighteen months, with the freedom thereafter to renew. It fell to Barbara Castle to get the necessary legislation through, which she loyally undertook to do; and there was formed between the Chancellor and the new Secretary of State for Employment and Productivity – hitherto known as a fiery left-winger – a surprising but remarkably close alliance. The trouble was that the policy had no friends, even in the Cabinet. It was forced through the Commons in July 1968 against the combined opposition of the Labour left and the Tories (the former outraged, the latter taking opportunistic advantage of the Government's unpopularity); it was overwhelmingly rejected by both the TUC and Labour party Conferences, and by the end of the year it was generally admitted that the norm was politically unsustainable.

'It's fair to say', wrote Crossman, 'that Roy never believed in the policy, but he realized at that moment that he couldn't take the lid off the pressure cooker because the mere removal of the lid is in itself dangerous.'⁵⁴ In his 1969 Budget, Jenkins had to announce that the

1968 powers would not be renewed. He was still alarmed by the danger
of an inflationary spiral when the lid came off, and tried to keep open
the option of taking further powers in the autumn if necessary; but he
effectively surrendered that possibility when he agreed to support Barbara Castle's industrial relations legislation instead. There was no way
the Government was going to be able to take on the unions on two issues
at once. The outcome was that they gave up any serious attempt to
control incomes, and were then defeated on trade union reform, ending
up with neither. In December 1969, with wages out of control, Jenkins
could announce no more than a 'declaratory' norm of $2\frac{1}{2}$–$4\frac{1}{2}$ per cent,
in the knowledge that no-one would stick to it. Between the last quarter
of 1969 and the last quarter of 1970 wage rates and average earnings
rose by 13 per cent, compensating for some of the earlier misery and
helping to put Labour within sight of winning the General Election in
1970, but undermining a good deal of what had been achieved in other
directions since 1967, and storing up inflation for the 1970s. It was a
serious failure, for which Jenkins bears the responsibility and to which
he contributed by weakness and a critical misjudgement; but the political forces which defeated Labour's incomes policy — the unions, the left
and particularly the Tory Opposition – can take little credit from their
victory.

The Government's bruising confrontation with the unions over Barbara Castle's White Paper *In Place of Strife* was another episode from
which Jenkins emerged ingloriously. It was not in origin his Bill, but he
was persuaded to go along with it as an alternative to statutory wage
restraint, and once committed to it, he argued strongly in favour of
putting it through quickly, in order to fill the gap left in his Budget by
the dropping of incomes policy. Proposals to tackle the problem of
unofficial strikes by giving the Government the power to impose a 28-
day cooling-off period and the power to enforce a settlement in inter-
union disputes (which was all the Bill contained in the way of 'penal'
legislation) really had nothing to do with the Budget. But Jenkins went
out of his way to identify himself publicly with the Bill by insisting on
announcing it himself in his 1969 Budget speech. From the point of view
of getting the Bill through, this was a mistake, because it made it look
like part of the Chancellor's 'two years' hard slog', imposed by the IMF.
('Law Courts do not make exports', was Vic Feather's response.) From
Jenkins' personal point of view it was still more of a mistake, contradicting the image of the aloof man coolly calculating his own interest,
as Peter Jenkins wrote in his book on the whole saga:

It was an odd political decision ... by a Minister who was beginning to get the reputation for "keeping his head below the parapet". Did the IMF care who announced the policy? By making the announcement himself Roy Jenkins committed himself to the short Bill to a degree which he was subsequently to regret.... Nobody was asking him to go to the lengths of mingling his blood publicly with Barbara Castle's. He was exceeding by far the terms of their demarcation agreement [by which each supported the other's policies].... Chivalry to a lady colleague was verging upon the quixotic. It was a political error for an ambitious man.[55]

As opposition to the Bill mounted both in the Cabinet and in the Parliamentary party, posing the most serious challenge to Wilson's authority in five years, Jenkins – having committed himself to Mrs Castle – found himself by the same token committed to the Prime Minister. In the Cabinet the rebels were openly led by Jim Callaghan, backed by his old supporter Tony Crosland – leading to speculation that Crosland was hoping to get the Treasury if Callaghan succeeded in toppling Wilson. But if there was one man Jenkins would 'fight to the death' (as he had told Crossman the year before) to prevent from replacing Wilson, it was Callaghan. There had been no love lost between them since their exchange of jobs in 1967: Jenkins was appalled by Callaghan's illiberalism as Home Secretary, and came close to despising the man. 'You know', he told Crossman, 'there is nobody in politics I can remember and no case I can think of in history where a man combined such a powerful political personality with so little intelligence.'[56] Intelligence in the sense of keeping his ear to the grass roots of the Labour movement, however, Callaghan had in abundance, and it was soon clear that Barbara Castle's Bill could not be got through the Parliamentary party. Wilson and Mrs Castle fought almost to the last, Wilson all but staking the survival of the Government on it and pulling out all the stops in demanding loyalty to himself; but at the crucial Cabinet on 17 June 1969 they were isolated, as Minister after Minister bowed to Bob Mellish's advice that he could not get the Bill through the House. If there were going to be any resignations, it was Wilson who would have to go, leaving Callaghan his undisputed successor. Throughout this meeting Jenkins sat silent, not supporting the rebels but withholding his support from Wilson and the ally to whom he had hitherto been loyal, Mrs Castle. At the end, in Peter Jenkins' words, he 'slid elegantly onto the fence'.[57] Looking back six months later, Crossman still thought this was the decisive moment when Wilson realized the game was up.[58] Of Jenkins' final defection, it can only be said that it was realistic; it was not heroic. *In Place of Strife* was an issue he

misjudged from the start. For it, he had given up the option of a renewal
of incomes policy; his argument in favour of putting the Bill through
quickly, without consultation and before the union conferences, proved
exactly the wrong way to go about it – there might have been a better
chance of success with a gentler approach; he over-committed himself
personally to a Bill which was not primarily his concern; and finally, he
backed down, when it came to the crunch, from the commitment he
had entered into, seriously damaging his reputation for unimpeachable
integrity. This sequence of errors calls in question his political skill
(though not as much as it does Wilson's, usually considered the subtlest
of political operators). It also lends support to the view that he was too
absorbed in his own department to give sufficient weight to the political
restraints within which the Government had to work in other fields. He
was out of touch with the party.

Nevertheless, as the next election began to cast its shadow, it was
Jenkins who was seen to hold the party's future in his hands. Towards
the end of 1969 it was clear that the balance of payments was coming
into healthy surplus, and that that must be the basis of the Government's
appeal to the country. Jenkins was personally determined that his
hard-won victory should not be thrown away in an irresponsible pre-
election boom, and the Cabinet had no choice but to agree. 'It's quite
true', Crossman quoted Barbara Castle supporting him in September.
'We must simply go for the balance of payments because any other
policy would be seen through and would fail. There are no gimmicks
we can use.'[59] At the party Conference in October, Jenkins took pleasure
in reciting the statistics of success, but insisted that this was 'no reason
for premature relaxation. . . . We can and shall win on the basis of real
achievement and not on a bogus boom.'[60] The opinion polls were
beginning to give some support to this optimism: the Tories' lead was
down to single figures.

Still, his colleagues increasingly saw the Chancellor's coming Budget
as the factor that could win or lose them the election, and felt themselves
helpless to influence it. While obliged to accept his broad strategy of
'responsible' stewardship, several members of the Cabinet – Crosland,
Crossman, Peter Shore, even Barbara Castle, her instincts reasserting
themselves against Jenkins' caution – and many more of the Parliamentary party, anxious for their seats, persuaded themselves that he could
surely risk a few vote-winning goodies in the form of reflationary tax-
cuts. As Jenkins kept his own counsel, Crossman chafed with frustration:

He can be cautious and conventional and keep his reputation as Chancellor, making an election defeat absolutely certain and keeping himself in a position to seize the leadership afterwards, or he can conceivably take the other risk and have a more expansionist budget, which could give us a chance of election victory but could also ruin his reputation if it went wrong.[61]

Crossman even wondered whether Jenkins *wanted* to win the election, or whether he was not calculating that he would have a better chance of succeeding Wilson after a defeat. 'I . . . think he feels that if the election is a success, the whole thing will continue in the same way with Harold and Jim at the top and Roy as number three.' He discussed what was to be done with Barbara Castle, Peter Shore, Nicholas Kaldor and Thomas Balogh.

> We decided that we had to persuade Roy that his future depends on a really good budget, that a high-minded Iron Chancellor's budget would ruin his chances of the leadership of the party. This I think to be true. In one sense Roy is in such a weak position with the party, so remote from it, that there would be a tremendous revulsion against him if he produced a budget which couldn't win the election.[62]

A few days later Crossman was wondering whether Jenkins could be bribed with the promise of the Foreign Office if Labour won![63] From his diary in these first few months of 1970 one gets the impression of the whole Government – the Prime Minister as much as any of them – nervously in suspense, simultaneously fascinated and infuriated by the spectacle of the upright Chancellor quietly deciding their fate. ('Roy, don't be a Stafford Cripps', Mellish begged him.)[64] They all felt uncomfortably in the power of 'this strange inscrutable young man, this extraordinary mixture of ingenuousness, feminine petulance and iron determination.'[62]

In the event, Jenkins' political judgement proved better than theirs. On 14 April he brought in an impeccably responsible Budget, giving away only £220m, mainly in tax relief to the lower paid and other needy groups, taking two million people out of tax altogether. ('Correct, prim and proper', Crossman called it, but also 'positively socialist.')[65] There was as he had foreshadowed no strong stimulus to expansion, on the ground that the wages boom was already giving a substantial boost to demand. If further stimulus were needed, he argued, making a virtue of his caution, more could be done later; better too little at this stage than too much. The press response was mixed. 'A political non-event' (*Financial Times*);[66] 'Almost too cautious' (The *Guardian*);[67] 'to be frank, a dull budget' (*Daily Telegraph*);[68] on the other hand, the *Sun* hailed 'An Honest Budget',[69] and the *Daily Mirror* echoed 'Yes – It's an Honest

Budget – and Fair . . . It is not a Bribing Budget'.[70] One thing the papers were agreed on was that an early election could now be ruled out. In fact Wilson was itching to go to the country at the earliest favourable moment; and the national reception of the Budget, measured in the opinion polls, gave him encouragement. For the first time since 1967, Labour moved into a small lead over the Tories. 'It has become evident', Crossman admitted on 23 April, contradicting all his previous forebodings, 'that not having an election budget might have been electorally the cleverest thing to do. It is clear that Roy's posture has paid off.'[71]

There is still argument over whether Jenkins' Budget was economically right. It is said that the forecast on which it was based actually overstated the demand already in the economy, so that he could have safely risked a stronger stimulus which might have won the election for Labour and might, more importantly, have averted the recession of 1971–2 and thus made unnecessary the wildly inflationary measures which Anthony Barber took to get out of it. On the other hand, Jenkins felt strongly that he must do nothing to endanger the balance of payments, which was Labour's one clear election-winning card, its dearly-bought platform for export-led growth in the second term. The overall surplus was not yet proof against an aberrant bad figure (as the May figure, unluckily, was to show), and he did not think he could take any risks. On the political side, it is argued that his caution made voters feel that there must be more wrong with the economy than he was letting on (particularly when Wilson did call an early election). But the opinion polls would seem to show that his refusal to buy votes struck a greater response from the electorate than his more cynical colleagues could allow themselves to believe. It was on the basis of these polls, followed in early May by substantial Labour gains in the local elections, that Wilson felt justified in taking the plunge in June. This did not, however, prevent Jenkins, for having failed to produce a giveaway Budget, being-cast as the scapegoat when Labour did not win the General Election after all.

Jenkins also took much of the blame for the unadventurous and 'unsocialist' manifesto on which Labour fought the election, particularly for having personally knocked out of it a commitment to a wealth tax: he now believed strongly that over-taxation was one of the problems of the British economy, and was deeply opposed to Labour being seen as the party of high taxation for taxation's sake. He wanted future redistribution to come from growth, which he now believed was within reach, not from taxation. It is heavily ironic that he, known

since the fifties as an ardent expansionist, should have been obliged as
Chancellor to preside over three years of severe deflation and increased
taxes; his success was not at all the sort of success he would have wished
himself five years earlier. (He never made the achievement of a trading
surplus an end in itself, however, and once it was achieved he looked
forward to the country now being able to adopt 'a more normal balance
of priorities'.)[72] At the same time it should be noted that, given the
externally imposed necessity of deflation, he was careful in his successive
packages to hit the rich hardest. In his first two Budgets, in addition to
the special levy of 1968, he struck several shrewd blows against inherited
wealth: he cracked down on discretionary trusts; he extended the qual-
ifying period for *inter vivos* gifts (thus making it harder to avoid estate
duty); and he aggregated children's income with their parents' for tax
purposes (an effective indirect assault on private education).[73] These
were, in most people's language, 'socialist' reforms. Against this it may
be said that Jenkins failed to institute the major reform of the tax
structure which he had long advocated to make it bear less heavily on
the only moderately wealthy, at the expense of the very richest. Some
redistribution there was during his Chancellorship, through tax changes
and increases in benefit; but he cannot be said to have pursued any
coherent strategy of redistribution. If the poor did not, as is often
alleged, actually grow poorer, they certainly did not get much richer.
The proportion of the GNP spent on both health and education did rise
significantly; on the other hand house-building was cut back well below
what Labour had promised in 1964.[10]

It is fair to say that the overall failure of the 1964–70 Government to
realize the hopes raised in 1964 was due to the mistakes of 1964–7.
Jenkins' Chancellorship, beginning in the pit of the post-devaluation
crisis, was relatively speaking, highly successful, certainly on the central
economic front on which he had to concentrate, restoring the balance
of payments and securing the pound. It was not the British economic
miracle; but he had got the economy back to a point where it was
reasonable to hope that another Labour Government could begin
cautiously to use the hard-won surplus for socially progressive ends. It
is not surprising, given the economic bunker they had been living in for
so long, that he and Wilson should have fought the election so conser-
vatively, emphasizing that single achievement and their proven economic competence in (at last) getting the economy right, rather than
on radical blueprints for the future (though Jenkins also put some
emphasis on his 'civilised society' theme). The remarkable thing is that
they were in a position to fight the election with a real hope, indeed

expectation, of winning at all. That they were in such a position by June 1970, after the unprecedented depths of unpopularity the Government had plumbed in 1968, was very largely Jenkins' achievement. For all the criticisms that can inevitably be made – of which the legacy of wage inflation is the most serious – no other Chancellor of recent years can boast a better record.

Jenkins himself would have preferred, until very late on, to have waited until October before going to the country, to give further time for the balance of payments surplus to keep on piling up beyond any possible Tory carping, and to avoid any impression that the Government was just trying to take advantage while the going was good. But Wilson, making the characteristic calculation that only Tories went on holiday in June and, rather optimistically, hoping for a boost from England winning the World Cup in Mexico, was determined to go early. The dissolution was announced on 18 May – polling day was 18 June. Throughout the campaign the polls were unanimous that Labour would win. The personality of the Chancellor was a major positive factor in Labour's appeal: whatever the left thought of him, he was established as the Labour politician most likely to attract the floating voter. On 9 June he made a television broadcast which the Tories' private polls found to be one of the most effective for any party, presenting a cautious, responsible but above all successful image,[74] and taking the opportunity to announce an overall surplus for 1969–70, declared that day, of £606m–£200m of it in the last quarter, January to March. Unfortunately the news was muffled by a newspaper strike. A week later, the strike had been settled when the trade figures for May showed, quite against the trend, a deficit of £31m. This was an unlucky freak, largely attributable to the ill-timed purchase of two jumbo jets costing £18m each, but it seemed to confirm the Tories' warnings that Labour's achievement was not as soundly-based as Jenkins claimed. It is impossible to ascribe the result of any election to particular causes, but this – coming the day after England were disappointingly knocked out of the World Cup by Germany – was a severe blow to Labour's air of confident invincibility. Wilson's clever timing had backfired. In the very last days of the campaign, too late for publication, the polls began to register a swing to the Conservatives which, to general astonishment, was translated in the early hours of 19 June into a clear majority of thirty seats. Labour was out. Within hours, Ted Heath's piano was being moved into 10 Downing Street, and Iain Macleod was moving into the Chancellor's residence at number 11. For Jenkins, six remarkable years which had brought him from the back benches and from the verge of leaving politics altogether to the second position in the Government and a place in the very front rank of politics were over. He now faced the very different and much less congenial challenge of holding his position and holding the Labour party to moderate courses in opposition.

SEVEN

The Struggle for the Labour Party Resumed, 1970–1974

Losing office after six years at the heart of government is a shock. Writing in 1971, Jenkins compared the experience to that of a prisoner released after several years 'inside'. 'There is a sense of release, but also a certain apprehension that the props of the familiar routine and the well-known jailers have been removed. A combination of greater freedom but greater responsibility for one's own life stares one sternly in the face.' Rehabilitation, he found, took three months. 'In July I felt lost. In August I had a holiday. In September I got back to normal.'[1]

'Normal', however, was a life very different from that he had lived prior to 1964. Not only was he an ex-Chancellor of the Exchequer and Labour's principal economic spokesman: on 8 July he was elected Deputy Leader, with a seat on the National Executive. The Deputy Leadership is not much of a job. Since it was invented to save Herbert Morrison's face in 1951, no Deputy Leader had ever succeeded to the leadership until Michael Foot in 1980; it has by no means invariably been held by the second man in the party. Nevertheless, when it is vacant it provides an opportunity for an important test of strength – between different wings of the party as much as between individuals. In 1970 George Brown had lost his seat at the General Election. Jenkins was now the obvious standard bearer of the right. Callaghan, his only possible rival, was content with the party Treasurership. A number of those who considered themselves Jenkinsites – including Bill Rodgers, George Thomson, David Owen, David Marquand and Bob Maclennan – met in Dick Taverne's flat and agreed that their man must run. Michael Foot stood for the left, and Fred Peart on an anti-Common Market ticket. In a three-way vote, the ease of Jenkins' victory caused general surprise. He won outright on the first ballot by 133 votes to 67 for Foot and 48 for Peart. Those observers who had feared that Labour would swing left in opposition breathed a sigh of premature relief. The result implied, wrote *The Times*, 'that the Labour Party has decided that it is going to continue in opposition to develop along the lines on which it was developing as a government. . . . It means that the Labour Party has not swung emotionally against Europe in the way that some people feared.'[2] 'Mr Roy Jenkins' election', wrote John Grigg in the *Evening Standard*, 'shows that Labour MPs are now definitely interested in power. The time has passed for mindless camaraderie or millenial dreams.'[3] All it really showed was that, three weeks after the election, the habit of Government-mindedness had not yet died, and that Jenkins' performance as a Minister was still fresh in the minds of Labour MPs.

Jenkins found the job of Deputy Leader in opposition just as time-consuming as being a Minister, to much less purpose; in particular, he was required to spend far more time in the House of Commons. 'As Chancellor', he wrote, 'I answered questions once a month, and made perhaps six speeches and six Ministerial statements a year. In opposition I find it necessary to be present for Question Time and part of the debate for at least three and possibly four days a week.'[1] For a man who likes to spend every minute of his day usefully, either on work or pleasure, hanging about the House of Commons listening to other people's speeches was intensely aggravating. He loves the atmosphere of big debates in the Chamber; but he does not like plotting and gossiping in the bars and tearooms, and when he is obliged to do it he does it awkwardly and unconvincingly – hence, in large part, his reputation for aloofness and élitism. In office this did not matter; he had a job to do. But opposition demands more backslapping and timewasting chat: Jenkins is not at his best in opposition.

He also had many more speaking engagements all round the country, with no official car to take him to them. He did not mind the latter deprivation, since he enjoys driving himself (and drives, when he gets the chance, frighteningly fast), but he found his precious evenings and weekends, if anything, less his own than as a Minister. On the other hand, when he was free he really was free, as a Minister – pursued everywhere by private secretaries and official boxes – never is. In what free time he had, Jenkins quickly got back to writing. He resumed book reviewing for the *Observer* (beginning with Bernard Levin's instant history of the sixties, *The Pendulum Years*). He wrote for the *Observer* and *Sunday Times* the special articles already quoted on the experience of being a Minister and the difference between the Home Office and the Treasury. He picked up again for *The Times* his political travelogue style from the fifties and reported his impressions after visits to the

United States, Africa, Australia and Bangladesh: he travelled now, of
course, as an experienced world statesman and pronounced more weigh-
tily. Most substantially he wrote, also for *The Times*, at the suggestion
of its editor William Rees-Mogg, a series of short biographies (10–
15,000 words each) published in 1974 as *Nine Men of Power*.

The nine subjects he chose to treat (there were meant to be ten, but
the 1974 election fortuitously intervened when he was stuck for the
tenth) shed a revealing light on his interests and political perspective.
Three were Labour figures: Hugh Gaitskell (written for the tenth anniversary of his death – 'For many of us there is a sense of long-term
deprivation which, as the years go by, persists and even increases');[4]
Ernest Bevin (of whom he wrote memorably that he became Foreign
Secretary 'with the qualification that there was no other position in the
Foreign Office, unless it was that of a rather truculent liftman on the
verge of retirement, which it would have been possible to imagine him
filling');[5] and Stafford Cripps ('almost the only post-war Chancellor' –
until Jenkins himself, one cannot help feeling – 'to depart with his
colours flying high', whose career additionally fascinated Jenkins, as a
student of careers, as one who 'for a short time exercised an authority as
great as it is possible to achieve without occupying the premiership
itself, and who came to it by a route which is one of the least obviously
charted in the history of British politics.'[6]

Three were American, reflecting an interest in the post-Roosevelt
Democratic Party which since the late fifties had become an increasingly
important influence on Jenkins' thinking about British politics. Franklin
Roosevelt, the architect first of the New Deal, then of the Marshall Plan
and NATO, was a hero of Jenkins' youth who remains a shining example
to this day: the ideal politician on whom Jenkins models himself would
combine the manner of Asquith with Roosevelt's drive and vision. The
Democratic Party of the fifties and sixties – a classless, progressive and
outward-looking party of energetic liberal reform, opposed to the conservative insularity of the Republicans – became for him a model of
what the British Labour party might be if it would shed its antiquated
commitment to fundamentalist socialism; it is equally one of his models
for the SDP. Two of the three Americans in *Nine Men of Power* are Adlai
Stevenson, the Democratic candidate for the Presidency defeated by
Eisenhower in 1952 and 1956, and Robert Kennedy, assassinated while
seeking the Democratic nomination in 1968. Stevenson is to Jenkins an
American Gaitskell: a civilized liberal who would not stoop to conquer,
a two-time loser who nevertheless 'inspired a generation'.[7] He got to
know him well in the early sixties, when he was frequently in Washing-

ton; Stevenson died in London in 1965, an hour after arranging to lunch at Ladbroke Square next day. Jenkins still quotes Stevenson probably more than any other politician. He admired both his modesty as a candidate ('I don't *have* to be President') and his grace in defeat ('He said that he felt like a little boy who had stubbed his toe in the dark.... He was too old to cry, but it hurt too much to laugh.')[8] Even his inability to decide whether or not to run in 1960 Jenkins portrays as part of his attraction as a man.

The Kennedys were very different. In the sixties Jenkins, like many others, fell under the spell of the Kennedy legend; even now he is still inclined to romanticize Teddy as the last of the line. Jack Kennedy he did not know well; but Bobby he came to know, and in *Nine Men of Power* he writes of him very movingly, first with the world at his feet before Jack's assassination, then 'completely disorientated' after it; finally, the last time they met, walking together on the sweltering four and a half-hour procession through Atlanta at the funeral of Martin Luther King in 1968, just eight weeks before he himself was shot. Like others, Jenkins saw in Bobby by then much more than the ruthless Irish machine politician he had once been, but wrote poignantly of his rapidly maturing statesmanship, his compassion, vision and rapport with 'the dangerously alienated elements of American society', his great potential had he lived.[9] There is love in this essay.

Jenkins felt no love at all for his third American, Senator McCarthy, the 'black joker' in his pack, of whom he could never have written a full biography but whom he thought a phenomenon worth the three to four weeks he spent on each of these studies.[10] The remaining essays were on Lord Halifax (a surprising choice but an instructive career); the French socialist Leon Blum (a nod to his father here?); and J.M. Keynes, the only non-politician in the nine and also the only one Jenkins never saw. ('It is a great deficiency which I wish I could retrospectively repair. There is no figure of the past generation (with the possible exception of Roosevelt) with whom I would more like to have talked.')[10] The interest of their subjects apart, these nine essays represent the consummation of Jenkins' mature style – polished, urbane and epigrammatic, not questioning but breathing a perfect confidence in his own political assumptions and historical judgement. The book is studded with passages of excellent writing; but one sentence from the essay on Blum may serve to illustrate both its quality and its limitations:

He was the one man who, from a dismal continent, with Hitler creating a new barbarism in Germany, with Mussolini grooming Italy for the role of predatory auxiliary, with Spain on the verge of eruption into the cruellest and most international of civil wars, with power in England about to pass from the fading benignity of Baldwin to the harsher defeatism of Chamberlain, might have sent back an answering light to the uncertain signals of encouragement which came across the Atlantic from Roosevelt.[11]

The long sentence is superbly structured, and reads most impressively; yet it contains no thought that is in the least original, rather a catalogue of solidly conventional judgements implicitly accepted as received facts. The effect is achieved by the arresting choice of words, particularly adjectives, and the final graphic image. Jenkins' writing, indeed – not least in his speeches – relies very heavily on pictorial metaphors, often extended to ingenious length: these make for vivid reading, but at the risk of running away with the meaning, so that content can come to be determined by style. Jenkins' facility with images carries the danger that once he has written something he is pleased with he is reluctant to alter it: he is not good at re-writing, because he thinks in images rather than in ideas. That said, however, his imagery (like that of those other Welshmen, Lloyd George and Aneurin Bevan – it is a peculiarly Welsh characteristic) is part of his force as a politician.

Labour's first two years in opposition were dominated by the re-opening, with a new urgency, of the old internal argument about the Common Market. For some years it had been in abeyance: on the one hand, since 1967 all three major parties were now officially agreed on the desirability of British entry; on the other, General de Gaulle continued resolutely to veto it. Labour's anti-Marketeers had not been too worried by Wilson's 1967 conversion since, for all his brave talk ('We won't take "No" for an answer'), his application never seemed likely to have much chance of success so long as the General ruled France. In 1969, however, de Gaulle had resigned, and his successor, Georges Pompidou, was known to look more favourably on Britain's entry. In this new situation, a Labour Government re-elected in 1970 would almost certainly have re-presented its 1967 application, and the Prime Minister would have remained committed to its success. As it was, the historic opportunity fell to Heath to renew the negotiations for which he had been responsible in 1962. For ten years Heath, equally with Jenkins, had been the most prominent advocate of joining Europe: now he lost no time in submitting a fresh application within days of the election. But almost as quickly Labour began to backtrack. All the party's old instinctive suspicion of Europe was fanned back to life by its loathing of Heath; and in the interest of party unity and the doctrine that the Opposition's job is to oppose, Wilson began to equivocate about what terms of entry Labour would find acceptable.

There now opened the critical battle of Jenkins' career – the battle that would destroy his position in the Labour party and eventually drive him out of it. The merits of the European argument became subsumed in the wider question of political morality and ultimately the very purpose and direction of the Labour party. On the first question he remained resolute. He refused to get bogged down in niggling about the terms of entry. 'I am in favour of strong bargaining', he wrote in *The Times* in May 1971, when the Tory negotiations were nearly complete. 'But we must not lose sight in the process of the purpose of the exercise', which was to get in. 'The terms themselves are not in any circumstances going to sound overwhelmingly attractive. An admission fee never does. . . . But anything will appear extortionate unless we have a lively idea of why we want to join.' Taking almost for granted that access to the European market would stimulate Britain's sluggish economy, he still emphasized the political and psychological benefits of membership: Britain's political opportunity in Europe as a counterweight to France and Germany, and a united Europe's power for good in the world as a counterweight to America and Russia, and as a source of aid to the poorer countries.

> Good transitional terms are necessary. So are honourable arrangements for those overseas who are economically dependent upon us. But necessary too is a full appreciation of the wider issues involved and a clear appraisal of the opportunities before us. What this country needs is a little more realistic self-confidence. Without it we face a future of narrowing horizons. With it we can find a new role as rewarding as any in our history.[12]

More impassioned now than such repeated statement of his old faith, however, was Jenkins' stand on the principle that Labour must not deny in opposition what it had upheld in office. Speaking in Birmingham on the first anniversary of the election, 18 June 1971, he was careful to begin by pinning on the Tory Government the blame for 'a rapid devaluation of the standards of British politics'. Elected 'on an utterly bogus prospectus' to reduce price rises and unemployment, it was now watching helplessly as both soared. But his point was that Labour must not mirror this duplicity, but make a stand for 'honesty and consistency' in public life. The week before, Jim Callaghan – his finger on the party pulse as always – had signalled his intention to oppose EEC entry not merely on the likely terms, but on any terms. Jenkins could see no basis on which members of the 1964-70 Government could follow this re-

versal – 'unless we believe that a party should take a different attitude
to the nation's interests and say different things in Government than in
opposition. I do not believe that.' Public opinion, he conceded, was now
against entry: but it had swung before. 'In any case', he added, with
heavy irony, 'I do not believe that it is always the duty of those who
seek to lead to follow public opinion.'[13]

Five days later, however, the National Executive voted 13–11 to hold
a special one-day party conference on the terms which the Government
published on 7 July: Wilson voted with Jenkins in the minority, but
they were beaten by the outright opponents of entry led by Callaghan
and Ian Mikardo. At the conference, held on 17 July in the Central
Hall, Westminster, the pro-Marketeers drew some encouragement from
the fact that an attempt to bring forward an early vote against entry –
which would certainly have carried – was defeated; on the other hand
Wilson edged nearer to outright opposition in a speech – which the
Jenkinsites ostentatiously did not applaud – not merely attacking the
'Tory terms' but at times bewilderingly hostile to the whole concept of
the EEC. The rug had been pulled out from under his attempt to limit
the argument to the terms by the testimony of George Thomson, the
Minister who had led Labour's 1967 negotiations, that he would have
accepted the terms now offered. Thomson was supported by all three of
the other Ministers who had had responsibility for negotiations with
Europe between 1966 and 1970, George Brown, Michael Stewart and
Lord Chalfont.

Jenkins did not speak at the special conference. But two days later he
made one of the most powerful speeches of his life at a meeting of the
PLP. He agreed not only that the Labour Cabinet would have accepted
the Tory terms, but that they were as good as anyone could realistically
have hoped to get: to suggest that Labour would not have accepted
such terms was to say that the whole 1967 application had been a waste
of everyone's time from the beginning. Specifically excluding Barbara
Castle, Fred Peart and Willie Ross, who had opposed the application
all along, he bluntly condemned Wilson's and Callaghan's cynicism
and derided the alternatives they now proposed. Wilson's 'kith and kin'
argument was mere sentimentality: Australia was 'the toughest, rough-
est, most self-interested Government with which I ever had to deal'.
Callaghan's alternative he dismissed with contempt:

> Jim Callaghan offered running the economy flat out for five years. That is
> not a policy: it is an aspiration. We were not lacking in aspirations in the
> early days of the last Government. What we were lacking was results.

The third alternative was the left's – 'Socialism in one country.' 'That is always good for a cheer. Pull up the drawbridge and revolutionise the fortress. That is not a policy, either, it's just a slogan' – unconvincing in itself and hypocritical when dressed up as Labour's contribution to international socialism. If Britain rejected the EEC, he ended, she would not have 'rugged independence' but merely greater dependence on the USA.

> I beg the party not to follow this recipe for disappointment and decline but to face problems realistically and to lift its eyes beyond the narrow short-term political considerations of the moment.[14]

This speech won a tremendous ovation, with great banging of desks, 'in which quite clearly many of the floating voters in the party joined'.[15] The last sentence in particular was widely interpreted as a challenge to Wilson and a signal to his supporters that he was going to fight. Wilson was alarmed, and replied next day with an ill-judged outburst alleging the existence of 'a party within the party' and wondering sarcastically how such Jenkinsites as Bill Rodgers and Roy Hattersley could sully their purity by holding Shadow office. Rodgers immediately sought a meeting with Wilson to clarify whether pro-Marketeers were now in-eligible to be front bench spokesmen. Assurances were given that this was not so, and a fragile front of unity was restored.[16] But relations in the party remained tense.

The critical moment on the horizon was the House of Commons vote on the principle of joining the EEC, to be taken at the end of a week-long debate at the end of October. At the beginning of the month, the full party Conference in Brighton overwhelmingly rejected the Government's terms and called upon all Labour MPs to vote against them. Jenkins and his supporters now came under tremendous pressure to toe the party line, or at least abstain. It was generally thought impossible that the Deputy Leader could defy Conference and vote against a three-line whip. At a fringe meeting of the Labour Committee for Europe, however, Jenkins firmly refused to accept that the flame of Labour support for Europe should be put out. Less provocatively than in July, he claimed 'no monopoly of rightness or sincerity'.

> I do claim that we are entitled to stick to the beliefs which we have long held. I do not apologise for doing so. I reject utterly the view that ... we are supporting the Tories. My aim is to increase the future opportunities and influence of the Labour Party.[17]

This was the clear lead needed to hold the pro-Europeans firm. At a meeting of his supporters shortly before the vote, at which they talked agonizingly round and round the trauma of voting against the party, Jenkins made it plain that he made no demands on anyone else, but he personally was going to vote for the principle he had believed in for fifteen years. He made it sound so simple, one of those present remembers: there could be no question of not following him. While Jenkins led by moral example, Bill Rodgers was leaning heavily on the consciences of potential backsliders. The result was that in the historic division on 28 October, 69 Labour members voted in favour of entry, with 20 more abstaining, more than enough to outweigh the 39 Tories who voted against the Government, giving an overall majority of 112, much larger than expected – a margin which was hailed around Europe as ending the argument over Britain's entry. This was Jenkins' finest hour. Faced with furious calls for his resignation and the widespread expectation that, as an honourable man, he must accede to them, he sat tight, taking the view that his convictions had been well known when he was elected: no more than Gaitskell in 1960 could he be expected to change his deepest beliefs at the dictation of Conference. Three weeks later his stand was dramatically vindicated when he was re-elected by 140 votes to 126 for Michael Foot, winning – to the astonishment both of his own supporters and of Foot's – *seven more votes* than he had got in 1970. The more faint-hearted of his supporters, led significantly by Hattersley (his campaign manager), who had thought his best chance lay in some conciliatory trimming, were overridden by the hard-liners, led by Rodgers, who would brook no compromise. 'Our strongest suit', one of the latter told the *Observer*, 'was the knowledge that Roy was a man of steel and, given that we were running against an india-rubber politician, we would have been very silly not to have led to it.'[18]

At this point Jenkins' position was very strong. The near-canonization he was receiving in most of the press as a man of courage and principle amongst a lot of tricky turncoats was admittedly a dangerous asset, if not positively counter-productive, with the party in the country. But his support in the Parliamentary Party had been shown to be formidable, reaching well beyond the sixty-nine who had followed him into the 'Aye' lobby on 28 October. He had stood his ground and he was still Deputy Leader: he had ensured that the Europeans in the Labour party could neither be disciplined nor ignored. Now, however, he faltered and began to lose his way.

He was subject to conflicting pressures – to widen the argument from Europe to the whole future of social democracy in the Labour party, even to the point of leading a breakaway party, as Taverne (already in trouble in his constituency) and, briefly in November 1971, Rodgers urged; to make explicit his challenge to Wilson for the leadership of Labour, as David Owen, David Marquand, Bob Maclennan and others wanted; or to rest on what he had already won and await events, in the interest of unity, as most of the rest of the party was begging him. At this crossroads of his career, the habit of loyalty to the party in which he had been raised – a hereditary loyalty for which his critics in the party never gave him credit but which was nevertheless immensely strong – overrode his half-formed doubts. He is not, temperamentally, a natural rebel. He chose, by default, the third course, the line of least resistance; and in doing so, by giving an impression of dithering where previously he had been firm, he dissipated a large part of the following he had built up – without, needless to say, gaining any compensating credit on the left.

For the sake of party unity, he decided – having made his stand on the principle of the EEC – to vote as a loyal Deputy Leader with the party against the Second Reading and subsequent stages of the enabling legislation, the European Communities Bill, required to make a reality of Britain's accession. This was utterly inconsistent, and a painful humiliation: it could be justified on the ground that it gave a public demonstration of his fundamental allegiance to Labour without in practice endangering the passage of the Bill. (There were never quite enough Jenkinsites in the Opposition lobby for that.) But the effect of their grand gesture of self-abasement was undercut by the strong suspicion on the left that they were in collusion with the Tory whips to ensure that there were no embarrassing defeats. This was an episode on which all the Jenkinsites today look back with a sense of shame.

Then, in April 1972, Jenkins did resign the Deputy Leadership – on an issue which most of his supporters now believe was peculiarly badly chosen: the Shadow Cabinet's decision to commit Labour to holding a referendum, when it returned to power, on Britain's continued membership of the EEC. In part, his reaction to the decision simply reflected a long-standing opposition to referenda. 'As Clem Attlee pointed out with terse force in 1945', he reminded Wilson in his resignation letter, 'it is a splendid weapon for demagogues and dictators.' Once introduced, there was no way the innovation could be confined to the single issue of the EEC: 'We would have forged a more powerful continuing weapon against progressive legislation than anything we have known in this country since the curbing of the absolute powers of the old House of Lords.' More specifically, Jenkins believed that a referendum on Europe, with members of the party publicly campaigning against one another on platforms up and down the country would be – far from a means of unifying the party – the most certain way of dividing it irreparably. 'It would in my view be incomparably more damaging than any difference between us in the House of Commons.'[19] (In fact, the 1975 referendum proved him quite wrong: Labour members, even Cabinet Ministers, *were* able to take opposite sides of the argument without splitting. Without the referendum, Labour must have been committed to withdrawal, which *would* have split it.)

Psychologically the most impelling reason for his resignation, however, was not his principled objection to the referendum, strong though this was, but his revulsion from the opportunist way the decision was made. The year before, the party had been firmly against a referendum. Benn could not even find a seconder for his proposal on the NEC, and Conference threw it out by over 2–1. On 15 March the Shadow Cabinet had decided not to support a Tory backbencher's referendum amendment. The next day Pompidou announced a referendum in France on the enlargement of the Community, and on 22 March the NEC voted 13–11 (with Wilson, Callaghan and Jenkins all absent) in favour of having one in Britain. Heath then announced a border plebiscite in Northern Ireland, which gave the idea further fashionable currency, and the following week the Shadow Cabinet narrowly reversed its decision of two weeks before, with Wilson and Edward Short switching sides. This performance, openly playing politics with a serious constitutional issue, was the last straw for Jenkins – the 'single incident', he called it, 'illustrating and accentuating a growing divergence'. In his resignation letter he condemned the 'relentless and short-sighted search for tactical advantage', 'this constant shifting of ground' which, he made it clear, he thought epitomized Wilson's entire style of leadership:

> This, in my view, is not the way in which an opposition, recently and soon again, I hope, the Government of the country, should be run.
>
> I want to see the present Government replaced by a Labour Government.
>
> But I also want to see that future Labour Government have a clear sense of direction. It is not easy at the best of times to preserve this through the buffetings of the week-to-week crises which are the lot of any Government.
>
> But if a Government is born out of opportunism it becomes not merely difficult but impossible.[19]

It was an enormous relief to Jenkins personally to resign. He had been deeply unhappy having to vote against the European Communities Bill and felt, rightly, that he was compromising his own integrity. He thought Wilson's whole conduct of the opposition in respect of

Europe both corrupt and corrupting, and he wanted to have no part in it. Encouraged by John Harris, he believed resignation to be the only honourable course, and he felt much happier and cleaner when he had resigned. Politically, however, it was a very doubtful move. If he was going to resign, the referendum was a very bad issue on which to go, exposing him to the charge that what he cared most about in politics was the vital principle of not consulting the people. To have resigned after voting to join the EEC in October, or rather than vote against the enabling legislation in November – either would have been stronger ground. But there were basic disadvantages in having resigned at all. Justly or not, it created the impression that he had not the stomach for a fight, and seemed to confirm the view of him as a thin-skinned literary *dilettante*, unwilling to get his hands dirty, more concerned for his personal honour than with winning. Not only his longstanding critics – who were undisguisedly delighted at his going – but many of his admirers concluded that he was not, after all, a leader. (This was, for instance, the beginning of David Owen's gradual loss of faith in Jenkins, which culminated in his standing against him for the leadership of the SDP in 1982.) More practically, it was an elementary mistake to give up a major position of influence in the party: not only the Deputy Leadership itself, with its seat on the NEC (which went to the dim Wilson loyalist Ted Short, who beat Foot by 145 to 116), but also the chairmanship of the party's Finance and Economic Policy Committee and the Shadow Chancellorship, which went to Denis Healey (Wilson again passing over Crosland). By resigning, Jenkins was cutting himself off from the policy-making process leading up to the next election. Nor was it only Jenkins himself who went: George Thomson and Harold Lever simultaneously resigned from the Shadow Cabinet (their places being filled by Reg Prentice and John Silkin, both at that time anti-EEC), and a few days later Taverne, Owen and Dickson Mabon resigned their front bench spokesmanships. (Shirley Williams hesitated and stayed; Roy Hattersley hesitated and accepted promotion – the beginning of his break with the Jenkinsites.) For the principle of not committing the party to a referendum, the social democrats who were most disturbed at Labour's leftward drift handed the future direction of policy over to those whose resistance to the left was weakest. To many it seemed an expensive principle, insisted upon in defiance of political sense.

The logic of resignation was that it freed Jenkins to launch an explicit attack on Wilson's leadership. But this he failed to do. Instead of pressing home his criticism, he was at pains to minimize the disruption caused in the party by his resignation. He had resigned to *prevent* a split, not to precipitate one. He even continued to vote with the party against the EEC Bill. At the prompting of Owen, Marquand and others, he delivered in the spring and summer of 1972 a series of major speeches on economic and social policy, widening the argument from Europe to the whole social purpose of the party. They were very good speeches, which sold a lot of copies as a paperback, *What Matters Now*. But they were largely written for him by David and Judith Marquand, and he delivered them without conviction. When the Sunday papers splashed the most provocative of them as a direct challenge to Wilson – which was exactly what it was meant to be – he went on *The World This Weekend* at lunchtime and played it down, denying that any challenge to Wilson was intended. In the autumn, Marquand and Maclennan wanted him to stand against Wilson for the leadership (as Wilson had once stood against Gaitskell): he would not have won, but he would have got not far short of 100 votes, and secured his position as still a major figure and an alternative leader in waiting. Again, he would not do it. He persuaded himself that his better way lay in loyalty, not rocking the boat but waiting in the hope that the party would come back to him. Whether he really believed that it would is very doubtful. In his heart he probably knew that he could never now lead the Labour party; he knew that it had already swung too far ever again to be the sort of party he would want to lead. But he could see no realistic alternative, so he simply kept on playing the Labour game according to the rules, honourably but unhappily and unconvincingly.

The Government was unpopular, but so was Labour: the Liberals were winning by-elections. *The Times* was calling for a centre party, and publishing opinion polls which showed huge potential support for an alliance of the Liberals with the Labour right. Jenkins was closely interested in these developments, but in 1972 he was still too deeply rooted in the two-party system to believe that this could be any more than newspaper-inspired mid-term froth. His colleagues were unanimous against any thought of a breakaway from the Labour party – with one exception. Since his vote for the EEC on 28 October, Dick Taverne had come to the parting of the ways with his left-wing constituency party in Lincoln. Rather than accept being dumped (as Bob Maclennan and others advised him was his only course), he determined to resign his seat and fight a by-election as an Independent: he would have liked to call himself a Social Democrat, but thought Democratic Labour would be more widely understood. Of all the Jenkinsites, only Jenkins himself thought that he had a chance of winning. Even so, he thought Taverne's action foolhardy and premature: he did not think the time was yet ripe, if it ever would be, for a mass breakout of the right from Labour.[20] Given that none of his other supporters was yet ready to contemplate the unthinkable, he was almost certainly right. This analysis dictated that he could not court expulsion from the party by going to Lincoln to speak for Taverne: but his heart was with him, and so, it was observed, in an advisory capacity, was John Harris. When Taverne won a momentous victory, beating the official Labour candidate out of sight with a majority of over 13,000, he felt bitterly that he had taken the coward's path. His unhappiness deepened; he has had Taverne's lonely, heroic fight on his conscience ever since.

1972-4 was an unhappy period altogether. While the Jenkinsites had been distracted by the Common Market argument, the left had got themselves into positions of power at all levels of the party and, taking advantage of the disappointment widely felt at the failures of 1964-70 – the reaction against *In Place of Strife* and the Tory Government's much stronger Industrial Relations Bill; and Wilson's temporary withdrawal to write his memoirs – were pushing through the policy committees documents tying the party more closely than ever before to the trade unions, and committing it to measures of sweeping nationalization of the type the former Gaitskellites thought they had consigned to the ideological dustbin in the fifties. For the latter development, while he was still Deputy Leader, Jenkins bears some responsibility: as chairman of the Finance and Economic Policy Committee he held few meetings, but preferred to make policy with his own circle of advisers – Taverne, Marquand, Lever, Jack Diamond, Edmund Dell. His speeches at the 1970 and 1971 party Conferences were statesmanlike and responsible, attacking the Tories' rapid squandering of the strong balance of payments surplus they had inherited (they had 'talked down the pound', he claimed in 1970, 'with a speed and accuracy which any air traffic controller would have envied'),[21] but not attuned to the desire of Conference to develop new radical policies for the seventies. He made a point of insisting that the next Labour Government, like the last, would need some sort of incomes policy. But he did little on the NEC or through its policy committees to win support for such realistic but unpopular policies or prevent the adoption of much wilder socialist programmes to fill the vacuum.[22] He was too preoccupied with Europe, and too alienated by that struggle from most of his natural allies on the right of the party, to give the attention that was needed to fighting the left for the control of future policy until it was too late. By the time the left's proposals – for the nationalization of banking, insurance, building societies, finance houses, building, road haulage, ship building and ship repairing, plus a National Enterprise Board to take over the twenty-five largest private companies – emerged as fully-fledged party documents, he was no longer a member of the NEC, and was able to criticize them only from the outside, and in public.

The division of the right was very personal and very painful. In particular the European issue had opened up a gulf of mutual incomprehension and recrimination between Jenkins and his oldest friend, Tony Crosland. Their relationship was already strained by Crosland's jealousy of Jenkins for getting the job he desperately wanted, and thought himself better qualified for, in 1967. But that was the luck of politics. Their difference over Europe was a matter of deliberate choice. Jenkins was disgusted by Wilson's about-face, but not surprised; he was disappointed at Denis Healey's denial of a policy he had supported in government, but Healey had never been more than a luke-warm European; he was profoundly shocked and felt personally betrayed that Crosland should have committed the same apostasy, remembering that in the late fifties he and Crosland had been Labour's two brightest young Europeans, joint vice-presidents of the Labour Committee for Europe, each seemingly as committed as the other, and both equally cast down by Gaitskell's opposition. Of all his colleagues, Jenkins felt that he should have been able to rely on Crosland's support against Wilson's backsliding. The Jenkinsites' explanation of Crosland's behaviour, of which they made no secret, was that he was moved by simple jealousy: his pride would not allow him to accept the leadership of one whom he had always regarded as a junior partner, but who had overtaken him so dramatically over the past five years. Susan Crosland's biography of her husband does not disguise that there is some truth in this: he clearly (and in human terms, very understandably) found the press adulation of Jenkins hard to stomach and, with characteristic perversity, went rapidly cool on Europe when it became Fleet Street's touchstone of integrity in politics.

At the same time Crosland's careful distancing of himself from Jenkins and Europe reflected a genuine and growing divergence from Jenkins' view of the Labour party. He now insisted that he had never regarded Europe as a matter of *principle*, overriding other issues in domestic politics. He claimed that he had always been in favour *on balance*, indeed that he still was; but that he regarded the unity of the Labour party and the defeat of the Conservative Government as higher priorities. It is fair to say that some old friends of both, like Philip Williams, confirm that Crosland was never as passionately committed to the EEC as Jenkins; while there was undoubtedly a case to be made, politically, for the strategy of abstaining in the critical vote on 28 October, as Crosland did, marking his dissent from the party's *volte-face* without going to the length of voting with the Government. The Jenkinsite answer was that it was necessary to stand up and be counted, not merely *for* Europe, but *against* the immorality of Labour cynically abjuring in opposition the policies it had pursued in government. But Crosland thought the Jenkinsites had got the issue out of perspective: that their self-image as a persecuted minority of the righteous had gone to their heads, and that they were blindly set on wrecking the Labour party for a cause that was not worth it. He himself was feeling his way towards the opposite response to the disillusion with 1964–70 years and Labour's leftward drift. He believed, with some reason, that the Jenkinsites were out of tune with the party in the country; and though this had not always been his own strength, he had now taken to idealizing his Grimsby constituents and was developing a line of grass-roots populism, modelling himself no longer on Gaitskell but on his new mentor Callaghan, trying self-consciously to stake out for himself a comparable position in the centre of the party, making loyalty to the party and the working class, rather than consistency of policy, his guiding principle. (Though he had no time for Benn's simplistic solutions, his political evolution – the middle class socialist's awakening to the unique virtue of the working class – is oddly similar.)[23]

Crosland was more than ever determined not to be a Jenkinsite by the crude bullying of Bill Rodgers and others – trying to make him feel like a pariah, even turning their backs on him at parties, 'punishing' him for not voting the right way by withholding their support from him in the Shadow Cabinet elections in 1971, so that he dropped from third place to eighth, and then backing Short for the Deputy Leadership in 1972 purely to keep him out. (He got 61 votes to Short's 111 in the first ballot: the Jenkinsites easily made the difference.) This was childish and self-defeating, in that Jenkins realized perfectly well that he needed Crosland and Crosland's small band of supporters if he himself was ever to have any hope of leading the Labour party, or if together they were to stop the left. They were still not far apart on policy; their difference was in style and the idea of the Labour party each wanted to represent. Ironically, while Jenkins still held to the Gaitskellite view of 1959–60, seeking to broaden the appeal of the party from its traditional and dwindling base of working-class support to attract the classless young and the whole left-inclined half of the nation, Crosland was rediscovering Labour's soul in its origins. Thus they curiously mirrored their early relationship at Oxford; then Jenkins, the upwardly-mobile working-class boy, had been putting Pontypool behind him as fast as he could, while Crosland, the academic middle-class socialist, had made the Jenkins household his home from home, learning the reality of the labour movement at the feet of Arthur. The memory of these early days gave an edge to their mature rivalry, sharper than the antagonism either felt for Denis Healey or Tony Benn. Susan Crosland vividly describes a meeting in 1973 when Jenkins proposed that they patch up their differences over a pre-dinner drink. First they quarrelled over a dinner held in January to mark the tenth anniversary of Gaitskell's death at which Jenkins had been rather tactlessly billed as the main speaker while Crosland was originally invited only as a guest.

> The second episode concerned Roy's recent speech berating Labour's collective leadership for giving way to the Left. Intense irritation was felt, Tony said, by those in the Party who were attending Committee meetings each week – in his own case, nine a week – to fight against the Left getting its way, while Roy stood on the sidelines and wrote elegant biographical pieces for *The Times* for a fat fee.
>
> The subject then veered. Tony was to blame for Roy's resignation. "You could have stopped me", Roy said.
>
> "How could I stop you when I was in Tokyo? In fact, your resignation cost us £50 in telephone calls".
>
> Two dogs with a bone came to mind.... A little later, when I returned from the kitchen to see how things were coming along, the combatants were re-engaged on episode two. The last words I heard as I retired again to the cooker were Roy's: "Well, you could resign too".

A few days later, Susan Crosland concludes the story, the two met in a House of Commons lift. 'Tony said, "We must have another of those conversations soon. Very enjoyable." Roy, surprised, immediately collected himself. "I suppose that any bridge-building must be preceded by major excavation", he said.'[24] For the moment, their occasional meetings only increased the distance between them.

Yet Jenkins and Crosland (to say nothing of Healey and Wilson) were equally and for the same reasons opposed to the lengthy shopping list of targets for further nationalization successfully pushed through the NEC by Tony Benn and his allies in 1973. They all thought it dogmatic in theory, unmanageable in practice and, above all, likely to be electorally disastrous. But his opposition to Benn's programme is not to say that Jenkins was yet, as he has since become, totally opposed to any extension of nationalization: far from it. In one of his *What Matters Now* speeches, to the north-western mineworkers in May 1972, he accepted that the experience of 1964–70 had shown that more direct Government intervention was necessary to correct the persisting economic imbalance between the regions. 'We relied principally on a mixture of bribery and cajolery – on lavish grants supplemented by some Government pressure on the more public-spirited or politically exposed businesses. These weapons were far better than no weapons at all, and their results should not be underestimated, but they have not nearly solved all the problems which we face in this field of regional policy.' He deplored the Tories' attempts to hive off parts of the nationalized industries and return them to the private sector. 'We should move firmly in the other direction. We should seek to hive on parts of the private sector to the nationalised sector, and encourage the nationalised sector to diversify wherever it sees a good opportunity.' To this end, he advocated a State Holding Company, backed by a Regional Development Bank, on the model of the Italian IRI and ENI. This was the same model on which the left based their National Enterprise Board. The difference was that Jenkins envisaged (as in the original revisionist debate of the fifties) a selective patchwork pattern of public ownership for the purpose of stimulating regional investment – *not* the wholesale nationalization of entire industries and major companies. 'I have always believed', he concluded, 'that public ownership should be judged more by the results it will produce than by abstractions and preconceived views.'

> I have not been convinced that it contains the key to the elimination of injustice between individuals.... But I am increasingly convinced that injustice between the regions cannot be dealt with except by a significant expansion of the public sector.[25]

Characteristically, he believed injustice between the regions to be bad, not merely in the abstract, but as a socially divisive force: 'If the South is allowed to suck away a disproportionate share of our country's prosperity there can be no real national cohesion.' National cohesion was becoming one of Jenkins' most insistent themes in the early seventies, in reaction against the left's increasingly strident appeal to the class war, which he found offensive in itself but also backward-looking and electorally unappealing. As in the fifties, he thought – with every support from the opinion polls – that nationalization was a vote loser. But what appalled him about the new 'hard' left was not the 'opposition-mindedness' that had so exasperated him in the old Bevanite left, but, on the contrary, the Bennites' ruthless and anti-democratic calculation that they could win an election and force their half-baked Marxist prescriptions on the country without winning the support of anything like a majority of the electorate: they had only to commit the Labour party to their programme and the swing of the pendulum would do the rest. Faced with this distortion of democracy as he understood it, Jenkins was beginning, for the first time, to question the two-party system and the winner-takes-all electoral system.

The party system as it had existed since 1945, he believed, only worked if the two major parties saw themselves as broad coalitions, respectively of conservative and progressive opinion, commanding between them the allegiance of almost the whole electorate and contending for the middle ground which would give them something near an absolute majority of the country. In 1972–3 it was not the fear that a left-dominated Labour party would lose the next election that worried him so much as the realization that it might win on a minority vote which gave it no democratic authority for the sort of bitterly-opposed measures it proposed to carry through. Speaking from the floor as an ordinary constituency representative at the 1973 party Conference – by his resignation he had given up the right to speak from the platform – he used most of his five-minute allowance to make this important point:

> It is not much good talking about fundamental and irreversible changes in our society and being content with a 38% Labour voting intention, which is what we have on the polls at the present time, but which is less than we had at the last General Election.
>
> Democracy means that you need a substantially stronger moral position than this to govern effectively at all, let alone effect a peaceful social revolution.[26]

Predictably, this warning did not go down well. The next speaker rebuked him for resuscitating 'the outmoded idea that this party can cater for the middle class, that we ought to fashion our policies to cater for the mythical floating voter'. But Jenkins – besides believing that it was simply common sense for any political party to seek to win as many votes as possible, not to congratulate itself on turning them away – believed passionately that the aim of a progressive party in particular must be to convert the country to its ideals. Society can only be changed in any real and lasting way by winning hearts and minds – not simply by passing Bills which the succeeding Government promptly repeals.

> If the next Labour Government [he wrote in the summing-up of *What Matters Now*] is to launch a more successful attack on poverty and privilege than did the last one, it will need the right policies, but it will also need something rarer and more elusive. It will need the conscious and active support of a majority of the British people – not just for a fleeting moment in the polling booths, but through all the doubts and setbacks which even a successful Government inevitably encounters.[27]

The goal Jenkins set for the next Labour Government in *What Matters Now* was nothing less than 'the elimination of poverty as a social problem'.[28] In one of the speeches, he dutifully set out detailed proposals for cutting into the cycle of deprivation by improved and better integrated tax and social security arrangements, by an expanded Urban Aid programme and by a fairer allocation of the Rate Support Grant.[29] But the heart of his political case was contained in another chapter, entitled 'The Call to Idealism', which faced the inconvenient fact for the Labour party that the poor were no longer the great majority of the working class, but a fragmented minority composed of several overlapping categories of people largely neglected by the trade unions in their search for bigger pay packets for their members, many of whom were now to be counted among the relatively well off. Labour had now a more complex and demanding task than fighting on behalf of the poor majority against a rich minority. 'It has to enlist the majority in a struggle on behalf of a poor minority.' This was why it was no longer any good simply invoking the class war and appealing to one section of society against another.

> We have to persuade men and women who are themselves reasonably well off that they have a duty to forgo some of the advantages they would otherwise enjoy for the sake of others who are much poorer than they are. We have to persuade motor car workers in my constituency that they have an obligation to low-paid workers in the public sector. We have to persuade the British people as a whole that they have an obligation to Africans and Asians whom they have never seen. It is a formidable task. We cannot hope to carry it out if we base our appeal on immediate material self-interest. . . . Our only hope is to appeal to the latent idealism of all men and women of goodwill – irrespective of their income brackets, irrespective of their class origins, irrespective in many cases of their past political affiliations.

Jenkins ended this speech with a phrase which ten years later was to become a cliché:

> We have to break the mould of custom, selfishness and apathy which condemns so many of our fellow countrymen to avoidable indignity and deprivation. In place of the politics of envy, we must put the politics of compassion; in place of the politics of cupidity, the politics of justice; in place of the politics of opportunism, the politics of principle. Only so can we hope to succeed. Only so will success be worth having.[30]

There is here a clear foreshadowing of the SDP. If Labour was irredeemably sunk in the outdated politics of class, as he already feared it might be, Jenkins' mind was now beginning to move in the direction of accepting the need for a new progressive party that would transcend class. In public, of course, he still denied entertaining any such thought. And it was true that even after Taverne's triumph, he did not yet see a new party as a practical possibility; nor did he yet finally accept that Labour was irredeemable. At the Gaitskell anniversary dinner in January 1973 he invoked, inevitably, the incantation that he would 'fight and fight and fight again to save the party we love'.[31] But the final paragraph of *What Matters Now* made clear the only basis on which he thought it could be saved. Labour, he wrote, bore a heavy responsibility as 'the only practical hope for those who have long been sceptical of Conservatism, and now, after half a Parliament of Mr Heath, see their scepticism turned to dismay.'

> The party is the repository of many hopes, both at home and abroad. In the past few years it has disappointed some of these. There is no need for it to continue to do so. A broad-based, international, radical, generous-minded party, aware of its past but more concerned with the future, could quickly seize the imagination of a disillusioned and uninspired British public.

How right he was shown to be, nine years later! The opportunity was there in 1972 if Labour could transform itself into the sort of party that could grasp it.

> Whatever we do we may win a negative victory at the next election. But what we need is a positive victory. For only that offers the likelihood of full success in government. Only that will enable us to carry through a programme which will give us pride in our party and confidence in our processes of government.

Decoded, the message is clear. The only victory worth winning would not be won by the present narrowly class-based, insular, backward-looking and intolerant Labour party. The sort of victory Labour was all too likely to win, on the other hand, would do nothing to inspire the disillusioned public, but only confirm the dominance of those forces within the party who were bent on further narrowing its broad appeal. Thus Jenkins found himself in 1973 in a peculiarly uncomfortable position. Deeply as he abhorred the Conservative Government and all its acts, excepting only Britain's entry into the EEC, the only chance of salvation he could see for his own party lay in its losing the next election.

Yet he had no option but to campaign loyally for the return of a Labour Government. In July he confirmed that he would be willing to serve in such a Government under Wilson's leadership. Late in the day, Wilson had come out of his shell and was beginning to exercise his influence against the wilder proposals of the left: in October he abruptly vetoed the commitment to nationalize twenty-five major companies, and persuaded Conference not to commit the party to coming out of the EEC, but only to 'renegotiate' the Tory terms and put the issue to the electorate either at a subsequent General Election or in a consultative referendum. On this basis – there was still the possibility that it might be the former – Jenkins rejoined the Shadow Cabinet, allowing his name to go forward for election in November and coming respectably fifth: he became Shadow Home Secretary, replacing Shirley Williams. There was then no expectation of an early election. But the situation was suddenly transformed by the miners' overtime ban against the Government's incomes policy (taking advantage of the massive rise in oil prices following the Middle East war, and the fact that coal stocks were desperately low). At the turn of the year, the Government imposed a three-day working week to save energy, but pay talks broke down and on 4 February the miners voted 81 per cent in favour of an all-out strike. Faced with this challenge to his Government, Heath felt he had no choice but to call a crisis election on the theme 'Who Governs?'

All the polls suggested that he would win. Jenkins rallied to the Labour cause like a professional, submerging his doubts about the wider implications of the election in the argument that it was Heath's mismanagement that had landed the country in an unnecessary crisis. In an article for the *Birmingham Mail*, for instance, he dwelled on the ways in which Birmingham suffered particularly heavily from the three-day week, and tried rather vaguely to identify Labour with an approach which would temper expediency with responsibility. 'It is relatively easy either to open the floodgates to still more inflation or to adopt a posture so rigid that great long-term damage is inflicted on our whole industrial machine. Statesmanship demands a solution which recognizes that the country has a special need for the miners and that others must not seek to exploit it so that we are all damaged in the process.'[33] Asked at a press conference what he thought of Heath, he replied diplomatically:

According to which way you look at it, Mr Heath has stubbornness or determination. Nobody becomes Prime Minister of this country without qualities. The tragedy is that he doesn't accompany those qualities with judgement, persuasiveness or the imagination to see across a chasm of disagreement and into the minds of others whose experience of life is different.[34]

He had much harsher words for Anthony Barber, whom he blamed for dissipating the gains of Labour's hard slog and depreciating the currency with unprecedented speed, calling him (in a speech for David Owen at Plymouth) 'a dated disaster, shot through with political viciousness'.[35] Recalling the fuss Heath had made in June 1970 about Labour's unlucky monthly deficit of £31m, he did not hold back from attacking the record deficit of £383m announced in February.[36] Barber's ill-judged consumer-led boom had sent imports soaring into the red again, and Jenkins was entitled to feel personally aggrieved. His more general theme, however, was that Heath's insensitivity had divided the country and it was Labour's task to heal it. Labour, he told his constituents the day before the poll, offered the only way out of Heath's 'blind alley of gloom, despondency, division, selfishness and frustration'.[37]

Whether he believed it is another matter. It is difficult for a lifelong politician not to want to win an election when the instinct of competition is aroused; but all the evidence is that Jenkins was deeply depressed by the result. Labour won exactly the sort of narrow victory he had feared, gaining 301 seats to the Conservatives' 297, with no more than 37.1 per cent of the votes cast against the Conservatives' 37.9 per cent. The Tories actually won 230,000 more votes: the Liberals, who had campaigned on an appeal to national unity and the need for a coalition (supported by Dick Taverne in Lincoln, who narrowly retained his seat), won over six million votes, 19.3 per cent, but were rewarded with only fourteen seats. The result seriously called in question the fairness of the electoral system for the first time since the 1920s. Of more immediate concern to Jenkins, however, it installed in office – once Heath's attempt to carry on with Liberal support had been rebuffed by Jeremy Thorpe – a minority Labour Government more than ever before in the pocket of the trade unions, and once again led by Harold Wilson.

The expected opportunity for a showdown was thus postponed. Had Labour lost, Jenkins intended to stand against Wilson for the leadership: he might not have won, but it would certainly have been the end of Wilson, and there would at least have been a new situation. A breakaway was undoubtedly in his mind: driving back from Birmingham to London with John Harris and Matthew Oakeshott (his personal adviser since 1972), he told Harris that if Labour lost he had better claim his expenses from Transport House pretty quickly to be sure of getting them. Labour's unexpected return to power shelved these calculations. But his supporters thought Jenkins had still a trump to play. The leading Jenkinsites met at Lord Walston's flat in the Albany and resolved that he should tell Wilson that the only office he would accept was the Chancellorship. With no majority, they believed that Wilson could not deny him: he could not afford to have Jenkins on the back benches as a focus of discontent. There was a difficulty that Denis Healey was Shadow Chancellor, but they thought that could be overcome if Jenkins held firm. Not for the first time in this period, however, Jenkins disappointed them. For one thing, he was not personally very keen to be Chancellor again: he had done that job already. Moreover, from his experience in the sixties he took the clear view that a man cannot be an effective Chancellor without the full consent of his colleagues: to force himself on colleagues who did not acknowledge his authority would be a recipe for conflict leading to an early and messy resignation. The position he would have liked – the third of the three great offices of State, and the only one he had not held – was the Foreign Office: but that was promised to Callaghan, and it would anyway have been impossible for Wilson, with the EEC renegotiation pending, to have appointed Labour's most ardent and least critical European to that of all offices. Jenkins, in fact, probably had a better idea of his own bargaining power than did his followers. By resigning the Deputy Leadership in 1972 he had abdicated his title to one of the top jobs. He had only rejoined the Shadow Cabinet four months before. It was politically out of the question, after the events of the past three years, far too provocative to a large section of the party, for Wilson to have thought of bringing Jenkins back to the second place in the new Government. The option remained of refusing to serve at all. But that would have been inconsistent with his actions of the preceding months in coming back into the Shadow Cabinet, and could only have been interpreted as ostentatiously disloyal. He might as well have walked out of the party there and then – but it would have been the worst possible moment to go. He had little practical choice but to take what he was offered, the job he had been shadowing in opposition. Nevertheless, there were several among the increasingly demoralized Jenkinsites who felt that yet another chance to assert himself and fight for the sort of party and policies they wanted had been missed.

Going back to the Home Office, though the most Jenkins could reasonably expect, was effectively a demotion for a former Chancellor. He had been there before; he had no enthusiasm for a second term of wrestling with prisons and the police – the liberalizing chapter of the sixties had been written. More seriously, the isolation of the Home Office, of which he had written in 1971 ('A man could, I believe, be a tolerable and even a good Home Secretary while not on speaking terms with most of his principal colleagues')[38] meant that he would be in a position to exert little influence on the central economic and political issues the Government faced. He went back to the Home Office with a heavy heart, quite unlike his original arrival there full of hope and energy, nine years before.

EIGHT

The Struggle for the Labour Party Lost, 1974–1976

Jenkins' second period at the Home Office, from March 1974 to September 1976, does not compare with his first in terms either of mythology or of tangible accomplishment. He came in with a sense of *déjà vu*, with no personal agenda of reforms he wanted to achieve, and his mind was to a considerable extent on other things. First, there was the state of the Labour party and his deep disquiet at the whole trend of the Government towards accommodating the trade unions and appeasing the left. Secondly, as a former Chancellor and the leader of a distinct faction within the party, he had a responsibility to bring his experience to bear as far as he was able on the major areas of policy facing the Government: part of his success in 1965–7 can be attributed to the fact that he was then a relatively junior minister able to give most of his attention to his own department. Third, he was deeply concerned to see that the EEC renegotiation and referendum resulted eventually in the right answer: this was still the single issue that mattered more to him than any other, and it took a good deal of his energy. Nevertheless, with all these distractions, Jenkins was still a very much better Home Secretary than most, and this second term too had its share of important initiatives.

One of the less important, but one which raised a few eyebrows in 1974, was the appointment among Wilson's second wave of junior ministers of John Harris to be Minister of State, for which purpose he was raised to the peerage as Lord Harris of Greenwich. By this means Jenkins was enabled to have his faithful henchman still beside him, but in a more formal capacity than previously, and with defined responsibilities of his own. It was said that Harris was the first peer ever created by a Home Secretary: but clearly his promotion from Jenkins' press handler to Minister in his own right suited Wilson admirably (while the elevation was a useful precedent for his similar translation of Marcia

Williams into Lady Falkender two months later). Harris's new status was initially viewed with profound suspicion in the Home Office, where he had been widely felt in 1965-7 to have been more concerned for Jenkins' political image than with interesting him in the sort of routine administration by which civil servants judge a minister. He was very quickly transformed, however, into the perfect Home Office Minister, so much so that he not only stayed on under Merlyn Rees when Jenkins went to Brussels in 1976, but was then appointed chairman of the Parole Board by William Whitelaw in 1979.

In addition to Harris, Jenkins also brought into the department with him his new young political adviser, Matthew Oakeshott: much of Oakeshott's time was spent keeping in touch with Brussels during the EEC renegotiation and briefing not only Jenkins but also Shirley Williams and the other leading Labour Europeans. Then, after a few weeks, he selected as his new Principal Private Secretary Hayden Phillips, with whom he quickly formed the same sort of special relationship he had enjoyed in the sixties with David Dowler: when Jenkins left the Home Office for Brussels in 1976, he took Phillips with him. Jenkins' second period in office was marked by the same need to surround himself with people he both trusts and likes that characterized his first.

Something that was quite new in the work of the Office since 1967 was the attention that had to be paid to combatting Irish terrorism. As the IRA spread its latest campaign of indiscriminate murder from Ulster to the mainland, London was becoming sickeningly resigned to regular bombing: the Home Secretary was increasingly confronted with convicted terrorists going on hunger strike. Two in particular captured the headlines – the sisters Marion and Dolours Price, aged twenty-three and twenty, sentenced in 1973 to life imprisonment for their part in a massive car bombing at the Old Bailey. For five and a half months up to May 1974 they had been forcibly fed in Brixton prison, until they withdrew the necessary minimum degree of co-operation, when on medical advice feeding was stopped. Their aim was to be allowed to serve their sentences in Northern Ireland. It was a relatively modest request, and because they were young girls it attracted noisy demonstrations and some public sympathy, despite the deaths they had caused. But Jenkins decided that he could not give way to moral blackmail; and on 6 June 1974, when they were near to death, he made one of the most memorable ministerial broadcasts ever, explaining his reasons. Quietly but unanswerably he set out the considerations which had to govern his decision. There were more than thirty IRA prisoners currently in British jails, of whom another four besides the Price sisters were on hunger strike. Was he to move

them all? Or only those who went on hunger strike? Or only those who
happened to be girls? There was simply no defensible principle on which
he could agree to move the sisters.

> In his judgement and explanation [wrote George Hutchinson in *The Times*]
> he has delivered, I think, one of the finest statements heard from any
> Minister in recent years, reflecting the deep personal consideration which
> has always distinguished the best Home Secretaries, and expressed, more-
> over, in words of such simple, compelling dignity as to elevate the public
> debate. This is Prime Ministerial language.[1]

Certainly this was Jenkins at his best, back in command as a Minister
after the uncertainties of opposition, applying the force of reason to an
emotionally charged situation. The next day the Price sisters ended
their hunger strike. In December they were moved, not to Northern
Ireland but to Durham top-security prison. From now on there was no
more force-feeding of hunger strikers. In February 1976 Frank Stagg
was allowed to fast to death in Wakefield prison. Jenkins had been
deeply relieved in 1965 that the grim shadow of the gallows had been
lifted from the Home Office just before he went there: in 1974 he found
that a new power of life or death had been handed back to the Home
Secretary by the IRA. But he would not be blackmailed.

The summer and autumn of 1974 saw an intense campaign of bombing following the breakdown of the 1973 power-sharing experiment in
Northern Ireland, killed by the Protestant workers' strike. Explosions
at Westminster Hall, the Tower of London, and soldiers' pubs in Guild-
ford and Woolwich were only the worst of a series of atrocities. Then on
21 November came the Birmingham pub bombing, in which twenty-
one people were killed and over one hundred injured. Hitherto, successive Home Secretaries had gone along with the insistence by the police
that they already had all the powers they needed to catch the terrorists.
But public reaction to the Birmingham outrage was such that something
more had to be seen to be done. Jenkins immediately announced an
emergency powers Bill to deal with the 'insensate killings'.[2] The Office
already had one prepared, which was finalized at East Hendred over
the weekend, published on the following Wednesday and rushed
through both Houses in twenty-four hours. The IRA was outlawed; the
police were given the power to arrest and hold suspected terrorists for
five days without charge; and the Home Secretary was given the power
to deport suspects to Ireland or bar them from mainland Britain. In
January 1975 Jenkins told the Commons that he had already signed
twenty-four exclusion orders. The Prevention of Terrorism Act was
intended as a temporary measure: but as is the way with such measures

it is still in force (indeed it was strengthened in 1976). It was under its provisions that in 1982 the Conservative Home Secretary, William Whitelaw, barred the two Sinn Fein leaders invited to London by the GLC leader Ken Livingstone. To many on the left, Jenkins' authorship of the Act – introducing the very un-British anomaly whereby men who can walk free in Belfast are not admitted to the rest of the United Kingdom – is a dark stain on his libertarian record. It is undeniable that it was brought in primarily as a gesture to public opinion, in unseemly haste; but no Home Secretary could have resisted such pressure, or would have been wise to try. It was as much as Jenkins could risk to stand firm against restoring the death penalty for terrorists: visiting the mutilated in Birmingham hospitals he was deeply shaken by the crowds of blood-crazed women screaming for revenge. On 11 December, the House of Commons voted 369 to 217 against restoring hanging. The following summer a *Sunday Times* profile commended Jenkins' 'sensitivity to the public mood' in his firm response to terrorism in all its forms. 'He has reacted without over-reacting, without relinquishing the need to lead.... At each stage he has taken account of the public response and then carefully articulated his own.'[3] The fault is the IRA's that the 1974 Act has been annually renewed.

On the more positive side of the ledger, Jenkins was responsible for two major pieces of legislation protecting citizens' rights. Neither has fulfilled all the hopes placed in them, but one made a start and the other took a further step towards guaranteeing equal treatment. The 1975 Sex Discrimination Act amended the 1970 Equal Pay Act, outlawed discrimination on grounds of sex in education, employment and other spheres, and set up the Equal Opportunities Commission. The 1976 Race Relations Act extended the scope of the 1968 Act initiated in Jenkins' first spell as Home Secretary (taking in, for instance, racial discrimination in clubs of over twenty-five members), and merged the Race Relations Board with the Community Relations Commission to form the Commission for Racial Equality. This merger, though advocated by Mark Bonham Carter (who had chaired the Board from 1966 to 1971 and the Commission from 1971 to 1977), has been widely criticized for confusing the quasi-judicial function of the one with the essentially propagandist function of the other: it is generally agreed that the new Commission combining the two functions under the former Conservative MP David Lane* has not worked well, though criticism is today directed more at its powers than at its structure. His handling of

* Ironically, Jenkins tried to persuade David Steel to take on the chairmanship of the new Commission. Fortunately he did not succeed.

race relations caused a rupture between Jenkins and his second Minister
of State, Alex Lyon, who wanted to pursue a much more actively
interventionist policy laying on local authorities a statutory obligation
to seek out problems caused by cultural differences and prepare programmes to tackle them, by language teaching and other means. Jenkins' answer to this was that, in the dire economic circumstances which
the Government faced, there was simply no money for such programmes. Advised by Anthony Lester (a human rights lawyer and old
associate: he was the editor of Jenkins' 1967 collection of *Essays and
Speeches*), Jenkins concentrated instead on the legal end of the racial
problem. Lyon also overreached himself within the Home Office by
using his discretion too freely in individual cases of immigration policy.
When Jim Callaghan became Prime Minister in 1976 he was abruptly
sacked. In his first bitterness he blamed Callaghan more than Jenkins.
('I have paid the price of trying to get justice for the blacks in this
country. Jim has never had much time for those who espoused that
cause.')[4] But the next month he was telling *The Times* that his experience
had disillusioned him with Jenkins too: from being an ardent Jenkinsite
he had ended up voting in the leadership election for Crosland and
eventually for Foot.[5] This was a conflict of style rather than intention,
since Jenkins actually operated the immigration rules as liberally as he
could. He changed the citizenship law so as to allow British wives to
bring in their husbands (a change reversed by the Tories in 1979, until
obliged by the European Convention on Human Rights to backtrack in
1982). He also announced in April 1974 an amnesty for immigrants
who had entered illegally before 1973, and brooked no Foreign Office
excuses for delay. In a vivid glimpse of Jenkins' force when roused,
Barbara Castle's diary records him dealing devastatingly with David
Ennals, Elwyn Jones and, in his absence, Callaghan, in the Home
Affairs Committee:

Roy gave the *coup de grace*, saying that he really couldn't have his policy
dictated by the fact that the FO had failed to man its posts adequately. Roy's
drawl always lengthens when he is angry, which heightens the effect of
contempt. Next he disposed equally effectively of Elwyn, who tried to make
out that Roy really ought to legislate. How the Lord Chancellor could argue
this, said Roy, was beyond his understanding, since the 1971 Act had
explicitly placed an administrative freedom of action on the Home Secretary
which he merely proposed to announce he did not intend to exercise.
Collapse of legal party.

Finally, when Roy declared the committee was agreed to proceed on the
lines he proposed, David caused another storm by announcing that in that

case he must reserve the Foreign Secretary's right to raise the matter in Cabinet. Roy went so cold with fury he could hardly speak. That was the most gross abuse of the procedures of Cabinet in his experience, he said icily. If one member of Cabinet, who had not even taken the trouble to be present, found himself in a minority of one on a committee and then claimed the right to reopen the matter in Cabinet, he really could not see any point in committees meeting at all. We all backed him up. 'You can tell the Foreign Secretary that this reaction is unanimous', I said tartly. Poor David looked as if he wished the floor would swallow him and merely said meekly that he would report the feeling of the committee to the Foreign Secretary. 'Do that', said Roy grimly. Altogether a good morning's work, for here is another election pledge we shall have kept and damn the consequences.[6]

Going back to the Home Office, Jenkins was confronted again with the problem of the prisons. If they had been overcrowded in the sixties, with the number of prisoners around 35,000, they were worse now, holding more than 40,000, in conditions that were increasingly becoming regarded by those who cared as scandalous. The measures he had taken in 1966 to try to reduce the prison population had had negligible effect. In 1974-6 he did what he could along the same lines to encourage the development of alternatives to prison: in August 1974, for instance, he extended the system of community service orders over the whole country. But the problem – beyond his control – was that crime was still rising inexorably, and the courts were not inclined to be sympathetic to suggestions that they consider 'soft' options or shorter sentences. William Whitelaw has met the same resistance. The 'hard' solution – building more prisons – cost more money than the Government could spare for a form of expenditure which wins no votes. In July 1975 Jenkins tried to draw the nation's attention to the crisis it was storing up by neglecting the prisons, asserting that if the prison population reached 42,000 'conditions in the system would approach the intolerable and drastic action to relieve the position will be inescapable.'[7] But that figure was passed in October 1976, a month after he left office; and Merlyn Rees had no more money for 'drastic action' than he had. The figure has continued to rise, and conditions to worsen. Prisons feature in Jenkins' record as a clear failure; but the failure belongs equally to every Home Secretary and every Government for the past twenty years.

Jenkins achieved slightly more with another intractable problem – complaints against the police, an increasingly live issue following the upsurge in mass demonstrations since the late sixties. In order to meet the argument that if complaints were to be seen to be fairly dealt with, the police could not be judge and jury in their own case, he was determined to introduce an independent element into the complaints procedure. When he first unveiled his Bill in July 1975, *The Times* thought he had done well to satisfy all parties.[8] In fact, he fell foul both of the civil liberties lobby on the left, who thought his independent element far too small, and of the police, backed by the Tories, who resented any outside interference in their disciplinary procedures at all. The answer to the former was simply that it was administratively impossible, without setting up an enormous bureaucracy, to have independent investigation of all of 17,000 complaints a year: the sensible balance was to have outside investigation only when the police enquiry proved unsatisfactory. Even this limited measure, however, was too much for the Commissioner of the Metropolitan Police, Sir Robert Mark, who was proud of his own internal efforts to stamp out corruption, and believed strongly that the morale of the force depended on discipline remaining entirely in the hands of the chief constables: he took early retirement rather than work the new Act – thus bringing to a sad end a remarkable relationship of mutual admiration between the Home Secretary and himself.[9] Jenkins had first spotted Mark when he was Chief Constable of Leicester in 1965 and was 'immediately struck by his exceptional quality'.[10] He was against hanging, in favour of majority verdicts, and strongly in favour of the modernization and amalgamation of police forces, even at the cost of his own job. The Home Secretary has no power of appointment over provincial forces, but while redundancy hung over Mark, Jenkins used him on the Mountbatten enquiry and on the Advisory Council on the Penal System. Then in 1966 he saw a chance to appoint him an assistant commissioner at Scotland Yard, in defiance of what he characteristically called the Yard's 'mercantilist' tradition. (It likes to export officers to the provinces, but not import them.) Mark was at first ostracized in London, but eventually made a powerful impact: he was nearly promoted Commissioner by Callaghan in 1968, before he was given the job by Maudling in 1972. He welcomed Jenkins' return to the Home Office in 1974; but then felt bitterly let down when Jenkins chose to interfere, as he thought clumsily and counter-productively, in police discipline. For his part, Jenkins stuck firmly to his middle way, and reviewing Mark's memoirs in 1978 expressed his bewilderment at Mark's objection to 'political' appointments (that is, made by a Minister) to the Police Complaints Board set up under his new Bill. 'Who does he think appointed him?' he asked. Why should Lord Plowden be any more intimidated than he was himself?[10]

Mark's objection was the reason why Jenkins in 1976 could take no more than the first step towards making the police fully accountable to the public. The Home Secretary has to retain the confidence of the force and, as in 1966, he was regarded with suspicion or even hostility by many policemen who judged him, by his reputation, to be 'soft' on crime. Then he had outfaced them and won their respect; but in 1975–6 he once again met with noisy interruptions when he addressed the Police Federation conference. Again he did not shirk the confrontation, telling the delegates straight that their campaigns for the death penalty and longer sentences defied the evidence that neither had any effect in deterring crime. The rule of law did not mean simply 'our own pet prejudices'.

> It means, in a democratic society, the law as passed by an elected Parliament and applied by impartial courts. You cannot have a rule of law while dismissing with disparagement Parliament, the courts and those who practise in them. That is not the rule of law. It is exactly what the pressure groups you complain about seek to achieve by demonstration. Your job, and mine, is to uphold the law as it is, and not to decry it.

Of the Federation's 'pet prejudices' he declared bluntly:

> I respect your right to put them to me. You will no doubt respect my right to tell you that I do not think all the points in sum amount to a basis for a rational penal policy.[11]

Jenkins had given early evidence of his determination to assert the rule of law in an area where the duties of his department brought him directly into conflict with the extremists of his own party: picketing. Under the terms of the so-called 'Social Contract', the Government gave the trade unions practically everything they wanted in return for the promise – not kept – to restrain wage increases. As part of the Government's side of the bargain Michael Foot (brought in for the first time from the back benches to the Department of Employment) proposed in his Trade Union and Labour Relations Bill, which replaced the Tories' hated Industrial Relations Act, to give official pickets the right in law to require drivers to stop to listen to 'persuasion', or require the police to do it for them. It was actually to be a criminal offence not to stop for a picket. When he heard of this preposterous proposal Jenkins immediately sent for Foot's Minister of State, Albert Booth, and told him that if they proceeded with it they would have to find a new Home Secretary. He also arranged a meeting between senior police officers and Foot's civil servants to explain to the latter how unworkable (quite apart from morally indefensible) such a law would be. The clause was withdrawn. 'We were fortunate indeed in our Home Secretary', wrote Robert Mark.[12]

Secondly, Jenkins was absolutely firm in the face of Labour protests and demonstrations on behalf of the famous 'Shrewsbury Two', imprisoned for picketing offences in December 1973. To the left they were martyrs, 'political prisoners', victims of the vicious Tory establishment, and any self-respecting Labour Home Secretary would make it his business to release them. He was petitioned by the NEC, called on by the entire Finance and General Purposes Committee of the TUC, repeatedly questioned in Parliament and heckled everywhere he went by chanting demonstrators. Steadfastly, Jenkins insisted that their case was a matter for the courts and it was not for him to interfere: not until September 1976 was the more recalcitrant of the two released, after thirty-one charges of misconduct and non-co-operation had reduced his normal remission. His principled refusal to waive the processes of law at the dictation of his party contrasted sharply with the Government's lifting in October 1974 of the penalties incurred by the Labour councillors of Clay Cross for refusing to implement the Tories' Housing Finance Act. 'It was the first time', one Jenkinsite junior minister told the *Sunday Times*, 'that this Government had told the Labour Conference and the TUC where to go.' His stand was loudly applauded, of course, by the Tories, which made him more than ever a marked man to the left; while the very fact that such things were demanded of Ministers, and more often than not conceded, increased his despair at the way the party was going. He felt desperately isolated in Cabinet, where he was regularly supported only by Shirley Williams; he was particularly sickened by the lack of support from Tony Crosland, who was actually the Minister responsible for the Clay Cross amnesty, disliked it thoroughly, but swallowed his qualms and did the party's bidding for the sake of 'unity'.[13]

He made a determined stand against the left in a well-publicized speech to the Pembrokeshire Labour Party at Haverfordwest in July 1974, in which he once again hinted at his growing belief that the two-party system could not long survive Labour's retreat into sectarianism. He was careful to dismiss 'febrile' talk of coalition, and insisted that the country was better governed by the present Labour Government than by the Tories.

At the same time one should not doubt that there is in Britain a great body of moderate, rather uncommitted opinion, and that unless substantial sectors of such opinion can feel happy in supporting one or other of the major parties the result will be an intolerable strain upon the traditional pattern of politics.

This uncommitted opinion, Jenkins believed, had been repelled by 1970-4 and rejected the Tories; but it had not given Labour a mandate either, so the country faced another election very soon.

> The stalemate will not be broken unless and until we can move over to the Labour party a sizeable part of this potentially progressive, but non-extreme opinion. I do not think that has happened yet.

The left's assumption that they alone possessed 'a monopoly of wisdom, the solution of every problem and the right to treat anyone outside their own ranks as either a knave or a fool' both alienated the mass of ordinary voters and produced 'the rigid division of the country into opposing and uncomprehending armies'. This was Heath's mistake, and the negation of true democratic leadership.

> If we are to get through the immense problems of the next few years we need to heal and not to deepen the wounds of the nation. That can, I believe, be done upon the basis of party government, with the coherence of policy and the offering to the nation of effective choice which that makes possible.
> But it cannot be done upon the basis of ignoring middle opinion and telling everyone who does not agree with you to go to hell.

Jenkins' commitment to the two-party system, and hence to Labour, was very strong. But it increasingly seemed to him that Labour's basic identity as a democratic party, the democratic values taken for granted by the party of Attlee and Gaitskell in which he had grown up, were being on the one hand systematically undermined by elements who would not previously have been admitted to the party, and on the other allowed to go by default by a leadership afraid to spell out what until very recently had been platitudes. On four fundamental questions, he now insisted, Labour's position needed to be 'crystal clear'. First, thinking of Clay Cross and the picket lines:

> No-one is entitled to be above the law. If we weaken on that principle, we can say goodbye to democratic socialism, because what is sauce for the goose will be sauce for the gander.

There was already a lot of wild talk in the press of 'private armies', ready to take advantage of any suspension of the rule of law. Secondly, Britain must remain fully committed to the Atlantic alliance built up by Bevin and President Truman after 1945:

> If anyone wants a Britain poised uneasily between the Western alliance and

the Communist block they can, in the immortal words of Mr Sam Goldwyn, 'include me out'.

Economically, by the same token, Britain lived by trade: the 'alternative strategy', promulgated by the left, of retreating into a siege economy was 'fantasy'. Third, Labour must live with the mixed economy, even though he still conceded that the mix might change:

> I am in favour of sensible and well-argued extensions of public ownership ... But I am also in favour of a healthy, vigorous and profitable private sector.

Finally, less an underlying principle than the overwhelming fact of the moment: 'The greatest threat to the cohesion of our society today is the still increasing rate of inflation', due partly to the Tories, partly to the rise in world commodity prices. Again Jenkins stressed the danger to democracy itself:

> The country will not for long put up with it. If we cannot solve it by tolerable and civilized methods, then someone within a few years will solve it by intolerable and uncivilised ones. And we shall all – Government and Opposition and other parties alike – look irrelevant and ineffective.

To restore stability it might be necessary to make 'sacrifices both of dogma and materialism': curing inflation was now even more important than securing growth. Though he commended Healey for recognizing this priority, Jenkins did not think the party had yet faced it.

> There is no point in pretending that we are not facing an economic crisis without precedent since the growth of post-war prosperity. It makes even the problems with which I had to deal as Chancellor in 1967–69 look small. There is nothing for the Labour party to be ashamed of in this. We left a relatively healthy situation, and we came back to desolation and decay....
>
> We need only begin to feel ashamed if we were to cover the problem up, to pretend that things are easier than they are, and encourage a reversion to the previous mood of dalliance in the face of danger.[14]

This was to be Jenkins' repeated refrain, in Cabinet and in the country, for as long as he remained in the Government.

His supporters were delighted with this speech, long-gestated but worth waiting for: he had at last broken the shackles of collective responsibility and spoken out plainly. Shirley Williams and Reg Prentice backed him unequivocally: so did George Brown. But Ian Mikardo, Eric Heffer and others on the left attacked him furiously; Neil Kinnock denounced 'Jenkins the splitter',[15] and Barbara Castle feared that by reopening the party's wounds he had lost Labour the election.[16] The

Tories indeed had a field day. Peter Walker was not alone in wondering how Jenkins could remain in a Government whose attitudes respectively to Clay Cross, the Common Market, nationalization and incomes policy violated each of his four basic principles.[15] But Jenkins had learned from his resignation in 1972 that he had to stay in office to fight his corner. Beyond sounding occasional trumpet calls, however, there was little, in his isolation, that he could do. The October 1974 election found him, as in February, condemning Heath's divisiveness and Barber's incompetence and doing his best to endorse Labour's 'Social Contract' – 'not perfect, not copper-bottomed, but the best hope for the future' – as a true partnership between Government, the people and the unions.[17] More often he followed his own line. 'Mr Jenkins', reported *The Times*, has pitched his campaign at a high level, speaking with almost religious zeal about political morality and the broad-based conscience and re-form approach for which the Labour party "does, and must stand".'[18] At Horsham he painted a rosy picture of the party which had little to do with the reality of 1974, but which, in its complete lack of ideological definition, perfectly encapsulated that vaguely benevolent view of political purpose which had sustained him since 1945 but was now leaving him politically homeless. Labour, he suggested, 'embraces the best part of the liberal tradition.'

> It is socialist because it puts the community first. It is national because it can secure a strong Britain, which the alternative has signally failed to do. It is internationalist because it recognizes that humanity does not stop at the shores of this country. It offers a way out of the blind alley of gloom, despondency, division and frustration into which we were too long led.... It is a message of humanity, justice and hope.[19]

Labour won an overall majority of just four, taking a slightly increased share (39.2 per cent) of a significantly lower poll (only 72 per cent of the electorate, compared with 78 per cent in February). It was another messy and uncertain result, confirming Jenkins' analysis that neither party commanded much enthusiasm in the country. (The Liberals also lost ground slightly, but still took 18 per cent of the vote, while the Scottish and Welsh Nationalists gained seats.) But Labour was confirmed in office. Now the question of the EEC came back centre stage to be resolved one way or the other. Since April, Callaghan had been engaged on the 'renegotiation' of the 1971 terms, truculently at first, then more positively. During the election he and Wilson maintained a hard negotiating posture, but it was clear that, back in government, they were preparing to reverse themselves again and defy the party Conference by recommending that the marginally improved terms should now be accepted. Shirley Williams created a stir at an election press conference by announcing that she would leave politics if the country voted to come out of Europe, which obliged Jenkins to say that he too would not remain in a Cabinet committed to withdrawal.[20] But he joined loyally in the renegotiation charade, declaring that there was after all 'substantial scope' for renegotiation ('I am optimistic ... that a position will come out which will be more favourable to this country and more helpful to the Community generally') and, after a last rearguard action, reconciled himself to a referendum. His objection to it as a regular feature of British life remained; but 'I accept on a broader plane the desirability of reconciling British public opinion to membership of the EEC.'[21] The battle was now to win the decisive vote.

In January 1975 Jenkins agreed to become President of Britain in Europe, the all-party umbrella organization set up to co-ordinate the campaign for a 'Yes' vote. But it was thought prudent not to publicize the fact until March, when the majority of the Cabinet officially approved the renegotiated terms and Wilson announced the constitutionally unprecedented 'agreement to differ'. (William Whitelaw kept the seat warm for him in the meantime.)[22] Then Jenkins overcame the misgivings which had formed a large part of his opposition to the referendum in 1972, and took the lead in insisting, against Wilson's cautious reservations, that Ministers must be free to speak on joint platforms with Conservatives and Liberals.[23] The experience of doing so gave him another significant push out of the Labour party. (To this extent his 1972 fear proved well-founded.) The 1975 referendum campaign was an important staging post on the road which eventually led to the formation of the SDP. It showed that co-operation between politicians of different parties to achieve a common goal was a real and practical possibility, and unexpectedly refreshing. It opened the eyes not only of Jenkins but of Bill Rodgers, Shirley Williams and others who were eventually to leave the Labour party to the degree of common ground they shared with Heath and Whitelaw, Jeremy Thorpe and David Steel, which made much of the old party battle seem suddenly artificial and irrelevant. A politician's habits of thinking easily become fixed in the particular rhetoric of his own party, even when he is as disillusioned with that party as Jenkins was by 1975. The referendum campaign had the effect of tearing off the mental blinkers, making it that much easier to contemplate a departure hitherto almost unthinkable.

The freedom to appear with lifelong opponents was enhanced by the

wicked pleasure derived from openly attacking colleagues. On 27 May
the newspapers were able to make gleeful play with Jenkins' cutting
dismissal of Tony Benn's wild claim that membership of the EEC had
already cost Britain 500,000 jobs: 'I find it difficult to take Mr Benn
seriously as an economics Minister.'[24] (Benn was Secretary of State for
Industry.) It was widely pointed out that Benn's figure amounted to
arguing that, but for the EEC, Britain would be enjoying, in the middle
of a world recession, the lowest unemployment since the war. Jenkins
suggested that Benn's method was simply to think of a number and
double it. On television on 2 June, he and Benn met in a head-on
debate, unprecedented between two Cabinet Ministers. It was an open
question which came over best, as John Whale graphically noted in the
Sunday Times:

> The contrast between the two men's styles was complete: Jenkins rapid in
> speech, Benn measured; Jenkins qualificatory, parenthetical ("Curiously,
> on a point of reminiscence ..."), Benn simple ("Be commonsensical, Roy!");
> Jenkins anxious to deal with everything that came crowding into his head
> ("Well, there are a lot of points there, and I'd like very quickly to run
> through one or two, if not three of them"), Benn banging one point repeat-
> edly ("This erodes the importance of the vote"); Jenkins eager to peg out
> common ground ("I don't think Tony would disagree with this ..."), Benn
> quite prepared to come through with the moralising rebuke ("A joke about
> weather is not really right when we're talking about people's jobs"); Jenkins
> worrying about truth, Benn intent on making a case.

Whale felt that on the printed page, Benn's evasion of Jenkins'
repeated questioning about jobs and alternatives might have looked
shifty; on television, however, 'it seems likely that his single point will
have stuck in more viewers' minds than any of Jenkins' did.' Television
is not really Jenkins' medium. He was much more at home on a platform:

> At the Newcastle meeting he tried physically to keep his chairman from
> intervening so that he could deal with his hecklers himself; at the Philhar-
> monic Hall in Liverpool he totally outshone his fellow-speakers, Jeremy
> Thorpe and Reggie Maudling, laying an incantation on his audience with
> his most characteristic gesture, right arm outstretched, hand tilted up,
> fingers spread; in an ill-filled Birmingham Town Hall, on the last weary
> night before polling, he could still speak with such verve as to prompt a
> woman in the gallery to call out as he sat down: "I'm glad he's my MP,
> anyway".[3]

Jenkins enjoyed the referendum. Once the Government had given its
endorsement to the renegotiated terms, and the campaign was seen to

pit (with a few exceptions) the most trusted and popular politicians, plus most of the press, against the least trusted and least popular, the opinion polls swung decisively from hostility to clear support for staying in. He was reinvigorated, speaking from the heart again after years of coded weasel words, and confident of the outcome. His theme was what it had always been, with the additional point that the country was now already in the EEC.

> I believe that both the security and the prosperity of the country depend upon a Yes vote. Not to have gone into Europe would have been a misfortune. But to come out would be on an altogether greater scale of self-inflicted injury. It would be a catastrophe. It would leave us weak and unregarded, both economically and politically.[25]

'Let us vote decisively', he urged at Britain in Europe's final press conference, 'to settle the issue overwhelmingly and to free us from the continued debilitation of being hesitant and reluctant partners.'[26]

Three days earlier he had coined a new image for his oldest argument. To leave the EEC now, he suggested, would be to go into 'an old people's home for faded nations. . . . I do not think it would be a very comfortable old people's home. I do not like the look of some of the prospective warders.'[27] Since the anti-Market campaign (Enoch Powell and some other maverick Conservatives excepted) was overwhelmingly Labour, the implied rejection of his own party was clear. It was the last hope of the Jenkinsites that a resounding 'Yes' vote in the referendum would tip the internal party battle back their way, providing the springboard for a counter-offensive by the right against a chastened and discredited left. 'We are going to know conclusively who speaks for what', Brian Walden was reported as saying, 'and who can deliver which votes which way. The referendum may in that way have a very therapeutic effect.'[3] The result was as resounding as the most ardent pro-Marketeer could have hoped, an almost two-to-one majority for staying in, uniform all round the country on a reasonably high poll (64 per cent). 'For all who have worked in this European campaign in bad days as well as good', Jenkins celebrated, 'it is a day of satisfaction and jubilation.'[28] But the therapeutic effect, if any, was shortlived. Wilson took the opportunity to remove Benn from Industry to the politically less sensitive Department of Energy. At the same time Jenkins' position was sufficiently enhanced to enable him, by threatening resignation, to prevent the Prime Minister performing a characteristic balancing act by sacking Reg Prentice from the Cabinet.[29] But Prentice's future was very soon to be the subject of the right's next defeat.

Reg Prentice was not a Jenkinsite. He had never been a Gaitskellite or involved in CDS. He was a pugnacious trade-union sponsored right-winger who until very late in the day had been against the EEC; by virtue of defying categorization and appealing to both wings of the Parliamentary party he had come top in the Shadow Cabinet elections in 1972 and third in 1973. In 1974 he had been appointed Secretary of State for Education. But he was in deep trouble in his constituency, Newham North-East, due to a combination of his own neglect and the organized 'entryism' by the left. In July 1975, just after the referendum, the local party voted to drop him for the next election: he thus became a test case for what was happening in the party nationally. With Taverne still on his conscience,* Jenkins determined that he must go into battle for Prentice. In September he, Shirley Williams and Tom Jackson, the leader of the post office workers, braved 'Free Des Warren' demonstrators from the left and flour bombs thrown by National Front protestors from the right to speak for him in his constituency. Jenkins was 'magnificent', Prentice told the press. 'He was angry, but he showed his scorn and contempt for these people and delivered his prepared speech.'[30] He specifically instructed the stewards not to bring in the police, believing that the demonstrators made his point for him. Promising over the uproar to 'fight and fight and fight again as long as we have political breath in our bodies', he spelled out the implications for the party as a whole if individuals like Prentice could be driven out by a few extremists.

> If tolerance is shattered, formidable consequences will follow. Labour MPs will either have to become creatures of cowardice, concealing their views, trimming their sails, accepting orders, stilling their consciences, or they will all have to be men far to the left of those whose votes they seek.
>   Either would make a mockery of parliamentary democracy. The first would reduce still further, and rightly reduce, respect for the House of Commons. It would become an assembly of craven spirits and crooked tongues. The second would, quite simply, divorce the Labour party from the people.[30]

Unfortunately Prentice turned out personally to be a bad cause to make a stand for: rejected by Labour, he crossed right over the political divide and joined the Conservative party, found another seat and in 1979 accepted office in Mrs Thatcher's Government, leaving those still in the Labour party who had supported him exposed to the charge of having sheltered a closet Tory, while the left crowed in triumph. No-one could have foreseen this outcome, however, in 1975, when the NEC

* Taverne had lost his seat in the second General Election of 1974.

not only refused to involve itself in Prentice's case but resolutely turned a blind eye to the wider implications. An investigation by the national agent, Reg Underhill, into the infiltration of the party by extremist groups was not even discussed, but simply shelved. Shirley Williams, Tom Bradley (Jenkins' PPS 1964-70) and the handful of other embattled right-wingers on the Executive were helpless, frustrated, increasingly subjected to insult and near to despair. Belatedly the right was trying to organize some resistance. The previous December some of the younger backbenchers had set up the Manifesto Group as a counterweight to the Tribune Group within the PLP: the leading spirits were the nucleus of those who eventually, in 1981, broke away to form the SDP - John Horam, Ian Wrigglesworth (Jenkins' PPS, 1974-6), Dickson Mabon, Neville Sandelson and others. March 1976, however, was to show up how weak they were.

In January 1976, Jenkins took another significant step in distancing himself not merely from the fundamentalist socialism of the left, but even from one of the cardinal tenets of revisionism as formulated by Gaitskell and Crosland in the fifties and taken for granted, until quite recently, by himself. Speaking in Anglesey, he dramatically challenged the orthodoxy of both wings of the Labour party that ever higher public spending was an unqualified good and the solution of all society's ills. Since 1964 the proportion of the GNP taken up by Government expenditure had risen from 44 per cent to 60 per cent - for no commensurate improvement in public services or social welfare. 'I do not think that you can push public expenditure significantly above 60 per cent', he announced, 'and maintain the values of a plural society and adequate freedom of choice. We are here close to one of the frontiers of social democracy.'[31]

'How these people come out in their true colours!', Barbara Castle had exclaimed in her diary when Jenkins had tried out this line in Cabinet the previous summer.[32] His argument was that inflation (which peaked at 26.9 per cent in August) was the overwhelming danger to society, that higher unemployment (which passed the million mark in December) was no cure for it, and that high public spending, paid for by taxation, was itself inflationary. Healey had in fact been forced, for economic reasons, to accept this logic and apply a squeeze on spending which made even Jenkins' own measures in 1968-9 look mild. But Jenkins was practically alone in the Labour party in arguing - as he now did at every opportunity - that public spending had reached its *politically* tolerable limit. This was an important moment of truth, reflecting his growing concern with the cohesion of a divided society and

carrying with it an implied rejection of *any* further nationalization – a
key step towards the SDP idea of a truce in the 'frontier war' between
the nationalized and private sectors. To some former supporters like
Roy Hattersley, it afforded, just in time, the doctrinal excuse they had
been looking for to sever an association that had become a liability to
their ambitions.

On 16 March 1976, with warning only to the Queen and a few close
friends, Harold Wilson stunned the political world by suddenly announcing his resignation. Ten Downing Street and the leadership of the
Labour party were open to election. This was the moment Jenkins had
been waiting for since 1968 or earlier, when he had first begun to be
spoken of as Wilson's natural heir. Now, however, the opportunity came
too late. He had been given an inkling of Wilson's intention as long ago
as December, but he had done nothing to prepare his position. He was,
on the contrary, already considering the suggestion that he should leave
British politics to become President of the EEC Commission, and had all
but decided to accept. Yet he had to throw his hat into the ring. Few
observers outside the editorial offices of *The Times* seriously thought he
had much chance*; but the 317 members of the PLP were not the party
in the country – he had a strong base of support in the Manifesto Group
and more might be won over in ten days of intensive canvassing. It was
just possible, if the arithmetic fell right. Six candidates declared themselves – Callaghan, the favourite; Foot, the principal champion of the
left; Jenkins, Healey, Benn and, quixotically, Tony Crosland, who was
infuriated by the suggestion that he would merely take votes from
Jenkins, insisting that he had 'always had a rather distinctive position
in the party which is well recognized'.[33] Most forecasts put Jenkins a
close third on the first ballot with 70–80 votes, in a position to gather
votes on the second ballot from the eliminated Healey and Crosland
supporters, who could not face the idea of either Callaghan or Foot as
Prime Minister in an economic crisis. In the event, however, Jenkins
won only 56 votes. Foot got 90, Callaghan 84, Benn 37, Healey 30 and
Crosland 17.

This was a deeply disappointing result, which showed how far Jenkins' stock had slipped since 1971. On the one hand, he had become too
exclusively identified with the EEC for most of the party: but at the same
time he had disappointed many of the pro-Marketeers who had looked
to him in 1972–3 for a leadership he had been unable to give. Analysis

* In *The Times*, both William Rees-Mogg's editorial and Bernard Levin in two extravagant
articles fulsomely endorsed Jenkins, ignoring the sound advice of Marc's cartoon: 'If you really
want Roy to win, what about *not* announcing your support?'[33]

of the result showed that Jenkins won only just over half (49) of the 90 MPs reckoned to be strongly pro-EEC; and *only* 7 of the other 227.[34] It was additionally calculated that he received the votes of only two of the 1974 intake: what appeal he still had rested on the memory of his 1966–70 performance as Home Secretary and Chancellor. There was a not unreasonable fear that, had he been elected, he could not have united the party. In the event of his victory, one northern MP told *The Times*, 'the PLP would embark on a period of disruption never yet experienced';[35] while at the 1978 Conference the Welsh left-winger Neil Kinnock told the story of 'an elderly Yorkshire member who was sitting in the Tea Room, and was approached by one of Roy's acolytes – sorry, I mean supporters – and asked: "Will you be voting for Roy Jenkins?" And the Yorkshire member said: "No lad, we're all Labour here".'[36] There was also the old criticism of his allegedly indolent lifestyle. Wilson contributed to this in his resignation letter with an extraordinarily feline remark, unmistakeably directed at Jenkins, that his successor would have to be prepared to work at the job: 'These are not the easy, spacious, socially-oriented days of some of my predecessors.'[37] Finally, many Labour MPs outside his charmed circle felt that Jenkins was personally too remote, not so much because of his fondness for grand dinner parties as because his basic shyness and his overdeveloped fastidiousness inhibited him from conducting himself with a false heartiness just because there was an election on. It was indeed his acolytes who had to do the canvassing. One senior Minister 'whose views very similarly resembled those of Roy Jenkins' told Gerald Kaufman that 'he would vote for him provided that before the close of the poll the candidate said "Good evening" to him in the Division Lobby; his vote was cast for someone else.'[38]

For a mixture of all these reasons, Jenkins received twelve votes fewer than his supporters' most pessimistic prediction. He immediately decided to withdraw from the race – to the consternation of several of his supporters, the relief of the Callaghan camp, who feared that he might still get enough of the Crosland and Healey votes to pip their man on the second ballot,[34] and the contempt of Barbara Castle. 'This further display of political daintiness', she wrote in her diary, 'proves conclusively what I have always known: that Jenkins will never lead the Labour party. I bet Denis stays in the ring, despite his derisory thirty votes. But then, he's a pugilist, not a patrician.'[39] Healey did stay in, announcing pointedly 'I am not a quitter',[40] though he only received another eight votes as Callaghan went on to defeat Foot, on the third ballot, by 176 to 137. Jenkins' decision was only realistic: he saw no point in pretending that he had not suffered a severe defeat. He thought it important that the choice of a Prime Minister should not be delayed any longer than necessary and, little as he liked Callaghan, he was determined to free his fifty-six votes as quickly as possible to move against Foot. He had stood with little expectation of winning – rather to carry the tattered Gaitskellite standard; having lost, he had another job to go to in Brussels. Moreover at least one of his supporters, David Owen, lost no time in telling him bluntly that he had become a liability to their cause and should go at once. Characteristically quoting Adlai Stevenson ('It hurts too much to laugh and I'm too old to cry') he prepared to bow out of British politics with dignity.

Yet he might have stayed if Callaghan had offered him the Foreign Office. This was the remaining major office he had never held, and there was an important job to be done, now that Britain's membership of the EEC was finally confirmed, consolidating the connection and making sure that the Government played a full part in Community affairs. Instead, Callaghan gave the job to Crosland – an ironic final twist to their lifelong rivalry, since Crosland knew, and admitted that he knew, nothing about foreign affairs, having never taken any interest in them. If Crosland had been on paper better qualified than Jenkins to be Chancellor in 1967, the roles were reversed in 1976. But Crosland's backing for Callaghan, going back to 1963, now had its reward; the Foreign Office was too valued a prize to give to such an object of suspicion to the party as Jenkins now was. Besides, from Callaghan's point of view, he was likely to be more useful safeguarding Britain's interests as a British President of the Commission than taking too 'European' a view as British Foreign Secretary.

Had he been offered the Foreign Office, Jenkins admitted in a television interview in October, when he had finally resigned from the Government and the House of Commons, he might have found it difficult to refuse. On reflection, now that he had definitely accepted the Brussels job, he was glad the choice had never been posed, since 'my own deeper seated judgement was and is that this job as head of the European Commission is in present circumstances more important than the British Foreign Secretaryship.' 'It's not more important than the British Prime Ministership', he added, spelling out his order of priorities quite clearly, 'but more important than the British Foreign Secretaryship. . . . I certainly don't approach the European job in any sense of it being third best.'[41] The impression was widespread, nevertheless, that he was going to Europe only because he had reached the end of the road in British politics, 'thus confirming', *The Times* regretted, 'a popular view of the Commission as a well-paid grazing ground for played-out politicians.'[42] David Dimbleby suggested on television that Jenkins had been 'expelled' from domestic politics.[41]

Jenkins himself was at pains to deny that he was leaving under a cloud or with any feeling of bitterness. In a valedictory survey of the domestic scene he gave his full endorsement to the Callaghan Government, which was now 'on the right lines' and 'showing signs of dealing with things', with public expenditure and the money supply under control and 'the most successful incomes policy since Stafford Cripps.' At the same time his resignation freed him to express more openly than ever before his doubt whether either party on its own could offer the way out of Britain's difficulties.

> I have perhaps a more detached attitude than some politicians at the present time, and I don't believe that all right lies with the Labour Party and all wrong with the Conservative Party.... I think there's too much formal party dogfight in British politics at the present time.

Coalition, he admitted, was a taboo word which both parties shied away from: there was no sign that it was a practical possibility at present, nor was it – without a definitely agreed programme – a 'magic recipe'.

> At the same time I can't take the view which so many politicians do that one must shy away from any suggestion of party collaboration and it would really be better to see the degradation of our currency and the impoverishment of our people than to ... embrace any greater degree of collaboration between parties. I am not sure that a coalition is likely or desirable by any means. I would like to see a position in which in the House of Commons, in politics, people instead of trying to disagree as much as possible with the other side ... try to seek out some areas of agreement.[41]

Leaving the House of Commons after twenty-eight years was a wrench: in particular giving up the seat he had held since 1951 was more painful than he had expected when he accepted the Brussels job. He had had his difficulties with the constituency in the early days, notably over German rearmament in 1954; but it had backed him loyally in the sixties, and he had suffered surprisingly little trouble from the left in the seventies. He had grown, in his own way, fonder of the place than his critics imagined: at a farewell dinner he said that leaving Stechford felt like handing his wife over to another man. (He did not imagine that in the consequent by-election it would be won by a Conservative on a 17 per cent swing.) Old associations apart, he knew very well how difficult it would be to find another seat if he should want one on his return – a possibility he was not prepared to rule out. History, *The Times* warned, suggested that hopes of a comeback from Brussels were illusory.[42] But Jenkins knew that history was no guide to what unforeseeable openings might exist in four years' time. 'I don't for a moment expect to do this job for more than four years', he told Dimbleby.

> I never believe in looking too far into the future but I can tell you one thing for certain, I am not going to preclude sitting on the bench in the House of Commons by sitting on the bench of the House of Lords.

With that half-promise that he might be back, Jenkins went off to tackle what he called 'the most difficult job open to me at the present time . . . in fact the most difficult I have ever done, but I regard it as a crucial next stage in my life.'[41]

NINE

President of the EEC Commission, 1977–1980

The Presidency of the EEC Commission is an impossible job. Indeed it can hardly be called a job at all – the President has a number of conflicting responsibilities, but no power. By no stretch of imagination does it resemble the Prime Ministership of Europe. Appointed by the governments of the nine (now ten) member states of the EEC, he is the chairman of twelve (now thirteen) fellow-Commissioners similarly appointed by their respective countries: he does not choose his colleagues, and he cannot sack them. The Commission administers the Community. Its job is to propose policy, and to carry out policy decisions: but it does not *take* decisions. That function is reserved to the Council of Ministers, which may be composed of the Presidents and Prime Ministers of the member nations or, at a lower level, of the Foreign, Finance or Agriculture Ministers. These decisions must be taken unanimously: they are therefore often not taken at all. The notorious immobility of the EEC is due not to the size or complexity of the Brussels bureaucracy (which is actually quite small – smaller, for example, than the Dutch Ministry of Agriculture), nor necessarily to lack of will on the part of the Commission, but to the inherent difficulty of getting nine or ten sovereign countries, each one holding a veto, to agree on any line of advance. The Commission, or most conspicuously the President, is charged with developing proposals to which the member Governments may be brought to agree and with attempting, through an eternity of horse-trading, to secure their agreement; he is blamed if they are unable to agree, and then held responsible for the Community's failure to evolve. But his only weapon is persuasion – public appeals to the shadowy forum of 'European opinion' or private words in the ear of the heads of government. The President has no bargaining position of his own, no sanctions at his disposal, no power to do or to decide anything. It is a job for a diplomat rather than a politician.

Yet it was for this very reason, paradoxically, that there was a strong feeling in 1976 that what the Community needed to lift it out of the difficulties into which it had run since the oil crisis of 1973 (which had coincided, unluckily, with its enlargement from six nations to nine with the admission of Britain, Ireland and Denmark) was a political figure of sufficient international stature to take on the Council of Ministers, raise horizons and restore the sense of momentum and hope to the adventure of a united Europe. This was the expectation which Jenkins' appointment aroused among those who wished the EEC experiment well. It was an ambition which he himself shared as he prepared that autumn – he resigned from the Home Office in September and worked for the next three months from a small room in the Cabinet Office – for an assignment for which he was in several vital respects thoroughly ill-suited. 'I don't regard myself as being a Civil Servant in Brussels', he told David Dimbleby on television in October. 'I have nothing against civil servants, but I am a politician.... I want to introduce some political content, to have direct contact with the Governments, with the peoples of Europe in a way that perhaps non-politicians have not been able to do to the same extent.'[1]

He started with an important advantage over his predecessors (none of whom, since the German Walter Hallstein in the formative fifties, had made much personal impact). Previously, all thirteen Commissioners had been appointed before one of them was chosen as President. In 1976, following a proposal by the Belgian Prime Minister Leo Tindemans, Jenkins was appointed to the Presidency several months before the outgoing Commission left office, with the idea that he should have a say in the selection of his colleagues – just a ghost of a Prime Minister's prerogative. In the event, however, this availed him very little. He toured the nine capitals, expressing his preferences to the respective heads of government; but Commissioners are generally appointed for domestic political reasons ('Whom can we get rid of?'), rather than for European ones ('Who would be the best man?'), and in most cases his preference was ignored. The Germans reappointed both their outgoing Commissioners, Wilhelm Haferkamp and Guido Brunner, although Jenkins had particularly wanted Haferkamp replaced. From Ireland, he was denied the Labour Minister of Industry, Justin Keating, and landed with the more conservative Fine Gael Minister of Justice, Richard Burke. Only in Britain, significantly, was he able to veto Margaret Thatcher's nomination of John Davies, assented to by Callaghan; he tried unsuccessfully to persuade his friend Ian Gilmour to take the job, but eventually settled for the quite junior Conservative MP, Christopher Tugendhat. For the first exercise of a new power this was not very encouraging. Nor was he able to reform the unwieldy structure of the Commission. Thirteen Commissioners (two each from France, Germany, Italy and Britain, one from each of the five smaller countries) were too many for the number of jobs actually to be done: but the big four rejected the simple solution of having only one Commissioner each, while the smaller countries refused to see the Commission regrouped into two tiers. The most the new President could achieve was some minor reallocation of functions between the thirteen portfolios (some of which were decidedly random). It was not even up to him to assign the portfolios among his colleagues. Each job has to be bargained for and voted on: all the President can do is to give a lead. The process, begun on the afternoon of 6 January 1977, when the new Commission formally took office, lasted fifteen hours and was not completed until 5.30 the following morning. This was not in the least like Cabinet-making at home, but a gruelling introduction to the reality of life in Brussels.

Jenkins' hope of being a political President, giving new direction to a distracted Europe, was quickly lost in a bewildering struggle to understand the Brussels machinery through which he had to work. It has been noted already that he tends to be a slow starter in any job – and this was a job to which, for all his years of ardent advocacy of the European idea, he came extraordinarily unprepared. The Europe for which he had risked his career was a noble abstraction: he had very little knowledge of how the EEC actually operated on the ground. Even with his six months' start, it took him another six months to begin to look as if he was in control and knew where he was going. Even then, he was never at home in the tortuous ramifications of the multinational bureaucracy. It was not merely that he had no feel for the detail of fisheries or sheepmeat policy: that could be picked up in time. More seriously, he had little patience for the tedious processes of pegging out, inch by inch, narrow areas of agreement between opposed positions. He was not a bureaucrat, after all, but a politician, a problem-solver, used to considering the options, making a decision, then sticking to it, explaining it and carrying it out. Moreover, it was as a politician that he had been appointed, to lift the Community's eyes above sheepmeat and fisheries. Yet he quickly came up against the fact that to achieve anything politically, to exercise any influence over the governments of the Nine, he had first to assert his authority within the Commission, to master the bureaucracy. Unfortunately running bureaucracies is not his strength.

This failure could have been foreseen by anyone with any knowledge of his way of working as a national Minister. He likes to work, not through the normal channels of his department, but through a few select associates: in Brussels the pattern familiar from the Home Office and the Treasury was repeated. To most of the members of the Commission civil service he was a remote figure. Somewhat tactlessly, four of the five members of his personal *cabinet* were British, with few continental connections. He brought over with him from the Home Office Hayden Phillips, who had no more experience of Brussels than he had himself; and he appointed as his *chef du cabinet* a very superior Foreign Office mandarin, Crispin Tickell (now British Ambassador in Mexico), who was eminently qualified by having been Geoffrey Rippon's Private Secretary during the 1971 negotiations for Britain's entry to the EEC and subsequently head of the Western Organisations Department in the Foreign Office, but whose manner unfortunately aggravated the impression created by Jenkins' own reserve. Tickell looked after his Minister and defended his interests as a British Permanent Secretary does: he did not muck in with his opposite numbers hammering out multilateral compromises in the way that Brussels expects. Jenkins admired his intellect, relied on him absolutely, but never understood that his quintessential Englishness rubbed a lot of French and Belgians in the Commission badly the wrong way.

He also brought over with him David Marquand, who gave up his seat in the House of Commons to become chief adviser in the Secretariat-General of the Commission, with special responsibility for liaison with the European Parliament: he was not a member of Jenkins' personal staff, but in practice he was always present at important meetings and was a close confidant. Jenkins' need to surround himself in this strange environment with familiar faces is, humanly speaking, understandable: for the first time in his life he was parted from Jennifer, who has throughout his career been of enormous emotional and practical support to him, yet has never regarded herself as a full-time political wife. She had her own interests to keep her in London: she had given up the chairmanship of the Consumer Council in 1976, but was now chairman of the Historic Buildings Council. The arrangement was that she came to Brussels two weekends a month, while he went to London (when he was not elsewhere in Europe) the other two. (Since all the children had now left home, they gave up the house in Ladbroke Square and made their London base a somewhat cavernous flat in

Kensington Park Gardens, overlooking the same private garden from the other side. Weekends, however, were generally spent at East Hendred.) Jenkins took with him to Brussels the stepdaughter of his old friend Mark Bonham Carter, Laura Grenfell, to act as his hostess-cum-housekeeper: there she met and married Hayden Phillips, completing the sense of a close circle of intimates, among whom friends and advisers were scarcely to be distinguished.

The impression that he was surrounding himself with English advisers, went to London for the weekend and spent as little time in Brussels as he decently could contributed in the first few months to the new President meeting a distinctly cool reception from the Brussels press corps. He committed a *faux pas* at the very outset by giving his first formal statement to the press in English and declining to repeat it in French: it was true that his predecessor, the Frenchman, Francois-Xavier Ortoli, had not repeated his similar statement four years before in English, but Jenkins' refusal was unnecessarily tactless and gave rise to the belief that his French was worse than it really was. He had actually been working hard at it since his appointment: it was unkindly described in *The Times* as 'painful but grammatically accurate', but it was perfectly serviceable. He soothed ruffled feelings by giving a television interview in French a few days later, and his staff gave it out that he spoke French at dinner parties![2] Little things, however – like the fact that his inaugural speech to the European Parliament on 11 January was given to the press in English only, because the translation into other languages was not ready – conspired to exacerbate the accident that the beginning of Jenkins' term coincided with the British Government for the first time holding the rotating chairmanship of the Council of Ministers (which meant a blustering anti-Marketeer like John Silkin chairing agricultural meetings). The impact of Jenkins' new European broom was unluckily marred by the fear in Brussels that the half-hearted and bloody-minded British were taking over. It was at this time that the French began referring to the new President disparagingly as 'Le Roi Jean Quinze'.[2]

So the first months after his arrival in Brussels were not an easy time, personally or politically. At times he must have wondered what he was doing there, especially when in February Tony Crosland suddenly died: beside his sorrow – for their old friendship had dramatically and significantly recovered as soon as their direct rivalry was at an end – he must have reflected that he might now have had the Foreign Secretaryship after all if he had stayed in Britain. Instead the 38-year-old David Owen was astonishingly promoted – and proceeded to make Jenkins' job harder by adopting a bullishly unhelpful negotiating posture towards Europe. Jenkins was quickly made to realize the limits of his influence. An early illustration arose when, on his initiative and in response to what he believed to be European (but was actually only British) public opinion, the Commission suspended the subsidized export of the EEC butter surplus to the USSR: the French, the Irish and the Danes – the butter producers – were immediately up in arms, and sales had shortly to be resumed. Imprisoned in the remote grandeur of the thirteen-storey Berlaymont building in Brussels, Jenkins actually seemed, after the initial burst of (generally bad) publicity, to disappear from view.

Ironically, he had made a particular priority, at the very outset, of raising the Commission's profile and of being himself more visible than his predecessors. To this end he personally took charge of communications and built a special television studio within the Berlaymont which was intended to broadcast his uplifting words around Europe. Yet his first press conferences were not inspiring, and in his first speech to the European Parliament he seemed hesitant and ill-at-ease. He made the expected noises, speaking elegantly of the need very soon to make fresh forays out of the citadel which the previous Commission had 'brilliantly defended';[3] but he disappointed those in all parties and from all countries who had looked for specific new departures, and received just seventeen seconds of applause. He was very quickly written down as a British pragmatist who had no idea of how, if at all, the Community should develop; there was even talk in the summer of 1977 that he might not serve longer than two years in Brussels.

Pragmatic he certainly was, as anyone who was familiar with his writings on domestic politics might have expected: a belief in progress, rather than a precise sense of destination, has always characterized Jenkins' thinking. He was bound to sound vague until he saw his way clearly; but he was determined not to be satisfied with the status quo. 'My wish is to build an effective united Europe', he told *The Times* on taking office.

> I've never sought absolutely to define exactly what I mean by this, but I've got an absolutely clear sense of direction. . . . I do not think it's terribly useful to lay down blueprints as to whether we will be federal or confederal in the year 2000 and beyond. I want to move towards a more effectively organised Europe, politically and economically, and as far as I am concerned I want to go faster, not slower.[4]

How, though? That was the question. He attached great importance, in his early speeches, to the move to a directly elected European Parliament (due in 1978), seeing the Parliament as an ally of the Commission 'against the national governments with their narrow preoccupations'.[5] But that was going to happen anyway, if the British did not block it. Another advance on the horizon was the further enlargement of the Community to bring in Greece, Portugal and Spain, possibly even Turkey. This could not be resisted, for political reasons, if the goal was a securely democratic and united Europe; but it would make economic convergence more difficult than ever. He repeatedly emphasized the *need* for economic convergence, but in a speech at Fontainebleau shortly before taking office he rejected the 'overschematic' approach to economic and monetary union (EMU) optimistically charted in the early seventies but now abandoned, only warning – in a phrase which must have taxed the translators – that it would be 'an enormous mistake to throw out the baby of economic convergence with the bathwater of monetary union'.[5] In his first months he seemed too overwhelmed by the difficulties in the way of any advance to suggest concrete new ways forward.

He concentrated instead, as a necessary preliminary, on establishing his right, as President of the Commission, to attend the economic summit meetings of Western leaders. The EEC was, after all, the largest single trading bloc in the Western world, with a distinct view of world problems broader than any of its nine component nations. At the same time his presence at the international top table would enhance both his personal prestige and the Commission's prestige *vis-à-vis* the Council of Ministers. Jenkins' case was strongly backed by the smaller nations of the Community (particularly the Dutch and Belgians) who would otherwise be unrepresented, and also received the support of President Carter, with whom he had lost no time, even before taking office, in establishing excellent relations. (Carter's four-year term in Washington ran exactly concurrent with Jenkins' in Brussels.) But it was equally strongly opposed by Giscard d'Estaing, who saw no need for a supranational EEC presence and thought Jenkins was getting above himself. A year before it was Giscard who had first proposed that Jenkins was the heavyweight President the EEC needed: now, under Gaullist pressure at home, he lost no opportunity to block Jenkins' every attempt to increase his influence. Chancellor Schmidt was at this stage little friendlier, as was shown by his reappointment of Haferkamp and Brunner. In March it seemed that Jenkins had won his battle to attend the forthcoming May summit in London of the top seven economic nations (USA, Canada, Japan, France, Germany, Britain and Italy). Then, on the eve of the meeting, it turned out that he was to be allowed to attend only half of it (the Sunday session on the North-South dialogue and energy, not the Saturday session on the world economy generally); and Giscard administered a further snub to both Jenkins and Callaghan by declining to attend the Friday evening dinner at Buckingham Palace. The Dutch and Belgians were furious, not least at Jenkins' meek acceptance of the rebuff: they urged him to walk out altogether. He characteristically thought it was more sensible to attend what he could, to assert the precedent, while pointing out the illogicality of the arrangement. He suffered a string of petty humiliations – not being allowed to sit with the heads of government at dinner, being given a place at the closing press conference but no microphone. But he did establish the precedent and demonstrated, so far as he was allowed to, both the value of having the EEC represented and his own ability to make a contribution. There was no question of his not being present at subsequent summits, and this stubborn victory was one of the major achievements – from the point of view of giving political leadership – of his Presidency.

Henceforth, he was treated with markedly increased respect by Schmidt and Giscard. Among other things, Jenkins put a great deal more effort than his predecessors into the thrice-yearly EEC summits, the so-called Council of Europe, composed of the nine heads of government, both playing a major part himself and making sure that the Commission sufficiently prepared the ground in advance to get the results it wanted, which had seldom been the case in the past. One example of his increased effectiveness was an imaginative scheme for a £650m loan facility to boost industrial investment in the EEC: when he originally proposed it at the London summit both Schmidt and Giscard turned it down, but a year later, by patient diplomacy, he got all nine governments to agree to it.[6] His greatest success, however, which turned out to be the principal legacy of his Presidency, was his resurrection of the idea of economic and monetary union, leading in less than a year to a large step towards its realization.

Here was Jenkins' answer to his critics who said he was failing to give a lead. By the autumn of 1977 he had determined that the time had come for a major foray out of the citadel. Since 1973 the goal of a European monetary union had suddenly become distant and utopian. As he characteristically expressed it in the speech in Florence on 27 October, in which he unveiled his plan, what had previously appeared as a reasonably close mountain top viewed through powerful binoculars was now seen with the binoculars both the wrong way round and out of focus. Without suggesting that EMU could be achieved overnight, he had decided that the goal must at least be brought back into focus. Those who secretly did not want to see closer economic convergence, and who were relying upon the enlargement of the Community to make it impracticable, must be flushed out into the open. 'The prospect of EEC enlargement', he argued, 'will face us with a clear choice either of strengthening the sinews of the Community or of tacit acceptance of a loose customs union, far removed from the hopes of its founders, and without much hope of recovering momentum.' In place of the mountaineer, he proposed a new image. 'Let us think of a long jumper. He starts with a rapid succession of steps, lengthens his stride, increases his momentum and then makes his leap.' EMU was such a leap: the run-up could begin with small steps, but the leap would have to come if the EEC was to continue to develop.

The stumbling block for sovereign nations was the requirement that they should give up an important degree of economic independence. But Jenkins argued, as he had always argued in the debates on British membership of the EEC, that this independence was largely illusory. Britain and other EEC countries were already obliged to accept 'very sharp surveillance' from the IMF, a body far more remote than the EEC: it was more realistic to see monetary union 'as part of the process of recovering the substance of sovereign power.... At present we tend to cling to its shadow.' He denied that EMU need involve an unacceptable degree of centralization, envisaging

> a highly decentralised type of monetary union in which the public procurement of goods and services is primarily in national, regional or other hands.... The public finance function of such a community would be stripped down to a few high-powered types of financial transfer, fulfilling special tasks in sectors of particular community concern.

There was 'no need to contemplate developing Community expenditure of a traditional federal scale', since the present nine nations already spent similar proportions of their income on social and welfare services. (He here left out of account the three less developed prospective members.) He postponed questions about balancing poorer countries with richer with his formula that the eventual arrangements would probably correspond to no existing federal or confederal prototype.

The great benefit of EMU was that it would 'help establish a new era of price stability in Europe and achieve a decisive break with the present chronic inflationary disorder.' At present, each nation was inhibited from expanding its economy for fear of sparking off speculation against its currency. By binding the European economies together in a single currency, a stable base would be created for controlled joint expansion to alleviate unemployment. The only necessary institution was an EEC

monetary authority issuing a new single currency and pursuing a determined and relatively independent policy of controlling note issue and
bank money creation, starting with the adoption of target growth rates
for monetary expansion consistent with a new European standard of
monetary stability. The Bretton Woods system which had been the
foundation of postwar prosperity had broken down: by creating 'a
major new international currency backed by the economic spread and
strength of the Community' which could serve alongside the dollar as
'a joint and alternative pillar' of a new monetary order, Jenkins concluded, Europe could lead the world out of recession.[7]

This, the *Economist* commented, was 'an astonishingly bold idea for
Mr Jenkins, himself nursing a thousand political cuts in his new Brussels
role, to espouse.'[8] *The Times* was equally surprised that Jenkins should
have 'attached himself so firmly and so personally to the idea' of EMU.[7]
The Times was clearly against it. The *Economist* was in favour in principle,
but thought his initiative unrealistic. (Even within the Commission
Jenkins' predecessor, M. Ortoli, now holding the economic affairs port-
folio, was said to think it ill-advised.) But the *Economist* gave him credit
for his courage.

> Mr Jenkins is right to be radical. It is, or should be, his job. Every road
> towards further European integration is strewn with land mines and the role
> of the Commission president is to give an intellectual lead: at the very least
> he is giving a little spark of that leadership in the midst of economic crisis
> that national governments are manifestly failing to give. Whether that will
> make him friends in the chancelleries and treasuries of Europe must be
> doubted. Brave though he is to attempt it, monetary union in the absolute
> form Mr Jenkins is suggesting is all too likely to prove a bridge too far.[8]

But the *Economist* was wrong. In defiance of the sceptics, Jenkins had
picked a propitious moment to fly his kite. Both the major continental
currencies, the Mark and the franc, were reasonably stable and both
Schmidt and Giscard, for different reasons, were prepared to consider
tying them together – Giscard to associate the franc with the Mark's
strength, Schmidt to share the burden the Mark was increasingly being
asked to carry. At the Brussels summit in December 1977 – a particularly
constructive one in several ways, under Belgian chairmanship – they
were responsive to Jenkins' argument that movement towards a long-
term goal could help solve *current* problems. From here on, it must be
said, the momentum was theirs, not his. It was equally their mistake,
however, to fail to involve Callaghan early enough in their planning:
when they tried to bring him in, over dinner at the Copenhagen summit
in April 1978, he was nettled that so much had been agreed without

him, and thereafter he remained suspicious. At Bremen in July, never-theless, all nine heads of government agreed provisionally to set up, not yet a fully-fledged EMU, but a European Monetary System (EMS) based on a new European Currency Unit (ECU), to be used alongside the existing currencies, and backed by a $50m European Monetary Fund (EMF), into which the nine governments would each pool 20 per cent of their gold reserves to ward off speculation against any of the member currencies, which would all be brought into a narrow band of fluctua-tion against one another. (This would go much further than the existing 'snake', in which only Germany, Denmark and the Benelux countries participated.) Bremen was the high point of Jenkins' Presidency: he told the press that he had never dreamed, nine months before in Florence, that so much progress would be made so quickly.

The EMS came into operation in March 1979. Jenkins' sense of achievement was qualified, however, by the fact that Britain stayed out of it. Responding to the Labour party's reviving hostility to being in the EEC at all, Callaghan and Healey argued that the strain on the weaker currencies would be too great. For a moment it seemed that Italy and Ireland would stay out too, which would have seriously weakened the scheme; but their doubts were overcome, and Britain was once again the only country out of step. In opposition, Mrs Thatcher was in favour of Britain joining; but in office from May 1979 she too has always found the moment inopportune – a disappointment which Jenkins has felt deeply. 'Without sterling the system is frankly incomplete', he regretted in 1980. 'Without participation, Britain is not playing its full part in Europe.'[9] A year later, now back from Brussels, he spoke bitterly of 'the endemic British error of semi-detachment from Europe', standing aloof from every initiative at the formative stage – first the Coal and Steel Community, then the EEC itself, now the EMS – and then complaining later because the rules were not precisely attuned to Britain's interest. After two and a half years, he was able to claim, the EMS was an island of monetary stability in a volatile world: while Callaghan had pleaded the fear of higher unemployment and Mrs Thatcher the primacy of defeating inflation, 'we have had a worse combination of unemployment and inflation than almost any of the eight fully participating countries and have suffered more than any of them from the disadvantages of a sharply fluctuating exchange rate.'[10] His wider disappointment was that the EMS had not yet developed beyond the first valuable but limited stage of currency stabilization: the ECU has still only a shadowy exist-ence, the EMF has not yet begun to be established, and the Germans and French have increasingly dragged their feet over creating the central

reserve bank envisaged at Bremen. The half-success of the EMS graphically illustrates the dependence of the President of the Commission
upon others to carry forward his ideas. The momentum generated by
Jenkins' Florence speech in 1977 had run out by 1980, leaving the vision
but half-realized, and the President by himself helpless to finish the job.

In 1978, however, it seemed that Jenkins, by seizing the initiative,
had justified his appointment and now had the ball at his feet as none
of his predecessors had ever had. Despite his failure to weld the Commission into a coherent body, the *Economist* wrote that summer, 'Mr
Jenkins' part in the monetary debate has established him as a major
figure in EEC diplomacy. His habit of regularly meeting with prime
ministers and presidents has begun to pay off.... As he demonstrated
in the debate on monetary policy in Copenhagen, his intellectual grasp
of complex monetary issues gives him a head start.' The article was
headlined 'The Rising Star of Roy Jenkins'.[6] Yet, as *The Times* put it at
the conclusion of his term, 'Mr Jenkins spent himself on the EMS issue.
Nothing afterwards engaged his attention to the same degree.'[11] Part of
the explanation may be that he was increasingly distracted by what was
happening in British domestic politics, as the possibilities began to look
favourable, after Labour's 1979 defeat, for the formation of a new party
to fill the vacuum on the centre-left. (He gave his now-famous Dimbleby
Lecture in November 1979.) Mainly, however, it was simply that the
fundamental problems of the EEC were too intractable. The biggest,
which people in Britain particularly looked to him to solve, was the
whole interlinked problem of the Common Agricultural Policy and
Britain's contribution to the Community budget.

Despite his irritation with Britain's attitude – under governments of
both parties – of 'semi-detachment' from Europe, Jenkins was sympathetic to Mrs Thatcher's demand, in the autumn of 1979, for a reduction
of Britain's contribution, which in 1980 was due to make her the largest
net contributor to the Community, although one of the poorer countries.
(The reason was that the Common Agricultural Policy remained far
and away the biggest item in the Community budget, while Britain, as
a primarily industrial country, drew from it the least benefit. Britain
had also, for a variety of reasons, gained less advantage than expected
from access to the EEC's industrial market.) He was less sympathetic to
her methods. At an hour-long meeting before the Dublin summit in
November, 'during which Mrs Thatcher is reported to have done most
of the talking', Jenkins warned her that an 'all-or-nothing' approach to
Britain's claim would be counterproductive. He was trying to get the
other member countries to agree to refund £350m of Britain's proposed

1980 payment of £1,025m, as the first stage of a wider settlement. But 'the word in Whitehall was that "we have not been offered even half a loaf, let alone the loaf we want".'[12] At Dublin Mrs Thatcher rejected the Commission's proposal out of hand and threatened to bring the Community to a standstill by operating an 'empty chair' policy until she got 'our money' back. Her intransigence wrung from Britain's partners a much improved offer (about two-thirds of her 'loaf') at the Luxembourg summit the following April; but Jenkins was left badly exposed, while Giscard and Schmidt were practically speechless with fury, when at the last minute, when agreement seemed very close, Mrs Thatcher peremptorily rejected this as well. A settlement was finally achieved a month later, in May 1980, at a nineteen-hour Foreign Ministers' meeting brilliantly chaired by the Italian Emilio Colombo. Lord Carrington (a more soothing presence than his Prime Minister) agreed to a somewhat smaller settlement for 1980 than was offered at Luxembourg in return for a larger rebate in 1981 and provision for the 1982 contribution to be settled on similar lines if no wider settlement had been achieved by then. Though Jenkins gave credit to Colombo for 'the finest piece of sustained chairmanship I have seen in decades of public life',[13] insiders in Brussels gave the credit to Jenkins and Tugendhat for months of patient groundwork, finally rewarded.[14]

The 1980 settlement was only temporary, however, because the wider solution to which Jenkins looked forward has so far proved unattainable. The long-term strategy which he devoted his last year in office to promulgating was to reduce the proportion of the budget spent on agriculture, not primarily by cutting back on agriculture (politically impossible), but by extending Community activity into new fields – industrial, energy, social and regional policy – from which Britain could expect a more tangible return. This, he argued in a valedictory speech in Luxembourg in November 1980, was the next step forward for the Community, the only way forward 'commensurate with the vision of our founding fathers'. There was no future either in 'Europe à la carte', of which British non-participation in the EMS was a lamentable example, or in drift. 'Some governments', he warned, mentioning no names, 'will wish simply to patch things up, shrink from tackling the agricultural problem, and leave the imbalances of the budget to be settled by a continuing series of ad hoc arrangements for countries whose situation would otherwise be unacceptable.' 'The most difficult and the most desirable course', on the contrary, involved 'a substantial reshaping of both our revenue system and our expenditure system.' The size of the Community budget, he proposed, should be tripled – from 0.8 per cent

to 2–2.5 per cent of the Community's GNP – by transferring to the
Community industrial and social functions at present funded nationally.
The Community's revenue should be increased by raising from 1 per
cent to perhaps 3 per cent the proportion of VAT payable to it: there
might be a Community tax on imported oil (which would benefit
Britain), or perhaps on oil production. Though this would still be very
little compared with the United States (where federal expenditure runs
to 25 per cent of the GNP) it would be enough to transform the EEC from
'an agricultural community with political trimmings' into something
much more all-embracing. 'Here is the means', Jenkins suggested, 'by
which we can on the one hand deal with the problems of economic
divergence and the future industrial base, and on the other establish
that better balance within the budget which is indispensable.' Like the
EMS, it could not be done overnight. 'But I strongly believe that we
should set ourselves on the budgetary path which would permit the
development of a Community of this scale and function.'[15]

All the President of the Commission can do, however, is to urge: and
the member governments of the EEC were not ready in 1980 – nor have
they looked any readier since – for another great leap forward. So
Jenkins ended his four-year term in Brussels with a feeling of considerable frustration. More than ever, he was convinced by his gruelling
experience of the need for movement towards greater European unity,
particularly in fields like energy conservation and micro-technology in
which the national governments would not or could not act alone. But
equally he understood better than ever the difficulties in the way of
progress; and he knew that he had to a great extent failed in breaking
them down. In a time of economic recession, governments and people
alike instinctively retreat into attitudes of defensive nationalism – no
matter how powerful the evidence is that the problems can be solved
only by co-operation. He had spoken, on first coming into office, of
'grafting the idea of Europe into the lives of the people', so that the
individual citizens of the nine nations should become aware of the EEC
'not as an abstraction ... but as a continuum extending from world
influence to job opportunity.'[3] Four years later he confessed in his final
press conference that he had not succeeded in changing the image of
the Commission as a remote and irrelevant bureaucracy.[16] He was
criticized for having failed, after all, to make himself more visible:

> Those who had hailed his arrival in Brussels ... looked to him for more than
> the role of a clubbable honest broker. They were hoping for a President who
> would be prepared to court the wrath of member governments in defence of

policies that amounted to more than the lowest common denominator of what was politically acceptable in national capitals.

To the disappointment of many, Mr Jenkins seldom seemed to put his head above the parapet.[11]

Jenkins rebutted this criticism. He had learned the hard way, he said, that 'you have to proceed by persuading governments. It would be nice to think that you could operate by generating a tide of public opinion which would sweep governments aside. But that is an illusion'.[16] His successes were indeed achieved by working directly on the heads of government. From that point of view, his victory over Giscard in establishing the President's right to be present and play a role not only at EEC but also at international summits could be his most important legacy to his successors – presently Gaston Thorn, the former Prime Minister of Luxembourg. The problem now is that Thorn has not the intellectual nor political weight to make his presence felt in the way that Jenkins could. Assessing the final balance sheet, one comes back to the feeling that Giscard and Schmidt were right, in 1976, to press for a figure of international political stature to take on the Presidency (however much they then set out to thwart him). Jenkins was not a great success at running or reforming the Brussels machine (though here again it was the heads of government who in his last year blocked implementation of the Schierenburg report, which recommended a number of improvements). But the EEC had had faceless technocrats like Ortoli before, brilliant at oiling the bureaucratic wheels but without the ability or the ambition to do more. The man who could fill both roles has not been born. Jenkins was appointed as a politician, and as a politician he probably had as much success as could be expected with no independent power base of his own. He launched, in defiance of the conventional wisdom of the moment, one big idea and saw it at least partly carried into effect. That is not a lot to show in four years: but such is the nature of international organizations. It is really a waste of a major politician to condemn him to the frustration of Brussels; and yet it takes a major politician to achieve even as little as Jenkins did.

He gave his farewell press conference in Brussels on 5 January 1981. 'I am glad that I came', he told reporters, 'and glad that I did the job. I would not have wished to spend the past four years otherwise.'[16] The next day he returned to Britain to set in motion the biggest gamble of his political life.

TEN

The Formation of the SDP, 1979–1982

Jenkins' return from Brussels to British politics was awaited with extraordinary anticipation in Westminster and Fleet Street. More people – certainly at Westminster – hoped that he would fall flat on his face than wished him well. But the buzz of expectation, apprehension and derision was palpable, for by speeches and soundings over the past year he had left little doubt that he was coming back with the intention of forming a new political party, to split the Labour party and precipitate the long-discussed, repeatedly-postponed realignment of the centre-left. During his four-year exile, events in the Labour party had moved at an accelerating pace: many on the right – the Jenkinsites of 1972–3 who had then been adamant against a breakaway – were now close to the point of no return. Jenkins had played no part in fomenting these developments. But his return was – quite by chance – uncannily timed to give the final impetus needed to push them over the edge. Rather as, ten years before, the Labour Government had waited with bated breath for his Budget in 1970, so during the last weeks of 1980 the whole political world seemed to be 'waiting for Roy'.

For the purpose which he had now set himself, his years of withdrawal from domestic politics were in some ways a handicap, in others an advantage. On the one hand, it was widely assumed that when he left the House of Commons in 1976 that was the end of him: he had had a distinguished career, he had got close to the very top but he had failed at the last and had now retired to lusher pastures overseas, to be followed perhaps by a spell in the City or the Mastership of an Oxford college, before he wrote his memoirs. His withdrawal was linked with the death of Tony Crosland and John Mackintosh, Brian Walden's move into television and David Marquand's to Brussels and then to a chair of politics at Salford, and the 1974 defeat of Dick Taverne, to support a general thesis that the social democrats in the Labour party had accepted defeat and given up the fight. From 1977 to 1979 Jenkins was out of sight and largely out of mind, no longer a part of political commentators' calculations.

In so far as the public remembered him at all, it was more for the size of his salary than for anything else. As President of the Commission he received £57,000 a year, plus £18,000 housing allowance and expenses.[1] Allowing for the higher cost of living in Brussels and the higher level of real earnings in Europe, this seemed excessive to no-one but the British; but it was nearly three times what the British Prime Minister received, and the Labour left and the popular press – playing on hostility to the EEC itself – combined to represent it as a fantastic fortune, and pictured Jenkins himself wallowing at the (British) taxpayers' expense in idleness and luxury. His image was fixed as a fat cat who had done well out of Europe; if he returned at all, he would surely be too sated with cream to retain any serious ambition to descend again into the grimy back streets of British politics. If he thought any constituency would welcome him back – for whatever party – he should be warned by the fate of Christopher Soames, another distinguished fat cat who returned from Brussels in 1977 hoping to get back into the House of Commons, only to be everywhere rejected. A large trunk labelled 'Brussels' was thought, with some reason, to be the worst possible baggage with which a returning traveller could hope to appeal to the British electorate.

And yet, seen in the context of his whole career, Jenkins' absence from British politics between 1977 and 1981 was an interlude whose benefits outweighed these short-term disadvantages. It gave him, for one thing, time to think, an opportunity to reconsider Britain's insular domestic struggles in a wider perspective and rediscover the personal sense of direction which he had lost when too closely caught up in them. Politicians all too rarely get the chance to think in the hectic British party battle. Brussels gave Jenkins first-hand experience of how much more sensibly other European countries run their politics. Secondly, being abroad allowed Jenkins to withdraw gradually and painlessly from the Labour party, without the wrestling with his conscience and the public ordeal of resignation that the other leading defectors to the SDP had to undergo. He actually kept up his subscription until 1980; Jennifer wrote to *The Times* in 1978 to scotch rumours that their membership had been allowed to lapse.[2] But having given up his constituency, he had no institutional ties to break, which made it very much easier for him than for the others.

Third, Brussels did, for all the mockery, subtly enhance his prestige.

Even if no-one quite knew what he did there, editors at least had to
report him as a major personage of international importance – much
more than if he had simply been out of the country on private business,
more even than a rejected former Prime Minister crying in the wilderness like Edward Heath. His having a fixed term to serve and the
knowledge that he would be back the day it ended added very greatly
to the drama of his return. Above all – a combination of all these factors
– far from preventing Jenkins playing a part in the agonies of the Labour
party as the internal crisis came to a head in 1980, his absence from
Westminster actually freed him to give a lead to the forces making for
a break, and keep up the pressure from the outside on the waverers as
he could not have done had he been there wavering with them. Whatever he achieved or failed to achieve in the EEC, Brussels rescued him
when his career had run out of steam and gave him a launching pad to
begin again.

When he went to Brussels in 1977, Jenkins carefully left open the
possibility that he might try to return to British politics. He knew very
well that the odds were against a successful comeback. He knew, indeed,
that such a comeback was out of the question except as part of a drastic
shake-up of the party system caused by a major breakaway from
Labour. Yet his analysis had long ago convinced him that such a
breakaway could not be indefinitely delayed. So he kept a close watch,
from Brussels and on his frequent weekends home, on events in the
Labour party and developments in British politics generally. He still
had an unrivalled network of advisers and spies to keep him informed:
Matthew Oakeshott, who briefed him every time he came back to
Britain; David Marquand, who stayed only two years in Brussels but
remained a trusted confidant after his return; the ever-faithful John
Harris; and not least Jennifer, whose own political acumen should never
be underrated. Another supporter whose job – up to 1979 – as Under-
Secretary for Prices and Consumer Protection gave him regular opportunities to visit Brussels unobtrusively was Bob Maclennan, who found
Jenkins always eager for information, always questioning it, continually
weighing the chances and assessing who might be counted as allies and
who opponents.

He watched the experiment of the 'Lab-Lib pact' in 1977–8 with
interest and growing admiration for the clear-sighted leadership of
David Steel. That, however, kept Callaghan's Labour Government in
office, and with it David Owen, Bill Rodgers and Shirley Williams, all
members of the Cabinet. The moment of opportunity for Jenkins began
with the May 1979 election which installed in power a radical Conser-

vative Government dedicated to shifting the postwar consensus sharply to the right, and threw Labour back into opposition, stimulating a renewal of the party's rapid movement to the left – the party Conference in October voted both for mandatory reselection of MPs and to vest control of the party's next manifesto exclusively in the (left-dominated) NEC. From now on the remaining moderates in the Labour party were on the run, while nationally the centre ground of politics was left invitingly vacant.

Into this vacuum, on 22 November, Jenkins launched a weather balloon in the form of the 1979 Dimbleby Lecture which he had been invited to deliver, on television, by the BBC. The decision to make an overtly political speech, seizing the opportunity of a huge audience to lay a prospectus of political reform before the country, was very much his own: he did not even show it to several of his friends for fear that they would advise him against it or try to tone it down. But the response he evoked – from the public, not the press which was largely sceptical – justified his gamble and his judgement. It is from Jenkins' Dimbleby Lecture that the history of the SDP can be traced.

What he actually said was only a more elegantly developed form of the sort of analysis of the failure of the two-party system that he had been making five or six years before, when still an active leader of the Labour party – indeed, in the broadest terms, all his life. Even now he did not explicitly disavow the Labour party, merely the path on which it seemed irrevocably set. What he made was an 'unashamed plea for the strengthening of the political centre', returning to his 1973 theme that the tendency of both main parties towards the extremes was disenfranchising a large part of the electorate:

> In 1951 83% of the electorate voted, and no less than 97% of those who went to the polls voted for one or other of the two big parties. In the second 1974 election only 73% of the electorate voted, and only three-quarters of those ... voted Labour or Conservative. To put it another way: the Labour Party in 1951 polled 40% of the total electorate, including those who stayed at home, and it just lost. In October 1974 it polled 28% of the electorate and it just won. Even in 1979, with some recovery in the total vote and a substantial victory, the Conservatives polled only 33% of the electorate.

The missing voters, Jenkins argued, were alienated by the false hopes and unredeemed promises held out by both parties over the past twenty years, the alternation of governments each claiming a monopoly of wisdom and rushing onto the Statute Book a mass of ill-digested legislation founded on little popular support and promptly reversed by its successor. Good government demanded, not an avoidance of contro-

versy – characteristically he cited the great Reform Bills, the repeal of
the Corn Laws, the curbing of the power of the House of Lords and the
Beveridge revolution as measures bitterly contested at the time which
quickly became inviolable parts of the social fabric – but the assurance,
before embarking on any major reform, that it would last, because no
succeeding government would dare repeal it. 'All this implies a certain
respect by politicians for the opinions of their opponents.' Exaggerated
political partisanship, the pretence that everything is the fault of the
other side, was no longer convincing to most of the electorate, whose
aspirations, he believed, 'pull far more towards the centre than towards
the extremes.' 'The vocation of politicians ought to be to represent, to
channel, to lead the aspirations of the electorate.'[3]

That being so, he now believed that the case for proportional representation was 'overwhelming'. This was not a sudden conversion. In the
1974-6 Government he had infuriated most of the rest of the Cabinet
by trying several times to have the possibility examined by a Speaker's
Conference, supported only by what Barbara Castle called 'the hard
core of Jenkinsite coalitionists (Harold Lever, Shirley and Reg Prentice)
... beavering away ... until they have finally destroyed the Labour
party's ... power to govern single-handedly.'[4] In 1976 an all-party
National Committee for Electoral Reform was set up by a group including, from the Labour side, John Mackintosh and David Marquand,
Brian Walden and Anthony Lester: Jenkins did not join, but he gave it
tacit support. Now, in 1979, fortified by his experience in Europe, he
believed that the demands of equity could no longer be resisted by the
argument that the first-past-the-post system produced strong, effective
and coherent government, avoiding the weakness and instability of
coalitions.

> Do we really believe that we have been more effectively and coherently
> governed over the past two decades than have the Germans? ...
>   Do we really believe that the last Labour Government was not a coalition,
> in fact if not in name, and a pretty incompatible one at that? I served in it
> for half its life, and you could not convince me of anything else.

All democratic government, he now asserted, depended on some form
of coalition.

> The old Labour Party of Attlee and Gaitskell was a coalition of liberal social
> democrats and industrially responsible trade unionists. Willy Brandt and
> Helmut Schmidt have governed the Federal Republic of Germany with a
> coalition of Social Democrats and Liberals for the past decade. Sometimes
> the coalitions are overt, sometimes they are covert. I do not think the

distinction greatly matters. The test is whether those within the coalition are closer to each other, and to the mood of the nation they seek to govern, than they are to those outside their ranks.

Proportional representation might indeed produce coalition.

> I would much rather that it meant overt and compatible coalition than that it locked incompatible people, and still more important, incompatible philosophies, into a loveless, constantly bickering and debilitating marriage, even if consecrated in a common tabernacle.

The last word, incidentally, is straight out of the political vocabulary of the 1890s. Jenkins does not talk down even to a mass audience on television – for this he is criticized as 'élitist'. Unabashed, he went on to quote *Hamlet*:

> The great disadvantage of our present electoral system is that it freezes the pattern of politics, and holds together the incompatible because everyone assumes that if a party splits it will be electorally slaughtered. They may be right. They may be wrong. I am not so sure. I believe that the electorate can tell 'a hawk from a handsaw' and that if it saw a new grouping with cohesion and relevant policies it might be more attracted by this new reality than by old labels which had become increasingly irrelevant.

Coming specifically to the Labour party, he made the point that there was nothing inherently wrong with mandatory reselection of MPs, NEC control of the manifesto or an electoral college to elect the leader. These proposals were only contentious because they were the battleground between two incompatible views of the party. 'The response to such a situation', he believed, here making a clear call to the beleaguered social democrats to come out and join him, 'should not be to slog through an unending war of attrition, stubbornly and conventionally defending as much of the old citadel as you can hold, but to break out and mount a battle of movement on new and higher ground.'

By changing the political structure, by strengthening the political centre and ending the see-saw alternation of irrelevant dogmas, he concluded, Britain might go a long way towards restoring national prosperity. 'Our great failure, now for decades past, has been lack of adaptability': the economic system mirrored the political. 'The paradox is that we need more change accompanied by more stability of direction.' In particular he called for the acceptance of the broad line of division between the private and the public sector, and the necessity of both, to create as much wealth as possible in order to be able to use it 'both to give a return for enterprise and to spread the benefits throughout society in a way that avoids the disfigurements of poverty, gives a

full priority to public education and health services, and encourages
co-operation and not conflict in industry and throughout society.' He
looked forward to a free, less class-ridden and more decentralized society
discovering 'a renewed sense of cohesion and common purpose'; and
thought that these objectives could be assisted by 'a strengthening of
the radical centre'. Without specifically mentioning the formation of a
new party, he accurately forecast its success:

> I believe that such a development could bring into political commitment
> the energies of many people of talent and goodwill who, although perhaps
> active in many other voluntary ways, are at present alienated from the
> business of government, whether national or local, by the sterility and
> formalism of much of the political game. I am sure that this would improve
> our politics. I think the results might also help to improve our national
> performance. But of that I cannot be certain. I am against too much
> dogmatism here. We have had more than enough of it. But at least we could
> escape from the pessimism of Yeats's 'Second Coming', where
>
> > The best lack all conviction, while the worst
> > Are full of passionate intensity
>
> and
>
> > Things fall apart; the centre cannot hold.[3]

To most of the political commentators and professional cynics, Jenkins' thesis was as banal and hackneyed as his concluding quotation:
talk of realignment had been going on as long as any of them could
remember, and nothing had ever come of it. Certainly there was nothing
intellectually very original in his analysis: but his best friends would
never claim Jenkins as a penetrating creative thinker. What he possesses
is acute political judgement and an ability to give weight and shape and
the authority of common sense to ideas which may seem too hackneyed
to be worth stating but which actually express what a lot of ordinary
people deeply but incoherently believe. In this case, his judgement as to
timing was precise and his words struck a resounding response from a
public which had been waiting years for someone in his position to say
clearly what he had now said. 'I have never received before', he said in
a second speech six months later, 'a great batch of mail which was, first,
99% friendly; second, 99% sane; and third, revealed, often argued over
400 or 500 words, such a degree of desire for release from present
political restraints and for involvement in the future.'[5]

Yet the politicians and the pundits – the very people who habitually
condemned Jenkins as arrogant and out of touch – only sneered. After
reprinting his lecture on 29 November (it was also reprinted as a BBC
pamphlet), the *Listener* two weeks later invited a number of politicians,

journalists and academics to comment on it. All, from Enoch Powell and Paul Johnson on the right to Jack Jones and Professors Bernard Crick and John Griffith on the left, were contemptuous: the most respectful was in fact Neil Kinnock, who alone conceded that Jenkins' views had 'the appeal of reason and the authority of demonstrated commitment', but thought him misguided on the ground that the country had had centre government for the past thirty years. Even Jo Grimond was grudging, complaining that Jenkins' revelation was twenty years too late. The criticism was of two types – political and personal. Most of those asked thought proportional representation ir-relevant and the concept of a 'radical centre' woolly naivety. Bernard Crick quoted Jenkins' wish for 'the innovating stimulus of the free market economy without the unacceptable brutality of its untram-melled distribution of rewards or its indifference to unemployment' and added sarcastically: 'We need camels without smell and with feathers'. But most striking was the widespread assumption that Jenkins was not prepared to put his own career to the hazard but, as Paul Johnson put it, wanted 'the palm without the dust'.

> A call to battle from Jenkins might have been useful, even well-received. Instead he drops a hint that if the system is changed and provided the breakaway works and once the dust has settled – and always assuming he hasn't been offered a better job in the meantime – then he might consider accepting the leadership.

Jo Grimond took a similar view, listing some of the radical goals – not just a return to Keynes and Beveridge, but co-operatives and decen-tralization – which the Liberals had long ago identified:

> If Mr Jenkins agrees, let him come down into the battle. Let him shove with the rest of us. All too many social democrats have gone off into banking, consultancy, TV, academic life etc. It is Mr Steel who has been in the scrum. Will they join him? The opportunity is indeed great ... but time is very short.[6]

Jenkins was not in a position to show the doubters that he meant business: he still had a year to serve in Brussels. But he was already much more deeply committed than those who wrote him off as a dilettante realized. He was in close touch, first of all, with David Steel. He had first invited him to dinner, alone, in Brussels, shortly after the General Election; they had a second long meeting at East Hendred over Christmas. They did not thereafter need to meet often because they understood each other perfectly. Despite the difference in generation, their analysis of politics and, more important, their view of the correct strategy, was identical. Jenkins was quite ready to join the Liberals if that had been the best way forward; but they were both agreed that a new Social Democratic Party, working in alliance with but separate from the Liberals, would have a better chance, by attracting a significant breakaway of disillusioned Labour MPs and Labour voters, of breaking the two-party mould than the Liberal party by itself, even if strengthened by the adherence of Jenkins and the few others who might have taken that step. During the next year – indeed during the next three years, when the SDP-Liberal alliance was being forged and consolidated – Jenkins and Steel had, as Hugh Stephenson has written, 'the huge tactical advantage over their respective colleagues of having thought out together and long in advance the direction in which they wanted things to move.'[7] The SDP is almost as much Steel's baby as it is Jenkins'.

Secondly, following the Dimbleby Lecture there came into being an important group of other figures already determined to leave the Labour party and only waiting for the leadership and the right moment to go. Jim Daly, a former trade unionist and Labour councillor, now a polytechnic lecturer, and Clive Lindley, a wealthy businessman who had made his money in motorway catering, set up a somewhat shadowy Radical Centre for Democratic Studies (run from Daly's front room), and began simultaneously to meet with a number of ex-MPs who had lost their seats in 1979 or 1974 – Colin Phipps, Michael Barnes, Dick Taverne; also David Marquand, John Harris and Stephen Haseler, another polytechnic lecturer and author of a book on the Gaitskellites, who in 1975 had set up a militantly anti-left forerunner of the SDP, the Social Democratic Alliance. Jenkins met and dined with this group at Brooks's in December 1979 – they formed his vanguard.[8]

The troops he really needed, however, to create a serious fourth party were the increasingly desperate social democrats still within the Parliamentary Labour party (plus Shirley Williams who, though she had lost her seat in 1979, still sat on Labour's NEC). Of these, Jenkins was in the closest touch – as he had always been – with Bill Rodgers. Rodgers and Ian Wrigglesworth, with Marquand and Taverne (plus all their wives), dined with Jenkins the evening the Dimbleby Lecture was broadcast; and a week later Rodgers made an important speech at Abertillery giving the Labour party a year to come to its senses, or he and others might feel they had to leave. On his way back to London he stopped off, at Jenkins' suggestion, at East Hendred; Shirley Williams was there too, and the three of them discussed the future. At this stage, however, the 'Gang of Three' – Rodgers, Williams and David Owen – had not yet given up hope of saving Labour; and so long as they were still fighting within the party they had publicly to repudiate Jenkins at every opportunity. The least indication that they were tempted by what Owen, two days after the Dimbleby Lecture, called 'siren voices from outside, from those who have given up the fight from within',[9] would have completely undercut their position. Despite another traumatic Conference in May, at which the party adopted the hard left policy document *Peace, Jobs, Freedom* – anti-EEC, unilateralist, anti-incomes policy but enthusiastic for further nationalization and import controls – and Owen was humiliatingly booed, they still felt bound to keep on denying any thought of joining a party which Shirley Williams said – in a famous phrase which many observers at the time knew she would soon regret – would have 'no roots, no principles, no philosophy and no values.'[10] Even in August, when they wrote a long letter to the *Guardian* threatening that they might be driven to leave Labour, they emphasized that their alternative would be a *socialist*, not a centre party.[11] They were *not* lining up behind Jenkins.

Encouraged by the reaction to his Dimbleby Lecture, however, Jenkins delivered in June a follow-up speech to the Parliamentary Press Gallery which went considerably further towards announcing a new party – and in a memorable metaphor made it clear that he did not envisage simply a purged Labour party.

> As a basis for discussion of realignment it is inadequate to see British politics as two and a half bottles, one labelled Conservative, the next Labour, the third Liberal, and then to think in the fixed quantities of exactly how much you could pour out of each of the first two bottles and put alongside the third.
>
> We must think much more in terms of untapped and unlabelled quantities – and when you look at the low level of participation today ... there is no reason to doubt that they exist.

He was aiming at that presently unrepresented constituency which had rallied so eagerly to the standard he had planted the previous November. At the same time he concentrated his attack, point by point, on Labour's *Peace, Jobs, Freedom* ('not by any stretch of the imagination a social democratic programme'), and stressed the true radicalism of breaking away from Labour. Jim Callaghan had asserted that no new party could succeed, because it would not represent either of the great organized interests, capital or labour. This was 'very compelling *realpolitik*', Jenkins commented, but it no longer corresponded to the pluralism of modern Britain, while a political system built on such a rigid social demarcation offered no possibility of the national co-operation which alone could halt the country's decline into an industrial desert.

> It is a very conservative and very static view of politics, and one which hands over to the Tory party the whole business interest and those who sensibly believe they have an interest in the success of British private industry. It hands them over to a far greater extent than I would be willing to do. And it is one which leaves the Labour party far too dependent upon trade union support and control.

Since this was the view of the leader to whom Owen and Williams, who professed themselves radicals, were still loyal, this was a shrewd thrust. He did not doubt, Jenkins went on, the strength of political inertia. But he expressed his belief that it could be overcome in another metaphor which, he later admitted, was a gift to the cartoonists:

> The likelihood before the start of most adventures is that of failure. The experimental plane may well finish up a few fields from the end of the runway.... But the reverse could occur and the experimental plane could soar in the sky. If that is so, it could go further and more quickly than few now imagine [sic], for it would carry with it great and now untapped reserves of political energy and commitment.

He concluded with a less noticed prophecy:

> There was once a book more famous for its title than for its contents called *The Strange Death of Liberal England*. That death caught people rather unawares. Do not discount the possibility that in a few years' time someone may be able to write at least equally convincingly of *The Strange and Rapid Revival of Liberal and Social Democratic Britain*.[5]

The response from most of the press was another volley of hoarse laughter. 'Almost everything Mr Jenkins says is true', the *Economist* generously conceded. 'It is all magnificent, but it is not war.' The battle, it believed, lay within the Labour party: all Jenkins was doing was undermining the right.[12] The rudest was the *Spectator*, which pictured its former columnist as 'a fat, flabby and nearly-extinct bird endeavouring to fly but lacking the muscle and momentum to take flight. Mr Jenkins might soar: he is altogether more likely to crash.' In a spectacularly ill-informed leader – mistaken both as to Jenkins' personal calculations and the opportunity waiting for another party – the paper went on:

> When Mr Denis Healey describes the possibility of a new party as 'absolute bunk' he is surely being accurate for once. General and bye-elections have continually established that there is insufficient room between the moderate

wings of the Tory and Labour parties for the Liberal Party to enjoy a share of power. To insert another party in the middle would further weaken the centre. If this is what Mr Jenkins wants, let him go ahead. But if he is disillusioned with the Labour Party and cannot face belonging to the Tory Party (to which he naturally belongs), he would do best to join the Liberals and give them the helping hand they need. It can only be ambition and self-conceit which prevent him from volunteering to serve under Mr Steel.[13]

The writer would have been wiser to notice Steel's own comment on the general ridicule. 'Roy Jenkins', he wrote calmly, 'is simply ahead of his time.'[14]

In the last months of 1980, timing was crucial. Earlier in the year several of the Colin Phipps–Michael Barnes group had been anxious to move at once. Jenkins, who in any case preferred to wait until he himself returned from Brussels, was supported by Clive Lindley and David Marquand in believing that it was better to hang on for the 'Gang of Three', confident that they would in the end come out. By the autumn the 'Gang', with an uncertain number of others, were very close to the brink. In October the Labour Conference voted in favour of an electoral college to elect the leader, giving a share in the decision to the trade unions (though the precise composition of the college was left to another conference in January); then in November the PLP elected Michael Foot to succeed Callaghan. Had Denis Healey been elected, they would have felt bound to stay on and see if he were prepared to fight the left; under Foot they knew there would only be further compromise. Owen declined to stand for the Shadow Cabinet, and began holding discussions with possible defectors to see how many would join a new party; Shirley Williams announced that she would not be a Labour candidate at the next election. Now Jenkins stepped up the pace. With his own little group, he virtually decided to go it alone if necessary as soon as he returned to Britain, appealing to the constituency he had uncovered in the Dimbleby Lecture and seeing who would follow. Writing in the *Spectator*, Marquand threw down the challenge to the 'Gang': if they did not break very soon and set up a party, which Jenkins would have to join, Jenkins would set up his own which *they* would have to join. They were in a race to determine which group would shape the new party.[15] But the 'Gang of Three', and particularly David Owen, were antagonized by these tactics. Owen strongly resented Jenkins assuming the lead, both on political grounds and personal. Politically he believed that Jenkins had in mind a centrist, quasi-liberal party rather than an explicitly left-of-centre social democratic party,

and was suspicious of his understanding with David Steel. Personally
he had become disillusioned with Jenkins' leadership between 1972
and 1976, and their relations had deteriorated further between 1977
and 1979 when Owen as Foreign Secretary had adopted what seemed
to Jenkins a stupidly 'Gaullist' line towards the EEC; Owen thought
Jenkins a *passé*, middle-of-the-road grandee, a liability rather than
an asset.[16] Here were the ingredients of their open contest for the
leadership in 1982.

At the end of November, however, they both realized that they had
to work together. Owen came to lunch at East Hendred, and they
reached a concordat – they discovered that their ideas were not as far
apart as Owen imagined, and the 'Gang of Three' became a 'Gang of
Four'. Owen secured from Jenkins what he wanted: agreement that
Jenkins did not simply assume the leadership by virtue of experience
and seniority, but would accept a collective leadership in the early
stages until the party was sufficiently established to elect its leader.
Jenkins, for his part, was happy to have got Owen at least – Rodgers
and Williams still hesitated – committed to leaving Labour. As for the
leadership, he was still unsure how easy it would be for him to make the
transition back into British politics; he was quite diffident, accepting
that his Brussels image might be too great a handicap and content, if
that were so, to see himself as godfather and elder statesman. Several
times he repeated his favourite Adlai Stevenson quotation, 'I don't *have*
to be leader.' Nevertheless there was a sense in which, not so much by
age as by weight of personality and clarity of purpose, by the working
of a basic human chemistry between four people, quite apart from the
public's perception of him as the originator of the whole process, he was
naturally and inevitably the leader.

Once Jenkins and Owen had come together, the final steps towards
the brink were taken at a series of meetings during January 1981 – at
East Hendred, in Shirley Williams' flat in Victoria, in Bill Rodgers'
house in Kentish Town, finally and historically at Owen's house in
Limehouse. At all these meetings, Jenkins pressed for speed. Rodgers in
particular wanted to go slower, to wait until October. Shirley Williams,
too, wondered at the last if it might not be enough to set up a Council
for Social Democracy as a pressure group *within* the Labour party. It was
Jenkins who insisted that the Council must be no more than a staging
post on the road out of the party, to enable the defectors to shed their
obligations to Labour with decency. The last battle was over the word-
ing of the 'Limehouse Declaration', issued from Owen's house on 25
January (the day after Labour's special Wembley Conference had come

up with a formula for electing the leader which gave the unions an even bigger share than expected, 40 per cent – the very last straw for the 'Gang of Three'). Most of the document was directed specifically to Labour supporters who were disgusted by the 'calamitous outcome' of the Conference and the 'long process' of which it was the culmination ('politicians who recognize that the drift towards extremism in the Labour Party is not compatible with the democratic traditions of the Party they joined'); but it also appealed, in words which echoed Jenkins' analysis, to 'those from outside politics who believe that the country cannot be saved without changing the sterile and rigid framework into which the British political system has increasingly fallen in the last two decades.' It repudiated what Owen and Williams feared that Jenkins wanted: 'the politics of an inert centre merely representing the lowest common denominator between two extremes'; but the next sentence came straight from the Dimbleby Lecture: 'We want more, not less radical change in our society, but with greater stability of direction.' The critical sentence, however, was the last. In Shirley Williams' original draft the Declaration could even now have been read as a call to fight on within the Labour party: it ended 'We look for a new assertion of social democracy.' Jenkins was determined to make it clear that the Rubicon had been crossed. The final draft read, unmistakeably, 'We believe that the need for a realignment of British politics must now be faced.'[17]

As Jenkins had anticipated, the Limehouse Declaration was the point of no return. In addition to Owen and Rodgers, nine Labour MPs, then another two, plus one Conservative, joined the newly-formed Council for Social Democracy. A *Guardian* advertisement signed by a hundred varied but prominent supporters attracted 80,000 letters and £175,000 in donations, mainly small.[18] The public pressure to go on and form a party as quickly as possible was irresistible. Instead of waiting until after the local elections in May, the launch was brought forward to 26 March. Then, at the Connaught Rooms at nine o'clock in the morning, drawing consciously on the public relations razzmatazz that had so impressed them all in the EEC referendum campaign six years before, the four leaders faced the television cameras of the world before flying off – making the most of collective leadership – to eight secondary launches around the country; Jenkins went to Cardiff and on to Manchester. As the senior of the four, he spoke the first words: 'We offer not only a new party, but a new approach to politics.'[19] The Social Democratic Party was born. Within days it was registering, with the Liberals, 48 per cent in the opinion polls.[20]

In the first chaotic weeks of the new party's existence, as the press tried to weigh up whether it was really an important departure or just a flash in the pan, there was a general tendency, particularly in the popular papers, to see Shirley Williams as the most likely eventual leader. She was at this time the darling of British politics. It was her agonizings about leaving the Labour party that had made the best copy: it was she whom the party was most sorry to lose. Despite having lost her seat in 1979 to an above-average swing, she had a real following in the country and was regarded, with some reason, as the new party's greatest electoral asset. It was not yet recognized, outside the narrow circle of those who had worked closely with her, that, for all her qualities, she is not a leader. Of the 'Gang of Four' she had been the least close, personally, to Jenkins. Though passionately pro-EEC, she was not one of the inner group of Jenkinsites in 1971–2; but as a member of Labour's NEC from 1970 and a member of the Cabinet from 1974 she had emerged in the last five years as the most prominent and personally embattled opponent of the left, while Jenkins was seen to have taken himself off comfortably to Brussels. Now they were in direct competition, not in the first instance for the SDP leadership but to find a seat in the House of Commons, which was a necessary qualification for the leadership. Ironically, the game of musical chairs on which they now embarked did decide the leadership – but not in the way that might have been expected.

The first by-election that fell due was in Warrington – a rock-solid Labour constituency in industrial Lancashire, fifteen miles east of Liverpool. Despite the SDP's ambition of displacing Labour as the main party of the left, this was not the sort of seat it would have chosen for its first electoral test. The party was thought to be stronger in the south: the voters of Warrington seemed the least likely type of Labour voter to desert their traditional allegiance. If anyone could swing them it would surely be Shirley, though in the first few days after the vacancy occurred in late May – the sitting Labour member was appointed a judge – David Marquand, Professor at nearby Salford was mentioned as an alternative. The Liberals insisted that they would stand down only for one of the SDP's big names; but no-one imagined that it was the right sort of seat for Jenkins until, to universal astonishment, Mrs Williams announced that, for family reasons, she did not wish to fight a by-election before the autumn. From this decision her career and public reputation have never recovered; overnight – assisted, she bitterly believed, by some black propaganda spread by Jenkins' aides, though not by himself – her golden image was suddenly tarnished and the papers were full of nothing but her indecisiveness, her habitual lateness and her inability to catch trains. The long term loss has been the party's; but the short-term gain was Jenkins'. After a couple of days to think it over in the utterly incongruous surroundings of an international monetary conference in Switzerland, he determined that he would stand for Warrington. Almost instantly, the tedious 'claret' jokes which had mocked him since the Dimbleby Lecture and indeed long before, to the extent that some columnists seemed to have got out of the habit of taking him seriously at all, were replaced by exaggerated respect for his courage (as though Warrington were the Gorbals) and the recollection that he was after all a lifelong and highly professional politician, who had represented a not dissimilar urban Labour constituency for twenty-six years. 'By grasping the opportunity from which Mrs Shirley Williams flinched', wrote Ronald Butt in *The Times*, 'Mr Roy Jenkins has put himself in a position in which he will almost certainly become the SDP's leader if he wins, and quite probably even if he loses.'[21]

Few commentators gave him any serious chance of winning: an *Observer* poll on 8 June gave the SDP 25 per cent, Labour 64 per cent and the Tories 10 per cent.[22] But he had scarcely a moment's doubt that he should fight the seat. The party had to make a good showing in its first by-election. It would be absolutely fatal to be seen to be picking and choosing which seats to fight; it had to be willing to fight anywhere and everywhere, and to regard *no* seat as unwinnable. Personally, too, Warrington was exactly the sort of seat to blood him again in domestic politics and prove that he was not a superannuated Eurocrat but *was* willing to get his hands dirty. The caricature of a claret-bibbing sybarite quite overlooks Jenkins' intense competitiveness. He had come back from Brussels ready and expecting to have to gamble. In fact, once Shirley Williams had refused Warrington, he could not really lose.

In the event, he had a personal triumph, though he did not quite win the seat. Labour made it easier for him by selecting a left-wing former MP, Doug Hoyle, who varied between trying to ignore him and calling him a traitor to the Labour movement and a 'retired pensioner from the EEC';[23] the Tories by offering up a London bus driver as sacrificial victim. Both, the *Economist* wrote, were 'ghastly ... and their ghastliness got much greater coverage under the by-election spotlight than they would in a General Election.' Jenkins, on the other hand, 'worked hard and argued seriously.... He got credit for putting Warrington on the map.'[24] He surprised reporters by the vigour and apparent enjoyment with which he blanketed the housing estates, toured the working-men's clubs with Lord George-Brown and accepted vodka (not claret!) in the Vladivar factory.[25] 'Avalanche of Charm as Jenkins Sweeps in', *The*

Times reported; [26] while Frank Johnson found to his surprise that 'the grand, stupendously distinguished and largely incomprehensible magnifico from another world who has been introducing himself with a courtly bow of his smooth shiny head to incredulous passers-by in this town' actually went down rather well.[27] He fought on national issues, taking advantage of the fact that the SDP had so far no official policies to make them up as he went along. Most notably, he unveiled a detailed and carefully costed plan to reduce unemployment by one million in two years by the expenditure of £6,000m on employment grants, public sector investment, renovation and training schemes.[28] (Clive Jenkins of ASTMS called it 'economically illiterate ... derisory and arithmetically juvenile', and proposed to spend £20,000m.)[29] Above all, Jenkins had the help of an army of SDP and – even though the Alliance was not yet formalized – Liberal volunteers from all over the country: the same army which later moved on, with similarly sensational results, to Croydon, Crosby and Hillhead.*

A week before polling day, on 16 July, no opinion poll gave Jenkins more than 30 per cent.[31] He seemed to have taken most of the Tory vote (29 per cent in 1979), but to have made little dent in Labour's 61 per cent. (The Liberals had taken 9 per cent.) Not even the canvass returns picked up what was happening. As late as just before the count, Jenkins admitted privately that he would be happy with 35 per cent, which would have been a very good result, both personally and for a party less than four months old. In fact, on a high poll, he won 42 per cent to Hoyle's 48 per cent, squeezing the Tories to a humiliating 7 per cent: Labour's 10,000 majority was reduced to a bare 1,759. This was the 60th safest seat in the country; on this swing, the BBC computer crazily extrapolated, a General Election would give the Alliance 501 seats, Labour 113 and the Tories one! No wonder Jenkins exultantly proclaimed the result 'my first defeat in thirty years in politics' but 'by far the greatest victory I have ever participated in.'[32] Hoyle's bitter victory speech told the country that Labour was shaken to its roots.

For the rest of 1981 the SDP continued to ride high, powerfully assisted by the long drawn-out public contest for the deputy leadership of the Labour Party between Denis Healey and Tony Benn, and by growing opposition within the Tory party to Mrs Thatcher's unyielding reliance

---

* This army developed an extraordinary *esprit de corps*, and its members wear their campaign medals with pride. Veterans of Warrington adopted as their *motif* (incorporated in a campaign tie) a favourite Jenkins image, in which he compared a Labour-governed Britain trying to come out of the EEC only six years after voting to stay in to 'a squirrel in a cage'. The phrase was actually Churchill's, about the Attlee Government's 1949 devaluation; Jenkins first used it, with attribution, in 1962.[30]

on high unemployment to reduce inflation. A steady trickle of Labour MPS continued to come over, bringing the total by the end of the year to twenty-seven. The alliance with the Liberals was ratified by both party Conferences in October, the culmination of the strategy on which Jenkins and Steel had been intent since 1979; they appeared together at the Liberal Assembly at Llandudno, and Jenkins was triumphantly received. The momentum of success overcame minor difficulties. For the next by-election after Warrington, at Croydon North-East, the local Liberals refused, despite pressure from Steel, to drop their own candidate, the decidedly uncharismatic four-time loser in the seat, Bill Pitt, in favour of Shirley Williams; but Pitt went on to win a three-cornered contest by 3000 votes, proving that the Alliance was not wholly dependent on big names. Then Shirley Williams disconcerted the Liberals by jumping at the 19,000-majority Tory seat of Crosby, north of Liverpool; but she too won an even more astonishing victory, becoming the SDP's first MP elected under the party's colours. She had beaten Jenkins back into the House after all, yet even this victory could not erase the memory of her ducking Warrington. A poll of party members showed Jenkins now the clear favourite for the leadership – 49 per cent to 29 per cent, with 19 per cent for David Owen.[33]

This took some of the heat out of a dispute that was boiling up about how the eventual leader should be elected. As their last throw within the Labour party, Owen and Mrs Williams had committed themselves to the principle of election by the entire membership. Now, most vociferously supported by Mike Thomas, they elevated the acceptance of this principle by the SDP as the touchstone of the party's radicalism. Jenkins and Rodgers, giving more weight to the constitutional requirement, most prominently expounded by Marquand, that the leader must have the confidence of the party's MPS, preferred the established system in the Tory and Labour parties of election by the MPS alone. So long as it seemed that the party at large would choose Shirley Williams while the majority of the MPS would go for Jenkins, this division between the collective and aspirant leaders threatened considerable embarrassment. In the event, by a postal ballot of the membership in May 1982, the one-member-one-vote camp won the argument; but by then it looked as though Jenkins would win under any system.

First, however, it was essential that he get back into Parliament. The leadership was not due to be decided until October 1982 – there were considerable advantages in retaining the collective leadership, though Steel was continually pressing that the SDP get on with it; even so, by the end of 1981 there were only four or five months left for a suitable vacancy to occur. As they scanned lists of constituencies whose sitting members' health was poor, Jenkins and his supporters knew that he would have to accept practically any by-election that came up. His fate was outside his control. If he did not find a winnable seat by the autumn he would have to settle for the Presidency of the party in the country and the role of elder statesman after all. The real possibility which the opinion polls held out, that he might lead the Alliance into government at the next election, hung agonizingly in the balance.

Then, on the second day of 1982, the Tory member for Glasgow, Hillhead, Thomas Galbraith, suddenly died. The vacancy did not come as a complete surprise – Hillhead had been on every politician's list of likely by-elections for years, not because of any expectation of Galbraith's death but because his father, Lord Strathclyde, was over ninety and Galbraith was his heir. At first sight, a Scottish seat was the worst possible thing for Jenkins: the SDP had fewer members and less support north of the border than in England, and though the Scottish National Party had declined from its heady days in the mid-seventies it was still a dangerous fourth party capable of taking much of the anti-Tory, anti-Labour vote – particularly from an English, or at any rate anglicized, carpet-bagger such as Jenkins. Scottish politics are an entirely different world, pitted with traps for the unwary: the time when Gladstone, Asquith, Churchill and others could sit for Scottish constituencies was, most Scots believed, long past. Desperate though he was to get back into the House of Commons, there were many among his friends, including David Steel, whose first thought was that Jenkins should decline Hillhead, on the perfectly respectable argument that a Scottish seat should have a Scottish candidate.

Against that, however, Hillhead was a very untypical Scottish seat. It was the one Conservative constituency left in Glasgow; but Galbraith had been a poor MP and the Tory vote had been crumbling for years – in 1979 his majority had dropped to 2,002. More important, it is one of the most socially mixed constituencies in the whole of Britain. The north is very grand – wide streets of large detached stone houses built by the captains of industry and commerce who had made their own and Glasgow's fortune in the nineteenth century. The south, beside the Clyde, is typical of most of Labour Glasgow – depressed, decaying tenements, pubs and boarded-up shops. The key lies in the middle, where lives a large part of Glasgow's white collar and professional middle class, clustered around two hospitals, the Jordanhill teacher training college, the university (just outside the constituency) and eight independent schools: nurses, technicians, medical staff, lecturers and teachers.[34] With these voters in its sights, the SDP already fancied Hillhead as one of its target seats in Scotland. It was indeed the perfect SDP seat, its three-class structure – two entrenched old classes and an educated 'new' class alienated from both – neatly mirroring the division of the country which the SDP had set itself to break.*

It so happened that Bob Maclennan (one of only two SDP MPs in Scotland) had been brought up in the constituency; John Harris also knew it well. They advised Jenkins that, contrary to first appearances, Hillhead might almost have been tailor-made for him: he would make a uniquely wide appeal, not only to the highly educated middle section but also to large parts of the Tory north (which had been neglected by Galbraith and would respond to his international distinction) and of the Labour south (where his record would still win him friends among those who were worried by the progress of the left). Maclennan assured him that his Englishness – or Welshness – would not be an issue. With this encouragement, Jenkins decided to back his own instinct and take another gamble. This time he knew that if he lost he would be finished, at least so far as the leadership was concerned. But behind the judicious manner he is a gambler; he is also a historian. He knows and relishes the element of chance in politics. He knew that Hillhead was the last chance he was likely to get. He knew that he really had no choice. He also knew that he was very lucky it was not Glasgow, Queen's Park, or Beaconsfield.

Once the press had recovered from its initial astonishment (most London commentators really did think he was going to the Gorbals this time), once they had realized the true character of Hillhead, the general assumption was that he would win. ('Why Roy Should Romp It', *Sunday Times*.)[35] This was less than two months after Crosby, when anything seemed possible. Very soon, however, it became clear that he had an uphill battle on his hands; for the Alliance bubble had burst. Quarrels over the New Year about the allocation of seats between the two parties had dented the image of smooth co-operation. (Even at Hillhead, the adopted Liberal candidate was only persuaded to stand down after high level intervention by Maclennan and Russell Johnstone.) The level of support registered in November – over 50 per cent – was in any case bound to fall; but once it began to fall, it fell rapidly. Suddenly it seemed that Jenkins had made a terrible miscalculation.

It was one of the longest by-election campaigns ever, extending virtually from the moment he announced his candidature on 11 January

---

* The redrawing of constituency boundaries in 1983 will make Hillhead slightly more 'Labour' in complexion; but Jenkins is confident of being able to retain it at the General Election.

right up to polling day, eventually fixed for 25 March; and one of the most highly-publicized, as the press not only of Britain but of the world descended on Glasgow and dogged the candidates' footsteps wherever they went. In the early days, Jenkins was able to walk about quite discreetly getting to know the place; but by the end he and Jennifer could escape the cameras only by giving it out that they were taking a morning off – bad publicity, but the only way they could actually meet the voters. With four parties all entertaining a real hope of winning, the electors were canvassed more intensively than any electorate in the history of British politics; long before 25 March many of them were sick of it. The SNP, who made the most noise on the streets, perhaps significantly did much less well than they had hoped, despite an attractive candidate. Of the two old parties, Labour had a poor candidate – a nineteen-stone bearded Bennite with an ear-ring, lacking the personality or eloquence to convince any but the most committed loyalist; but the Tories selected a handsome and personable young solicitor, born and bred in the constituency, just the candidate to hold the Tory ladies of Anniesland to their traditional allegiance. During the campaign the opinion polls put first one party, then another marginally ahead. There was never much in it, but with less than two weeks remaining Jenkins seemed to have missed the bus. The sort of surge that had carried Shirley Williams to victory at Crosby had not materialized, and the papers, feeding on each other, began to predict a spectacular débâcle. Around 14 March the Jenkins camp, based in the unromantically named Pond Hotel, was sunk in gloom. The weather was cold and miserable, everything seemed to be going wrong, and the candidate, facing defeat, was in a filthy temper.

What turned the election round was sheer hard work, and the willingness of a serious-minded Scottish electorate to listen to the arguments. Jenkins pitched his campaign at a high intellectual level, yet his meetings – addressed also by the other members of the 'Gang of Four', by David Steel, Jo Grimond and other Liberals – were phenomenally well-attended. The crowds who packed the largest halls in the constituency to overflowing totalled 10,000 – a quarter of the entire electorate. He also used the technique of coffee-mornings to meet and talk with groups of ten or a dozen ladies or retired people in their own homes. Most were curious, then flattered and usually impressed to meet so famous a man in such circumstances, and told their neighbours. By the end there seemed to be few electors who had not either spoken to him themselves or knew someone who had. As Maclennan had promised, the carpet-bagger charge did not stick: most people understood that a politician needing to get back into the House of Commons between elections has no choice but to stand for whatever seat comes up, and as in Warrington were grateful that he had put their constituency on the map.* He undertook to buy a house in the constituency if he won,† but did not attempt to disguise that he intended to play a wider role than simply to represent Hillhead: he hinted that as a well-known name he would be able to do more for Glasgow than the city's twelve other, largely anonymous, Labour members. What he did have to do was commit himself and the SDP to Scottish devolution: devolution in general was already a plank of the party platform, but he had to come up more quickly than the party might otherwise have done with a detailed plan for an Assembly with revenue-raising powers. Fortunately he was able to prove, by quoting Barbara Castle's published diary, that this was not an expedient conversion on his part: though initially doubtful, by the last days of the Wilson Government in 1976 he was strongly in favour of recognizing Scottish aspirations.[36] That substantially disarmed the SNP, who were left to make as much as they could of his army of very English helpers.

One of them, a quintessentially Kensington lady, attracted satirical attention for running up and down some of the poorest tenements in shocking pink tights. Two days before polling day, Jenkins was able to tell her that he thought she could safely wear her pink tights again. In the last days the tide had turned. The canvass returns were telling a different story: the weeks of hard persuasion had done their work. The sun even came out – gay with purple crocuses, the constituency now looked nothing like the southerner's idea of Glasgow. Jenkins visibly relaxed, beaming broadly as he cavalcaded round the streets in a decorated Land Rover and plunging into the shopping centres to shake hands – Maclennan at his shoulder, Bill Rodgers ahead playing John the Baptist with a megaphone, Jennifer (her right arm in a sling because of a poisoned finger) gamely shaking hands with her left. A late Gallup poll in the *Telegraph* showing Labour ahead was brushed aside: it served to key up the final effort on the day, but Jenkins' professionals on the ground were certain it was nonsense. Three polls on the last morning all put him six points clear. A more nagging worry was a spoiler who had changed his name to Roy Jenkins to try to confuse the voters. In order to combat him, volunteers were posted at every polling station wearing sandwich boards proclaiming 'The *Real* Roy Jenkins is No. 5.'

* The EEC was not held against him as much as was predicted, either. The story was told of one man, strongly anti-EEC, who said he was going to vote for Jenkins. 'But he was President of the EEC!' 'Aye, but he jacked it in, didn't he.'

† He and Jennifer subsequently bought a four-room flat overlooking the Great Western Road.

The counterfeit Roy Jenkins polled 282 votes – which might well have decided a tight result. But the real Roy Jenkins' majority was 2,038. Given the four-way split (plus four fringe candidates) it was a handsome margin.

Roy Jenkins (*SDP/Liberal Alliance*)	10,106
Gerry Malone (*Conservative*)	8,068
David Wiseman (*Labour*)	7,846
George Leslie (*SNP*)	3,416

On a poll higher than at the General Election (76 per cent – remarkable tribute to the interest aroused), Jenkins took 33.4 per cent, to the Tories' 26.6 per cent, Labour's 25.9 per cent and the SNP's 11.3 per cent. Pledged as he was to proportional representation, it was ironic to win with twice as many votes against as for him: but that is the unreformed system. The swing in his favour (19 per cent) – at the expense almost equally of Tory and Labour – was actually less than at Warrington, which remains statistically the best of all the Alliance's parliamentary results. The difference was that at Hillhead, when he absolutely had to win, he won, against an ebbing national tide – leaving the commentators once again shaking their heads at his luck, his nerve, his unexpected vote-getting ability; above all his knack, time and again throughout his career when the chips are down, of coming out on top. On the anniversary of the SDP's foundation just one year before, the headlines hailed one of the greatest victories in modern politics: 'Reckless Roy Comes Out On Top: The Gambler Who Hit The Jackpot' (*Daily Mail*);[37] 'Jenkins Breaks the Mould' (*Glasgow Herald*);[38] 'The Second Coming of Saint Roy' (*The Times*).[39] And then on Sunday, 'The SDP Finds Its Leader' (*Sunday Times*).[40]

The leadership not only of the SDP but of the Alliance was now, it was generally assumed, sewn up. Moreover Hillhead, as well as a personal triumph, was surely the boost the Alliance needed to reverse its national slide in the opinion polls. But far away in the South Atlantic events were in train which drastically invalidated both these expectations. On 2 April – just seven days after the Hillhead result – the Argentines invaded the Falkland Islands and British politics were suddenly and lastingly transformed. Jenkins was extraordinarily lucky to have got Hillhead over before the Falklands swept everything else off the front pages and the television screens; a fortnight later he would have been submerged in the nation's emotional rally behind the Government. But the war obliterated the advantage the Alliance would in normal circumstances have expected to gain from the Hillhead victory; and it dramatically promoted the hitherto unfancied figure of David Owen as a serious rival to Jenkins for the leadership.

The Falklands crisis divided the British people into three groups, roughly but not exactly along the political spectrum from left to right: within parties the differences were as much temperamental as political. One group – mainly the Bennite left in Parliament, but a very much wider section of leftish opinion in the country, including many members of the SDP – opposed the war outright, thought the sending of the Task Force a post-imperial spasm and believed that the problem could be solved at the United Nations. Practically everyone else – that is, the great majority of the House of Commons, including the Labour Front Bench, and of the country – supported the sending of the Task Force and the necessity of meeting force with force. This majority, however, was divided between those, like Mrs Thatcher and the *Sun*, who embraced necessity with martial relish, and others, more like the *Guardian* and Michael Foot, who backed it with evident reluctance and a preference to negotiate if possible. This was where temperament came in. Jenkins, though absolutely clear that the Government must be supported, was a reluctant warrior who could not help giving the impression that the crisis was really not his style; Owen by contrast, though there was no difference between them in substance, seemed to be in his element. As one of the collective leadership and still the leader in the House of Commons, a former Foreign Secretary who claimed credit for averting a Falklands crisis in 1977, Owen was the SDP's principal spokesman on the only issue that mattered in British politics between April and July. Jenkins, within weeks of Hillhead, was totally eclipsed; when he was heard on radio or television, he tended to take a lofty historical perspective, explaining that the Falklands crisis was not like Suez, and that it was the responsibility of both Government and Opposition parties to ensure that it did not become like Suez. However much he backed Owen's tough line, he gave the impression of living in the past.

Suddenly, therefore, the leadership election was a real contest. Long before the Falklands crisis, before Hillhead, Owen had announced that he intended to stand, if Shirley Williams did not, if only to establish the principle for which they had fought that the leader should be elected by the whole membership and not 'emerge' by cosy agreement at Westminster. From the autumn of 1980 when he had made his definite decision to leave the Labour party, Owen had been determined that Jenkins should not be handed the leadership on a plate. Personal factors apart, there had been from the beginning a difference of emphasis between Owen and Mrs Williams on the one hand and Jenkins on the other on the nature and purpose of the SDP: it reflected more than anything else the different roads by which they had come into the new party, but so far Jenkins had held the initiative and from the Dimbleby Lecture through Limehouse to Warrington and Hillhead had carried all before him. Now, with the party's momentum falling away and his own stock boosted by the Falklands, Owen had the chance to challenge this dominance. With the agreement of the membership, the ballot was brought forward from October to late June: and there began a strange campaign, decorous in public but increasingly desperate behind the scenes, to woo an electorate of 65,000 whom nobody knew very much about.

The battle was all about image and strategy, not at all about policy. Jenkins once asked Owen if there was any specific policy on which he disagreed with him, but Owen could not think of one. If anything, Jenkins considers Owen's instincts more conservative than his own (as perhaps the Falklands illustrated). Their political personalities, however, convey the opposite impression – Owen young, handsome, brash, impatient; Jenkins nearly twenty years older, Home Secretary before Owen was in Parliament, still only sixty-one but presenting the image of a wise and experienced old owl; Owen a bit of a puritan, strongly anti-tobacco and personally sparing with alcohol; Jenkins famous for enjoying his pleasures. 'Abrasive David or Rounded Roy?' was Hugo Young's summary in the *Sunday Times*:[41] 'Bossyboots *versus* the Drinker's Friend' Alan Watkins' more memorable encapsulation in the *Observer*.[42]

At a more serious level, Owen was concerned to paint himself as offering the party a more radical direction. He had broken with the Labour party much more recently and more suddenly than Jenkins. His book *Face the Future*, when first published in 1980 had included frequent references to 'socialism'; these had to be changed, for a revised edition in 1982, to 'social democracy',[43] but he (with Shirley Williams and others) was determined that it was the Labour party, not they as social democrats, which had changed. It was important to them to keep emphasizing that the SDP was the true heir of the best tradition of the Labour party; their purpose was to vindicate this claim by taking on and displacing Labour as the party of the moderate non-Marxist British left. Before the SDP was founded, they had vehemently rejected what they believed to be Jenkins' aim of creating a centre grouping, rather than a party unashamedly of the left; even during the euphoria of 1981 they remained apprehensive that the alliance with the Liberals would blur the sdp's distinct identity. By the time the leadership election was held in 1982, Owen was afraid that this had happened. There was a difference here, but in reality a very slight one. Jenkins' experience from the Dimbleby Lecture onwards undoubtedly disposed him to attach greater importance to attracting into the sdp that 'untapped and unlabelled' reservoir of support for a new non-ideological party to end the sterile dogfight of the adversary system, rather than creating a 'Mark II Labour party' to ease the passage of those whose hearts were still with Labour. But much of the difference is simply playing with words. Of the two strategies, Jenkins' is strictly speaking the more 'radical'. Furthermore on a test issue which caused a lot of heart-searching within the party in February 1982, Owen was one of those in favour of voting for the Second Reading of the Tory Government's Employment Bill, so as not to appear 'soft' on union reform; of the leaders, it was Shirley Williams who was inhibited by her Labour past.[44] On a left-right scale, the difference in practice between Jenkins and Owen is minimal.

Jenkins did *not* want to concentrate on winning uncommitted and Tory votes, nor did he accept, after Hillhead and Warrington, that he was personally more likely to attract these than Labour votes. He believed simply that the party and the Alliance needed to win some of both to win the overall victory which was there to be won, while to aim exclusively at displacing Labour was to accept the limited and danger-ous target of merely establishing a bridgehead. He fully agreed, in a campaign article in the *Observer* on 13 June, that 'the historic role of the sdp – and indeed of the Alliance – is to push the Labour Party out of the arena of government, and to make ourselves the effective alternative to the Conservatives.'

> The dangerous and unnecessary limitation is that, as the Labour Party clearly will not disappear altogether, it recreates the scenario of the 1920s and offers the prospect of political realignment at the price of a period, maybe a generation, of Conservative hegemony. This has been the one aspect of 'breaking the mould' which has from the beginning given me pause. I do not wish to repeat this part of the political history of the inter-war years. I do not believe it is necessary. I cannot understand why it is regarded as the 'left-wing' strategy, for it is a gift to the Right.
>
> My view ... is that it should in the future be perfectly possible over the country as a whole to take approximately two votes from a terminally sick Labour Party for one vote from an inflated Conservative support, to add this to a significant Liberal base, and by so doing to create a new radical majority without the penalties of fifty or sixty years ago. This is the correct left-centre strategy. This is the true breaking of the mould.[42]

Did Owen not want to win Tory as well as Labour votes? Of course
he did. Both in practice were aiming at the same target – a broad
spectrum of the centre-left: they merely had different perceptions of the
image that would attract them. Similarly, if his regard for David Steel
was less warm than Jenkins', Owen recognized perfectly well the necessity of the Liberal alliance. Jenkins was suspected of looking to an
eventual merger, while Owen valued the separate identity of the SDP; in
the long run that might become an issue, but in practice the difference
was that Jenkins thought it electorally essential to emphasize the Alliance as a 'partnership of principle', not merely an expedient pact which
might break up immediately after the election. He had no more intention than Owen of an early merger, even had he thought it possible: the
whole point of the strategy he had agreed with Steel since 1979 was that
four parties would be better than three. The contest was in large part a
phoney battle, with Owen and his supporters erecting a false model of
Jenkins' intentions which they could then knock down.

Formally, they left it to the press to elaborate their differences. The
eight hundred word election addresses which were the only communication the candidates had directly with the electorate were masterpieces
of coded understatement. Each, without mentioning the other, under-
lined modestly but unmistakeably his own particular qualities, while
gently expropriating those of the other. Thus Jenkins' – much the better
written – launched straight in with a reminder of Warrington and
Hillhead and then looked back to the Dimbleby Lecture and the agonies
of 1980 to make the point that it was he, not Owen, who had originated
the SDP and borne the heat of its first campaigns. By the same token
Owen began with a reminder that the election was by one member, one
vote (which he had supported and Jenkins had opposed), called for 'a
spirit of adventure, "guts" and drive' (which by implication Jenkins
lacked) and was not afraid to beat a small drum for 'rational patriotism'
(the spirit of the Falklands). Jenkins denied that there was any left–
right distinction to be made between them, praised the 'partnership of
principle' with the Liberals, but stressed 'our distinct SDP philosophy
and membership'. Owen emphasized the distinctiveness, but was careful
also to mention 'our principled partnership' with the Liberals. Jenkins
stressed that the party's 'historical role will almost certainly be to take
over as the main political force opposed to the Conservatives.' The SDP
was 'a radical party, and must remain one.' But, he insisted, 'our
radicalism does not spring from the need to seek a particular segment of
votes. We are radical because the country is in desperate need of change:
constitutionally, industrially, socially. We need change that will stick,

not the largely irrelevant and too easily reversible changes of recent Governments which have paradoxically left us an almost uniquely hidebound and unadaptive society.' His message was contained in the two characteristic key words 'sense and hope', though he was more specific than Owen, listing unemployment, 'democracy in the voting system and in industry', 'a constructive commitment to Europe' and 'our determination to attack poverty and prejudice at home and abroad' as priorities, while Owen by comparison was wordy and surprisingly vague. Significantly Jenkins ended – while Owen pledged himself 'win or lose' to work hard for victory – with a leader's authoritative words of encouragement to the troops: 'We have come an immense distance in a very short time. If we keep our nerve and our sense of direction we can make the breakthrough at the next crucial General Election.'[45]

Jenkins was still *claiming* the leadership, while Owen challenged for it. Yet during the campaign there seemed a real possibility that Owen would win: some surprising newspapers came out editorially for Owen, including *The Times*[46] and the *Economist*,[47] on the argument, first, that it was a realignment of the left, not of the centre, that Britain needed; and second, that it was no longer a question, since the party's decline in the polls, of choosing the best Prime Minister but rather of choosing the more dynamic leader for the long haul of opposition. The latter argument had more substance than the former; but most of the political commentators still thought that Jenkins would be the party's more potent vote-winner. Four factors perhaps determined the result. First, the membership was successfully reminded, by a flurry of articles, letters and speeches by his supporters, of Jenkins' vision, experience and real distinction as an international statesman and potential Prime Minister. Second, he himself in his 'non-campaign' successfully identified the economy (rather than the Falklands) as the major issue which would decide the next election: Owen could not match his economic experience and expertise. Third, while preserving in public a strict impartiality, David Steel let it be widely known that he hoped Jenkins would win; Jenkins and Steel had shown that they could work harmoniously together – the same harmony was not expected of Steel and Owen. A Jenkins' victory was felt by many SDP members to be essential to the success of the Alliance. The fact that this was to so many a decisive factor implies a fourth: that in so far as there was perceived to be a real difference of strategy between the candidates, the majority of the membership actually preferred the 'centre' strategy to one that harped too much on the party's Labour origins. The 'untapped' new constituency brought into politics by the Dimbleby Lecture remained faithful to the man who had first tapped and labelled it.

In the result announced on 2 July, Jenkins won by 26,256 votes to Owen's 20,864 (56 per cent to 44 per cent on a 75 per cent poll). Visibly relieved, he told reporters with some exaggeration – a measure of how worried he had been – that he was getting used to 'winning from behind'.[48] It was a margin big enough to be thoroughly decisive, without in the least humiliating Owen; on the contrary, though he was desperately disappointed not to win, Owen had done more than enough to make his point, keep Jenkins on his toes and establish his own position as his deputy and heir apparent. Whether the contest had done the party good is questionable. On the one hand, an amicably-conducted election between two contrasting but outstandingly able candidates furnished a lot of free publicity which kept the SDP before the public. On the other, following the protracted constitutional debates about the system of election, positive discrimination in favour of women and other internal matters thrashed out at a special convention at Kensington Town Hall earlier in the year, it kept the attention of the party focussed for another three months on its own concerns (in the autumn there was another contest between Shirley Williams and Bill Rodgers for the Presidency); it concentrated the public's attention on the party's search for its identity, conveying the damaging impression of a more serious division between the two strategies than really existed; and it also, since the contrast in age and style was implicitly such a large part of the Owen campaign, did serious harm to Jenkins' standing in the country, undoing much of the hard work of Warrington and Hillhead by allowing him to be portrayed once again as an indolent fat cat, distinguished perhaps, but conservative now and ten years past his prime. It has been a major uphill task of his leadership so far to combat this impression put about in 1982 by members of his own party.

It was not going to be easy anyway. The Falklands war had wrought an astonishing transformation of the political landscape, raising the Conservatives' popularity to levels unprecedented for a party not only in government but presiding over massive and still rising unemployment. Despite the negligence which the opposition parties believed to have preceded the crisis, Mrs Thatcher's triumphant conduct of the war had rendered her apparently invincible in the polls. Labour and the Alliance alike seemed marginal, as the commentators began to take her return in 1983 practically for granted. But Labour was still the official Opposition, and despite the shambling leadership of Michael Foot, set about its familiar routine of pulling itself together just in time. The Alliance, once the allocation of seats was settled – heavily in the

Liberals' favour – ceased to be news and began to slip from public consciousness. Jenkins' famous 'experimental aeroplane', which had soared beyond all expectations in 1981, was losing height badly by the end of 1982. Jenkins himself, within a few months of becoming leader, was blamed for failing to arrest the decline: many who had voted for him began to feel that Owen might have been more vigorous after all. In fact Jenkins was working harder and speaking more continuously than ever before in his life: his difficulty was in getting reported, as the press and television repented of their saturation coverage of the party's early days and consciously applied a squeeze. There is truth in the gibe that a party which lives by the media dies by the media. A new party more than an old one is dependent upon generous coverage to tell the electorate that it exists: the press is very sensitive to trends – when a phenomenon is new it is all the rage, when it is suddenly old hat there is not a good word to say for it. So it was, at the end of 1982, with the SDP: Jenkins as leader could do nothing right.

He was sustained, in this period of intense anxiety, by the faith that the objective forces which had created the party and borne it aloft in the first heady months of its existence – forces which he more than anyone else had identified, analysed and harnessed – had not suddenly ceased to exist but would assert themselves again if the party and the Alliance only kept its nerve. All its victories, except Crosby, had been won in the face of initially discouraging polls. Whenever the Alliance has had the opportunity to put its case, under the full glare of publicity, to the electors, it has always performed far better than the most optimistic forecasts. The same could well happen at the General Election; past Liberal experience, too, gives ground for thinking that it will. Faced with the choice of another five years of messianic Thatcherism, pursuing a lost vision of a Victorian heyday, or a Labour party led by Michael Foot but deeply penetrated by the Trotskyist followers of Tony Benn, the electorate is likely to rediscover its preference for the moderate combination of hope and sense, the liberation from class-confrontation politics, offered by Jenkins and David Steel. Together they make a formidable blend of experience and youth. Jenkins has lived through too many violent swings of opinion in the last three years to believe that any momentary position of the pendulum is permanent. All was still to play for, he insisted at a packed Alliance rally in the Central Hall, Westminster, at the beginning of 1983. The major breakthrough remained as real a possibility as ever. It would be a very unwise commentator who was confident that Jenkins would not in the end, as he has so often done before, come out on top. Number Ten still beckons.

Epilogue:
Leader of the SDP

British political leaders can be divided into two groups – there is the classical tradition descending from Walpole and the younger Pitt, through Peel and Gladstone to Asquith; and the romantic tradition running from the elder Pitt through Fox, Palmerston and Disraeli to Lloyd George. Coming nearer to the present, the game gets more difficult to play: Churchill and MacDonald are unquestionably romantic, but it is somehow difficult to think of Attlee or Neville Chamberlain as classical, though they have many of the characteristics. The attributes of each group are easier to recognize than to define, but the classical politician is essentially a man of government, a rationalist, a believer in the cool and unhurried solution of problems as they present themselves rather than in fulfilment of any long-term scheme; the romantic is more of a visionary, more of a word-spinner, even a demagogue, with a tang of opposition about him even when he is in office. Effectiveness in government is not the distinguishing characteristic – Lloyd George is the supreme example of a romantic thoroughly at ease with power. The two types very often define themselves in pairs – Pitt and Fox, Gladstone and Disraeli, Asquith and Lloyd George: more recently one can oppose the romantic Macmillan to the classical Butler – but these examples underline that the distinction is not simply between right and left. It is overwhelmingly a matter of individual temperament. There are plenty of romantic Tories, and the line of classical radicals is a distinguished one. It is from this latter tradition that Roy Jenkins, the biographer in politics, exceptionally aware of historical continuity, self-consciously claims descent.

Jenkins' career has been made in government. He is a practical man with an orderly mind who likes doing things, getting them right and moving on to the next. He did not cut much of a figure in opposition in the late fifties and early sixties, mainly because he was more interested in other activities – writing and travel – than in hanging about the

House of Commons making and listening to the same speeches that he had made and heard before. It was in office that he shone, overtaking all his contemporaries and rivals in the rapidity of his rise to the Cabinet, the Treasury and the Deputy Leadership: office is a continuous series of the sort of challenges he most enjoys, problems to be solved on the run and speeches to be made specifically expounding and defending the particular course of action taken, never the same speech twice. As an accomplished man of government, no-one else in the Labour Cabinet could touch him. In opposition, however, his star faltered and he lost his way. Enjoying writing again, and politically preoccupied with the single issue of the EEC, he could not summon sufficient interest in the wearisome, repetitive and internecine drag of opposition to be effective, except in the occasional set-piece debate when he could still wipe the floor with his successor. This contrast between the sixties and the seventies needs to be remembered in the eighties. Today, as leader of the SDP, leader of a minority opposition party without access to the publicity opportunities enjoyed by the leader of the official Opposition, and heckled remorselessly by the Labour left in the House of Commons, he is out of his natural element. His idea of opposition is too responsible, too judicious to grab the headlines: he is not good at the sort of wholesale denunciation of the Government, the instant quote on the radio, the controversial interview that makes the television news, which the media and the voters expect and which a less scrupulous old pro like Denis Healey, for instance, can unblushingly provide. Pressed for a quick reaction, Jenkins is inclined to hedge, sounding pompous rather than incisive. He prefers to speak only when he has had time to think out and phrase what he is going to say. Since becoming leader in 1982, indeed since returning to British politics in 1981, he has made speeches up and down the country practically every night of the week; but they are measured, rather old-fashioned speeches, carefully deploying the same considered analysis of what is wrong with British politics and the policies of the Government and the Labour party. They read well on the rare occasions when they are reported; but they do not make news. When he strives for effect, however, he loses conviction and risks what is still his greatest asset with the public, his evident integrity. It is better, he believes, to keep on saying steadily what he thinks than to turn cartwheels in public in a frenetic attempt to catch the eye: the hope of his supporters is that the electorate will recognize, when the election comes, that the best Opposition leader does not necessarily make the best Prime Minister. The clever footwork which made Harold Wilson a brilliant leader of the Opposition served the country a good deal less well in government.

Jenkins is ill-at-ease in opposition because he is genuinely shy. The close-up probing of the television camera makes him visibly uncomfortable when it is his own personality he is trying to put across. Though as vain in his own way as any other politician, he would rather be judged by what he does than by what he is. He does not consider his personality politically relevant. (It is notable how rarely he stoops to personal gibes at others.) He is sometimes irritated but not deeply worried by his reputation for drinking claret; he is quite indifferent to mockery of his inability to pronounce his r's, to the extent that he sometimes seems to go out of his way to use, rather than to avoid, words which display it, and positively to emphasize the defective consonant (*RAD*ical, *RE*ealism, *RE*alignment). These things are like Churchill's cigars or Joseph Chamberlain's orchid – superficial trimmings for the caricaturists to identify him by; he is encouraged in his belief that a man's private character is irrelevant to his politics by the classical tradition – Gladstone, Asquith and (if he is included, as perhaps he should be) Attlee, the leaders of the last three successful reforming administrations in British history, were all in their private attitudes and social habits notably conservative men. He sees no reason why his accent, his taste for good wine, his interest in Edwardian politics or his enjoyment of the novels of Anthony Powell should be thought to debar him from being, in government, at least as radical as they. The trouble is the increasing tendency of political comment and even parliamentary reporting to concentrate exclusively on quirks of personality and style rather than on policy; the tendency to trivialize concerns Jenkins as much as it does Tony Benn – not merely because it is becoming increasingly damaging to himself, but for the lowering effect it has on the level of political debate in general.

And yet there is a paradox: here is this shy, private man of government, plainly out of his element in opposition, a classical politician if ever there was one, coming back from a comfortable and internationally prestigious job in Brussels to return to the bottom rung of the domestic political ladder, to create a new party and fight two hard by-elections in the face of Labour obloquy and press derision, in an attempt to smash the settled structure of British politics. Nothing could be more 'romantic'. Nothing could be less Asquithian. The nearest comparison, perhaps, is with Gladstone who, after a career devoted to dry economic reform, discovered late in life a driving mission to liberate Ireland and splintered the party system of his day in the attempt. Inside Jenkins there is a similarly surprising passion – surprising because he does his best to hide it behind a manner of Olympian rationality and effortless

Balliol superiority. There is a duality in his nature – perhaps there is in all the examples mentioned, which was what gave them their potency, though it spoils the categorization: inside his Asquith, a Lloyd George trying to get out (though he would probably prefer to say a Franklin Roosevelt, offering a New Deal to the British people). Something in him – ambition alone is not a sufficient explanation – drives him to spurn the quiet life he could so easily have come back to, the role of elder statesman, merchant banker, man of letters, enjoying his EEC pension, the nostalgic approbation of the press and the company of his friends, to get back into the raucous bear garden of politics, exposing himself to failure and ridicule by hazarding the memory of his past success on what is still a desperately uncertain gamble. He did not have to go for the leadership of the SDP himself. He did not have to fight Warrington. Most observers expected him to shrink from that ordeal: yet he embraced it with energy and considerable personal courage. He dislikes canvassing, he hates having to introduce himself to strangers, shake hands and seek their approval: his small talk is painfully limited to a few standard phrases. (He does not always get the right one: once when visiting a prison as Home Secretary the only thing he could think of to say to an inmate to whom he was introduced was 'How nice to see you here'!) Yet he forced himself, both at Warrington and Hillhead to do it, and actually did it very well, partly because he is a good listener, partly because his very awkwardness seems more genuine than many a more smooth-talking back-slapper. Nevertheless it is a strain, and the strain sometimes shows. He often resembles some large sea-creature flopping about on dry land.

Like a performing seal, in short, he is a classical politician forcing himself through uncongenial romantic hoops – unconvincingly, yet successfully enough already that, for all his achievements in government in the sixties, it will be for the creation of the SDP that history will now remember him. He was, in the dismal context of the time, a relatively successful Chancellor: historically he was more memorable as a liberalizing Home Secretary in a period of revolutionary social change. He played an important part in taking Britain into Europe, and he was probably the most effective President the EEC Commission has had. But these were the achievements of a Butler or an Austen Chamberlain – the grey 'nearly men' of British politics. He is now engaged on a bolder adventure than either of those two ever attempted; one which, if he has not entirely misread the development of politics, will rank him with Joseph Chamberlain or even Keir Hardie (romantic figures both) as one who – whether he personally wins the prize or not – changed the face of politics itself. Such are the improbable metamorphoses that tides in the affairs of men can wreak in political careers.

The paradox is that he is *not* a visionary. He is in reality – a classical characteristic again – a somewhat unimaginative politician, doggedly pursuing the course he believes to be right by the light of a set of beliefs and assumptions imbibed early in his life and never seriously questioned. This is why the charge that he has 'betrayed' the Labour party is absurd. He has always believed in the same programme of improving the lives of the worse-off with the consent of society as a whole, within a domestic framework of personal freedom and social order and a world framework of co-operation with democratic allies in Europe and the United States to resist tyranny and alleviate poverty. For thirty years he thought the best vehicle for reaching these broad goals was the Labour party; but in the fifties he was already alarmed by the minority within the party who clung to extreme, socially divisive and utopian ideas of socialism, and signalled clearly that he thought the party had no future if that minority were to come to dominate. In the seventies the left did come to dominate, and Labour became progressively committed to more and more positions that he could not accept: neo-Marxist in relation to nationalization and the class war; isolationist in relation to the EEC; unilateralist or even neutralist on defence; subservient to undemocratic trade unions; and dedicated to a concept of party democracy which would undermine the independence of Parliament. He resisted these developments as best he could; but it is crass nonsense to suggest (as some who should know better, like Barbara Castle, do) that because he was born in the Labour party, because he owed his career to the Labour party, he was bound to stay in the Labour party when it had adopted a whole spectrum of policies with which he was in fundamental disagreement. That view makes a political party an end in itself – 'my party right or wrong'. But parties are only vehicles for achieving specified ends, bodies of individuals with a common view of the rough direction in which they wish to travel. If he finds out that the bus he is on is taking him where he very strongly does not wish to go, the rational man will naturally get off and find another going nearer to where he does want to go. That might be a purely private decision – Jenkins might have simply dropped out of politics – if he did not believe that a large proportion of the other passengers on the Labour bus were similarly being carried in a direction they did not wish to go. In that case it was his democratic duty, if at all possible, to find or provide an alternative bus to give them the choice. The argument that he, and Shirley Williams and David Owen and the rest, should have stayed in

the Labour party, standing for election on policies in which they did
not believe while fighting to reverse them, as the left always had, is –
beyond a certain point which they had long passed by 1981 – specious.
The left swallowed policies they did not like because they preferred
moderate Labourism to Toryism, hoped to convert the party to their
policies but in the meantime knew that they had no chance of electoral
survival except on the back of the despised moderates. This was simply
good politics, not loyalty. By the same token, it would have been
ludicrous for the social democrats to allow what they believed to be
their popularity to be hijacked by the left for purposes they did not
agree with. It was not only honourable, but the only rational political
decision, once they saw no hope of regaining control of the Labour
party, to get out and offer themselves to the electorate under different
colours. There was no 'betrayal', except of a sentimental idea of mindless
tribalism which has nothing to do with serious debate about how the
country should be governed.

This is not the place for a discussion of what the SDP is and stands for:
enough to say that, even at its lowest point in the polls, it has tapped a
substantial well of dissatisfaction with the old parties and the distorting
mould of adversary politics. Policies apart, it reflects a sociological shift
in the structure of British society which the traditional two-party division is no longer able to represent. The Alliance may or may not break
that rigid mould at the next election; but it has already shown that the
mould is ready for breaking in the next few years. It is necessary,
however, to ask what Jenkins himself stands for in 1983. It is certainly
arguable that the two causes to which he most particularly attached
himself and which he made his own are largely spent. First, Britain is a
much freer society today than when he first took up the running on
homosexuality, hanging, censorship, divorce, Sunday opening and the
rest of the liberal agenda: there is some backlash against 'permissiveness', but no-one seriously wants to go back to the days of Henry Brooke,
'guilty parties' and the *Lady Chatterley* trial. Second, Britain is in the
EEC, and even the Labour party is beginning to accept that it will not
be an easy matter to come out again. There is still much to be done in
persuading the British people of the benefits of membership, and bringing Britain and the other countries of the Community to pool a greater
degree of sovereignty, just as there are still anachronisms to be cleared
up in the libertarian field; neither, however, now rates high in the
priority of urgent political issues. From a third theme with which he
started his political career, Jenkins has to some extent retreated over
recent years: that is equality, or rather the enforced egalitarianism of

Fair Shares For The Rich. His view of that pamphlet today is that it was too 'mechanistic'. He is still concerned to achieve a society of equal human rights and greater equality of opportunity; but he long ago ceased to believe that confiscating the wealth of the few was any help to the many, and gives more value than in 1951 to freedom and variety in promoting a society in which all can flourish. Taxation is only one weapon, and not one whose use can be confined to a few plutocrats. Since his Chancellorship – most explicitly in *What Matters Now* – his view has been that equality involves taxing the comfortable majority, including many skilled workers, to raise the level of the underpaid, ununionized and unfortunate minority which still exists beneath society's consciousness. And that involves persuading the majority of their obligations.

Three themes, all interrelated, sum up Jenkins' political concerns today. The first follows from and goes beyond the above, involving the whole rationale of founding the SDP. This is his alarm at the break-up of the social cohesion of Britain, the decline of traditional tolerance under the stress of recession and the return of mass unemployment after a generation of prosperity and rising expectations. The harsh economic climate has bred a mood of selfishness, resentment, a search for scape-goats and a heightening of class antagonism which is exacerbated, he – and many others – believe, by an outdated political system which creates and amplifies conflicts of interest, in politics as in industry, instead of assisting their resolution. This is the relevance of 'breaking the mould'. So long as Britain is led by one or other of two class parties, each of which implicitly or explicitly regards half the population as class enemies to be bashed or cowed into submission to the other, there is no prospect of lifting this mood or recreating any sort of social co-operation, trust or sense of belonging to one community. Improving race relations is something to which he attaches great importance in this respect; abolishing poverty and alleviating inner city blight are equally central. But the big symbolic breakthrough of creating a political framework which will reflect the true pluralism of British society, not the false dichotomy of sixty years ago, remains the precondition of everything else.

Secondly, unemployment itself: to anyone of Jenkins' generation and Jenkins' politics, the return of mass unemployment is the most terrible thing. It was the greatest boast of the Attlee Government, which was where his political career began, that Labour had created full employment. Too optimistically, the Labour revisionists in the fifties believed that Keynesian techniques had abolished unemployment for ever. Its recrudescence has damaged their credibility and confidence, as monetarists and socialists have arisen to claim that Keynesianism no longer has the answer, but was rather part of the problem. On the defensive, Jenkins would still argue that demand management still contains more of the answer than the quack remedies of left or right. The programme he unveiled at Warrington is still the basis of the SDP's unemployment policy. Though full employment on the fifties pattern may never again be possible, while it is urgently necessary to develop new forms of partemployment, self-employment and job-sharing, he believes passionately that much can and must be done by a battery of measures to create work and stimulate employment, without either excessive borrowing or renewed inflation. The planned restraint of incomes, in which he has believed since the forties, is the key, but that will only be secured by a party which has advocated it from the outset, not been driven to it by events. Similarly he believes that only the SDP/Liberal approach stands a chance of bringing both sides of industry to work together – encouraging business, by rewarding enterprise, to revive investment (not frightening it off, like Labour), but not relying on the market alone (like the Tories). One of his favourite images is the need to use *all* the available controls, not just one or two. Both old parties seem to a pragmatic problem-solver self-defeatingly hidebound by their theories. Jenkins' record as Chancellor showed what he can do with a specific technical problem in his sights. He turned a massive balance of payments deficit into a healthy surplus: if anyone can conquer unemployment, there is sound precedent for thinking it is he. What is certain is that Mrs Thatcher's iron indifference to what unemployment is doing to the country angers him more than anything in politics today.

His third personal theme is the international one: his deep belief, enhanced by his experience in Brussels, that lasting economic recovery can only be achieved by all the western countries acting together. The instinctive isolationism of both Margaret Thatcher and Michael Foot appals him. Getting Britain into the EEC was only a first step and only one aspect of a general continuing need to pool sovereignty and coordinate decisions – both with the EEC and with the United States and Japan – in order to recover any real independence and control over the world economy. In particular Jenkins continues to believe that the European Monetary System which he did so much to create is one of the keys to lifting the recession: not only would the pound be more stable inside the EMS, but a 'tripod' (as he characteristically calls it) of the dollar, the yen and the European Currency Unit (including the pound) would give much increased stability to the world money market, reducing speculation against any currency and allowing each national economy a margin to stimulate growth. A second aspect of internationalism is his belief – deeper than that of most British politicians, but something he shares with David Steel – in the need to help the Third World, on the lines proposed by the Brandt Commission, not simply out of generosity or in the form of 'aid', but from enlightened self-interest. The world economy is a single economy. Britain is a trading nation: it is in the interest of trading nations that the underdeveloped countries should be enabled to buy goods in a buoyant market. The third aspect of internationalism is peace, suddenly in 1983 the issue of the moment. Jenkins has surprised some who remember Gaitskell's passionate advocacy of the British bomb by his readiness both to abandon the Trident programme and to see Polaris included in disarmament negotiations. But he could never be a unilateralist, just because he believes as a matter of principle that Britain is part of the western alliance and must negotiate as part of that alliance. He has been fighting all his life against those who think Britain should go it alone, whether in disarmament or trade, mistaking grand, self-important gestures for real politics. Here again, not through any visionary insight but simply by common sense, he has arrived at a middle position which regards as equally foolish the strident inflexibility of Mrs Thatcher on the one hand and the simple-minded posturing of Labour on the other. He believes, on this as on so many other issues, that he is closer than either to the real attitudes and preferences of the British people, could they only break out of the two-party straitjacket to express them.

Is he, then, a radical? In the sense of offering the British people a vision of a new heaven and a new earth, maybe not; he believes that he is offering them what they really want, but cannot at present have. But as he wrote back in 1953, the need is to be 'radical in the context of the moment'; and the radicalism of the moment is the radicalism of busting the adversary system in the name of democracy and common sense. That by itself would release enough energy into the political arena to keep two or three reforming Governments busy for years to come, modernizing, decentralizing and democratizing all the institutions of the country as well as tackling poverty, unemployment and the whole rusty industrial infrastructure. He has a powerful historical belief that the time is ripe. At the Alliance rally at Westminster in January 1983 he pointed to the extraordinary rhythm by which reforming Governments have come to power at intervals of thirty-eight or thirty-nine years over the past century and a half: 1830, the Whig Government of the Great Reform Bill; 1868, Gladstone's first Liberal administration;

1906, the great Liberal landslide that heralded the Liberal Governments of Campbell-Bannerman and Asquith; 1945, the Labour landslide that brought Attlee to power at the head of the only thoroughly
successful Labour Government. Thirty-eight years on is 1983. The
country's need is desperate for a new beginning under a new type of
government, combining more than one party in an alliance for national
regeneration after the locust years of Labour–Tory alternation. Can
Jenkins be blamed if he believes that he is the man to lead it, the
destined heir of Gladstone, Asquith and his father's old leader, Attlee?
He is still only sixty-two, politically in his prime. The country will have
cause to blame itself if it fails to put its most gifted man of government
back in office before it is too late.

Notes

Chapter One: From Pontypool to Oxford, 1920–1945

1 Leo Abse, *Private Member* (MacDonald, 1973), pp. 34–6.
2 Kenneth Harris, *Attlee* (Weidenfeld & Nicolson, 1982), p. 58.
3 *Daily Herald*, 27 April 1946.
4 *Monmouthshire Free Press*, 19 April 1952.
5 *South Wales Argus*, 26 April 1946.
6 *The Observer*, 3 December 1967.
7 Roy Jenkins, article written for Cardiff University magazine, 1982.
8 Andrew Roth, *Heath and the Heathmen* (Routledge & Kegan Paul, 1972), p. 39.
9 *Isis*, 25 January 1939.
10 *Sunday Times*, 20 February 1977.
11 *Oxford Magazine*, 23 November 1939.
12 *Ibid*, 6 June 1940.
13 *Ibid*, 28 November 1940.

Chapter Two: Industrious Apprentice, 1945–1953

1 Roy Jenkins, *Mr Attlee* (Heinemann, 1948), p. 217.
2 *Ibid*, p. 274.
3 *Western Mail*, 26 April 1946.
4 *Monmouthshire Free Press*, May 1946.
5 *Sunday Express*, n.d., quoted in Douglas Bence and Clive Branson, *Roy Jenkins: A Question of Principle?* (Moat Hall, 1982).
6 Jenkins papers.
7 *Manchester Guardian*, n.d. (Jenkins papers).
8 *Observer*, 25 April 1948.
9 Roy Jenkins, *Nine Men of Power* (Hamish Hamilton, 1974), p. 83.
10 *Hansard*, Vol. 451, col. 1254 (3 June 1948).
11 *Ibid*, col. 1255–6.
12 *Ibid*, Vol. 453, col. 93–8 (5 July 1948).
13 *Ibid*, Vol. 458, col. 132–7 (15 November 1948).
14 *Ibid*, Vol. 474, col. 208–13 (19 April 1950).
15 *The Sphere*, 23 August 1952.
16 Jenkins papers.
17 *Labour Party Annual Conference Report 1949*, p. 143 (7 June 1949).
18 Roy Jenkins, *Fair Shares For The Rich* (Tribune Pamphlet, 1951).
19 *Birmingham Gazette*, 28 April 1951.
20 *Encounter*, January 1964; reprinted in Roy Jenkins, *Essays and Speeches* (Collins, 1967), p. 63.

21 *Tribune*, 4 May 1951.
22 Jenkins to Gaitskell, 3 October 1952. Gaitskell papers, quoted in Philip Williams, *Hugh Gaitskell* (Jonathan Cape, 1979), p. 303.
23 *The Backbench Diaries of Richard Crossman* (Hamish Hamilton & Jonathan Cape, 1981), pp. 280–1 (3 December 1953).
24 *Times Literary Supplement*, 17 April 1953.
25 Roy Jenkins, *Pursuit of Progress* (Heinemann, 1953), p. 96.
26 *Ibid*, p. 105.
27 *Ibid*, p. 104.
28 *Ibid*, p. 24.
29 *Ibid*, pp. 44–5.
30 *Ibid*, p. 37.
31 *Ibid*, p. 161.
32 *Ibid*, p. 174.

Chapter Three: Widening Horizons, 1954–1964

1 *The Times*, 30 November 1967.
2 *Ibid*, 11 September 1971.
3 *Spectator*, 18 March 1960; reprinted in Roy Jenkins, *Essays and Speeches* (Collins, 1967), p. 45.
4 *The Times*, 23 October 1958.
5 *Times Literary Supplement*, 31 October 1958.
6 *Birmingham Mail*, 1958 (Jenkins papers).
7 *The Current News Magazine*, 26 September 1951.
8 *The Times*, 23 October 1956.
9 Roy Jenkins, *The Labour Case* (Penguin, 1959), p. 11.
10 *Spectator*, 11 November 1960.
11 *Ibid*, 22 January 1960.
12 *The Times*, 21 September 1961.
13 *Labour Party Annual Conference Report 1961*, pp. 215–16 (5 October 1961).
14 *The Statist*, 24 November 1961.
15 *Spectator*, 7 July 1961.
16 *The Times*, 7 December 1962.
17 *Encounter*, August 1961; reprinted in Roy Jenkins, *Essays and Speeches*, p. 123.
18 *Spectator*, 22 March 1957.
19 *The Author*, Autumn 1959.
20 *Spectator*, 14 August 1959.
21 *The Current News Magazine*, 28 December 1955.
22 *Encounter*, January 1964; reprinted in Roy Jenkins, *Essays and Speeches*, p. 59.
23 *The Backbench Diaries of Richard Crossman* (Hamish Hamilton & Jonathan Cape, 1981), p. 748 (14 May 1959).
24 *New Statesman*, 2 November 1959.
25 Roy Jenkins, *Nine Men of Power* (Hamish Hamilton, 1974), pp. 165–6.
26 C.A.R. Crosland, *The Future of Socialism* (Jonathan Cape, 1956).
27 *Labour Party Annual Conference Report 1958*, pp. 157–8 (1 October 1958).
28 Roy Jenkins, *The Labour Case*, p. 146.
29 *Ibid*, p. 7.
30 *Ibid*, pp. 73–4.
31 *Ibid*, pp. 11–12.

Chapter Four: Gaitskell's Fight for the Labour Party, 1959–1964

1 *Spectator*, 30 October 1959.
2 Douglas Jay, *Change and Fortune* (Hutchinson, 1980), pp. 273–5.
3 *The Times*, 5 November 1959.

4 *The Backbench Diaries of Richard Crossman* (Hamish Hamilton & Jonathan Cape, 1981), p. 796 (23 October 1959).

5 Philip Williams, *Hugh Gaitskell* (Jonathan Cape, 1979), p. 550.

6 *Spectator*, 27 November 1959.

7 *Ibid*, 11 November 1960.

8 *Encounter*, January 1964; reprinted in Roy Jenkins, *Essays and Speeches* (Collins, 1967), pp. 68-9.

9 Roy Jenkins, *Nine Men of Power* (Hamish Hamilton, 1974), p. 177.

10 *The Times*, 20 September 1960.

11 *Daily Telegraph*, 25 October 1960.

12 Lord Windlesham, *Communication and Political Power* (Jonathan Cape, 1966), pp. 265-7.

13 *Spectator*, 13 October 1961.

14 *Ibid*, 12 January 1962.

15 *Ibid*, 25 September 1959.

16 Roy Jenkins, 'British Labor Divided' in *Foreign Affairs*, April 1960.

17 *Labour Party Annual Conference Report 1962*, pp. 173-4 (3 October 1962).

18 *Labour Party Annual Conference Report 1960*, pp. 211-12 (6 October 1960).

19 Williams, *op. cit.*, pp. 708-9.

20 *Ibid*, p. 736.

21 *Encounter*, January 1964; reprinted in Roy Jenkins, *Essays and Speeches*, (Collins, 1967), pp. 71-2.

22 Roy Jenkins, *Nine Men of Power* (Hamish Hamilton, 1974), p. 161.

23 *Ibid*, p. 162.

24 *Ibid*, p. 164.

25 *Encounter*, January 1964; (*Essays and Speeches*, p. 72).

26 Crossman, *op. cit.*, pp. 978-9 (15 February 1963).

27 *Observer*, 3 December 1967.

28 *Birmingham Post*, 6 May 1971.

29 *Hansard*, Vol. 693, cols. 482-90 (15 April 1964).

30 *The Times*, 1 October 1964.

Chapter Five: Aviation and the Home Office, 1964-1967

1 *Daily Mirror*, 19 October 1964.

2 'How Not To Run A Public Corporation', *Observer*, 12, 19 July 1964; reprinted in Roy Jenkins, *Essays and Speeches* (Collins, 1967), pp. 182-96.

3 *The Times*, 6 November 1964.

4 Richard Crossman, *The Diaries of a Cabinet Minister*, Vol. 1 (Hamish Hamilton & Jonathan Cape, 1975), p. 58 (16 November 1964).

5 *The Times*, 21 January 1965.

6 'How Whitehall Grew Wings' in Jock Bruce-Gardyne and Nigel Lawson, *The Power Game* (Macmillan, 1976).

7 Crossman, *op. cit.*, pp. 152-3 (8 February 1965).

8 *The Times*, 10 February 1965; Jenkins, *op. cit.*, pp. 221-31.

9 Crossman, *op. cit.*, p. 191 (1 April 1965).

10 *The Times*, 14 April 1965.

11 *Ibid*, 23 November 1965.

12 *Ibid*, 17 December 1965.

13 Crossman, *op. cit.*, p. 100 (11 December 1964).

14 *Ibid*, p. 203 (18 April 1965).

15 *The Cecil King Diary 1964-70*

(Jonathan Cape, 1972), p. 23 (16 July 1965).

16 Harold Wilson, *The Labour Government, 1964–1970: A Personal Record* (Weidenfeld & Nicolson/ Michael Joseph, 1971), p. 66.

17 *Observer* Colour Magazine, 14 February 1965.

18 *The Times*, 23 July 1966.

19 *Ibid*, 15 July 1967.

20 Leo Abse, *Private Member* (MacDonald, 1973), pp. 252–8.

21 Crossman, *op. cit.*, Vol. 2 (Hamish Hamilton & Jonathan Cape, 1976), pp. 442, 445–6, 467–8, 590 (26, 27 July 1967, 7 September 1967, 24 November 1967).

22 *The Times*, 24 May 1966; Jenkins, *op. cit.*, pp. 267–73.

23 Crossman, *op. cit.*, p. 526 (19 October 1967).

24 *Ibid*, p. 684 (6 February 1968).

25 Roy Jenkins, *Nine Men of Power* (Hamish Hamilton, 1974), pp. 179–80.

26 *The Times*, 21 October 1966.

27 *Ibid*, 13 September 1966; (*Essays and Speeches*, pp. 243–51).

28 Sir Robert Mark, *In The Office of Constable* (Collins, 1978), p. 70.

29 *The Times*, 28 October 1966.

30 *Daily Mirror*, 1 November 1966.

31 *Daily Telegraph*, 1 November 1966.

32 *The Times*, 1 November 1966.

33 Crossman, *op. cit.*, p. 100 (31 October 1966).

34 See Abse, *op. cit.*, pp. 121–5.

35 Crossman, *op. cit.*, p. 577 (16 November 1967).

36 Lord Harris of Greenwich.

37 Crossman, *op. cit.*, p. 87 (22 October 1966).

38 *Ibid*, p. 297 (3 April 1967).

39 *Ibid*, p. 368 (7 June 1967).

40 Susan Crosland, *Tony Crosland* (Jonathan Cape, 1982), p. 171.

41 Crossman, *op. cit.*, p. 373 (8 June 1967).

42 *Ibid*, p. 393 (22 June 1967).

43 *Ibid*, p. 433 (19 July 1967).

44 *Ibid*, pp. 445–6 (27 July 1967).

45 *Ibid*, p. 462 (5 September 1967).

46 *Ibid*, p. 300 (3 April 1967).

47 *Ibid*, p. 159 (11 December 1966).

48 *Ibid*, p. 112 (6 November 1966).

49 *The Times*, 14 May 1967; (*Essays and Speeches*, pp. 278–88).

50 Crossman, *op. cit.*, p. 552 (3 November 1967).

51 *New Statesman*, 1 December 1967.

52 Crossman, *op. cit.*, p. 593 (27 November 1967).

Chapter Six: Chancellor of the Exchequer, 1967–70

1 *Economist*, 2 December 1967.

2 *Daily Mirror*, 30 November 1967.

3 *Financial Times*, 30 November 1967.

4 *Spectator*, 1 December 1967.

5 *The Times*, 30 November 1967.

6 *Sunday Times*, 3 December 1967.

7 *The Times*, 1 December 1967.

8 *Evening Standard*, 30 November 1967.

9 *Sunday Telegraph*, 3 December 1967.

10 See Michael Stewart, *The Jekyll and Hyde Years* (Dent, 1977); Wilfred Beckerman (ed.), *The Labour Government's Economic Record, 1964–70* (Duckworth, 1972); Robert Rhodes James, *Ambitions and Realities: British*

Politics, 1964–70 (Weidenfeld & Nicolson, 1972); Samuel Brittan, *Steering the Economy: The Role of the Treasury* (Penguin, 1971); Leo Pliatzky, *Getting and Spending: Public Expenditure, Employment and Inflation* (Blackwell, 1982).

11 The phrase was actually from his first Budget speech.

12 *Money Management*, September/October 1971.

13 Richard Crossman, *The Diaries of a Cabinet Minister*, Vol. 2 (Hamish Hamilton & Jonathan Cape, 1976), p. 633 (3 January 1968).

14 *Ibid*, p. 621–2 (27 December 1967).

15 *Ibid*, p. 652 (15 January 1968).

16 *Ibid*, pp. 646–7 (12 January 1968).

17 *Ibid*, p. 619 (27 December 1967).

18 *Ibid*, p. 697 (7 March 1968).

19 *Ibid*, pp. 777, 783 (11, 16 April 1968).

20 *Ibid*, Vol. 3 (Hamish Hamilton & Jonathan Cape, 1977), p. 43 (3 May 1968).

21 *Ibid*, pp. 97–8 (17 June 1968).

22 *Ibid*, pp. 109–110 (26 June 1968).

23 *Ibid*, p. 180 (4 September 1968).

24 *Ibid*, Vol. 2, p. 695 (7 March 1968).

25 *Annual Register 1968*, p. 5.

26 Crossman, *op. cit.*, p. 723 (19 March 1968).

27 *The Times*, 20 March 1968.

28 Crossman, *op. cit.*, Vol. 3, p. 24 (24 April 1968).

29 *Ibid*, p. 174 (26 August 1968).

30 *Observer*, 20 June 1971.

31 *Evening Standard*, 26 February 1970.

32 *Sunday Times*, 17 January 1971.

33 Roy Jenkins, *Nine Men of Power* (Hamish Hamilton, 1974), p. 103.

34 Roy Jenkins, *Asquith* (Collins, 1964), p. 334.

35 *Observer*, 18 October 1976.

36 *Birmingham Evening Mail*, September 1970 (Jenkins papers).

37 *The Times*, 9 January 1970.

38 *Ibid*, 13 January 1970.

39 Brittan, *op. cit.*, p. 51.

40 *Labour Party Annual Conference Report 1968*, pp. 135–8 (30 September 1968).

41 Crossman, *op. cit.*, p. 437 (14 April 1969).

42 *Ibid*, p. 440 (15 April 1969).

43 *Ibid*, p. 72 (21 May 1968).

44 *Ibid*, p. 250 (5 November 1968).

45 *Ibid*, pp. 539–40 (30 June 1969).

46 *Ibid*, p. 712 (3 November 1969).

47 Harold Wilson, *The Labour Government, 1964–1970: A Personal Record* (Weidenfeld & Nicolson/Michael Joseph, 1971), pp. 723–5.

48 *Evening Standard*, 3 May 1968.

49 Crossman, *op. cit.*, p. 57 (11 May 1968).

50 *Ibid*, p. 546 (2 July 1969).

51 *Ibid*, p. 269 (22 November 1968).

52 *Ibid*, p. 234 (22 October 1968).

53 *Ibid*, pp. 715–16 (4 November 1969).

54 *Ibid*, p. 260 (17 November 1968).

55 Peter Jenkins, *The Battle of Downing Street* (Knight, 1970), p. 94.

56 Crossman, *op. cit.*, p. 627 (5 September 1968).

57 Peter Jenkins, *op. cit.*, p. 154.

58 Crossman, *op. cit.*, p. 766 (31 December 1969).

59 *Ibid*, p. 629 (5 September 1969).

60 *Labour Party Annual Conference Report 1969*, p. 255.
61 Crossman, *op. cit.*, p. 819 (15 February 1970).
62 *Ibid*, pp. 824–5 (18 February 1970).
63 *Ibid*, p. 831 (22 February 1970).
64 *Ibid*, p. 649 (8 March 1970).
65 *Ibid*, p. 886 (13 April 1970).
66 *Financial Times*, 15 April 1970.
67 *Guardian*, 15 April 1970.
68 *Daily Telegraph*, 15 April 1970.
69 *Sun*, 15 April 1970.
70 *Daily Mirror*, 15 April 1970.
71 Crossman, *op. cit.*, p. 898 (23 April 1970).
72 Quoted in Beckerman, *op. cit.*, p. 60.
73 See John Grigg, *Evening Standard*, 9 July 1970.
74 David Butler and Michael Pinto-Duchinsky, *The British General Election of 1970* (Macmillan, 1971), p. 224.

Chapter Seven: The Struggle for the Labour Party Resumed, 1970–1974

1 *Observer*, 20 June 1971.
2 *The Times*, 9 July 1970.
3 *Evening Standard*, 9 July 1970.
4 Roy Jenkins, *Nine Men of Power* (Hamish Hamilton, 1974), p. 180.
5 *Ibid*, p. 64.
6 *Ibid*, pp. 83–4.
7 *Ibid*, p. 203.
8 *Ibid*, p. 197.
9 *Ibid*, p. 223.
10 *Ibid*, p. x.
11 *Ibid*, p. 29.
12 *The Times*, 10 May 1971.
13 *Ibid*, 19 June 1971.
14 *Ibid*, 20 July 1971.
15 Leo Abse, *Private Member* (MacDonald, 1973), p. 264.
16 *The Times*, 21–23 July 1971.
17 *Ibid*, 4 October 1971.
18 *Observer*, 14 November 1971.
19 *The Times*, 11 November 1972.
20 See Dick Taverne, *The Future of the Left: Lincoln and After* (Jonathan Cape, 1974).
21 *The Times*, 4 October 1970.
22 Michael Hatfield, *The House the Left Built* (Gollancz, 1978).
23 See Susan Crosland, *Tony Crosland* (Jonathan Cape, 1982).
24 *Ibid*, pp. 252–3.
25 Roy Jenkins, *What Matters Now* (Fontana, 1972), pp. 30–36.
26 *Labour Party Annual Conference Report 1973*, pp. 183–4 (2 October 1973).
27 Roy Jenkins, *What Matters Now*, p. 115.
28 *Ibid*, p. 18.
29 *Ibid*, pp. 38–57.
30 *Ibid*, pp. 20–22.
31 *The Times*, 17 January 1973.
32 Roy Jenkins, *What Matters Now*, p. 122.
33 *Birmingham Mail*, 14 January 1974.
34 *The Times*, 16 February 1974.
35 *Ibid*, 21 February 1974.
36 *Ibid*, 22 February 1974.
37 *Ibid*, 28 February 1974.
38 *Sunday Times*, 17 January 1971.

Chapter Eight: The Struggle for the Labour Party Lost, 1974–1976

1 *The Times*, 8 June 1974.
2 *Ibid*, 23 November 1974.

3 *Sunday Times*, 8 June 1975.
4 *The Times*, 15 April 1976.
5 *Ibid*, 10 May 1976.
6 Barbara Castle, *The Castle Diaries, 1974–76* (Weidenfeld & Nicolson, 1980), pp. 72 3 (5 April 1974).
7 *The Times*, 22 July 1975.
8 *Ibid*, 16 July 1975.
9 Sir Robert Mark, *In The Office of Constable* (Collins, 1978).
10 *Observer*, 15 October 1978.
11 *The Times*, 19 May 1976.
12 Mark, *op. cit.*, p. 152.
13 Susan Crosland, *Tony Crosland* (Jonathan Cape, 1982), p. 283.
14 *The Times*, 27 July 1974.
15 *Ibid*, 29 July 1974.
16 Castle, *op. cit.*, p. 156 (29 July 1974).
17 *The Times*, 9 October 1974.
18 *Ibid*, 4 October 1974.
19 *Ibid*, 28 September 1974.
20 *Ibid*, 27 September 1974.
21 *Ibid*, 5 October 1974.
22 David Butler and Uwe Kitzinger, *The 1975 Referendum* (St Martin's Press, 1976), p. 75.
23 Castle, *op. cit.*, p. 351 (25 March 1975).
24 Butler & Kitzinger, *op. cit.*, pp. 168ff.
25 Official 'Yes' leaflet (Butler & Kitzinger, *op. cit.*, p. 291).
26 Butler & Kitzinger, *op. cit.*, p. 188.
27 *Ibid*, p. 183.
28 *Ibid*, p. 274.
29 Castle, *op. cit.*, pp. 411–14 (9, 10 June 1975).
30 *The Times*, 13 September 1975.
31 *Ibid*, 24 January 1976.
32 Castle, *op. cit.*, p. 427 (20 June 1975).
33 *The Times*, 18 March 1976.
34 Peter Kellner & Christopher Hitchens, *Callaghan* (Cassell, 1976), pp. 170–2.
35 *The Times*, 22 March 1976.
36 Stephen Haseler, *The Tragedy of Labour* (Blackwell, 1980), p. 119.
37 *The Times*, 17 March 1976.
38 Gerald Kaufman, *How To Be A Minister* (Sidgwick & Jackson, 1980), p. 18.
39 Castle, *op. cit.*, p. 705 (25 March 1976).
40 *The Times*, 27 March 1976.
41 BBC 'Panorama' interview, 11 October 1976.
42 *The Times*, 27 April 1976.

Chapter Nine: President of the EEC Commission, 1977–80

1 BBC 'Panorama' interview, 11 October 1976.
2 *The Times*, 21 January 1977.
3 *Ibid*, 12 January 1977.
4 *Ibid*, 5 January 1977.
5 *Ibid*, 5 November 1976.
6 *Economist*, 8 July 1978.
7 *The Times*, 28 October 1977.
8 *Economist*, 24 September 1977.
9 *The Times*, 13 February 1980.
10 *Ibid*, 14 November 1981.
11 *Ibid*, 31 December 1980.
12 *Ibid*, 28 November 1979.
13 *Ibid*, 30 May 1980.
14 *Economist*, 27 December 1980.
15 *The Times*, 21 November 1980.
16 *Ibid*, 6 January 1981.

244 ROY JENKINS

Chapter Ten: The Formation of the SDP, 1979–1982

1 *The Times*, 2 December 1980.
2 *Ibid*, 20 October 1978.
3 *The Times*, 23 November 1979; reprinted in the *Listener*, 29 November 1979, and in Wayland Kennet (ed.) *The Rebirth of Britain* (Weidenfeld & Nicolson, 1982), pp. 13–29.
4 Barbara Castle, *The Castle Diaries, 1974–76* (Weidenfeld & Nicolson, 1980), p. 554 (18 November 1975).
5 *The Times*, 10 June 1980.
6 *Listener*, 13 December 1979.
7 Hugh Stephenson, *Claret and Chips: The Rise of the SDP* (Michael Joseph, 1982), p. 14.
8 Ian Bradley, *Breaking the Mould? The Birth and Prospects of the Social Democratic Party* (Martin Robertson, 1981), p. 73.
9 Stephenson, *op. cit.*, p. 31.
10 *Ibid*, p. 24.
11 *Guardian*, 2 August 1980.
12 *Economist*, 14 June 1980.
13 *Spectator*, 14 June 1980.
14 *Ibid*, 11 June 1980.
15 *Ibid*, 22 November 1980.
16 Bradley, *op. cit.*, p. 85.
17 Stephenson, *op. cit.*, pp. 40–41.
18 *Ibid*, p. 50.
19 *The Times*, 27 March 1981.
20 Bradley, *op. cit.*, p. 142.
21 *The Times*, 11 June 1981.
22 *Observer*, 8 June 1981.
23 *The Times*, 30 June 1981.
24 *Economist*, 25 July 1981.
25 *The Times*, 2 July 1981.
26 *Ibid*, 30 June 1981.
27 *Ibid*, 6 July 1981.
28 *Ibid*, 8 July 1981.
29 *Ibid*, 14 July 1981.
30 *Spectator*, 12 January 1962.
31 *The Times*, 15 July 1981.
32 *Ibid*, 17 July 1981.
33 *Ibid*, 10 October 1981.
34 See *The Times*, 15 January 1982, 15 March 1982.
35 *Sunday Times*, 17 January 1982.
36 Castle, *op. cit.*, p. 713 (1 April 1976).
37 *Daily Mail*, 26 March 1982.
38 *Glasgow Herald*, 26 March 1982.
39 *The Times*, 26 March 1982.
40 *Sunday Times*, 28 March 1982.
41 *Ibid*, 13 June 1982.
42 *Observer*, 13 June 1982.
43 Stephenson, *op. cit.*, p. 175.
44 *Ibid*, pp. 156–7.
45 SDP Leadership Ballot: Statements by Candidates.
46 *The Times*, 29 June 1982.
47 *Economist*, 26 June 1982.
48 *The Times*, 3 July 1982.

Bibliography

Leo Abse, *Private Member* (Macdonald, 1973).

Peter Bartram, *David Steel: His Life and Politics* (W.H. Allen, 1981).

Wilfred Beckerman (ed.), *The Labour Government's Economic Record, 1964–1970* (Duckworth, 1972).

Douglas Bence and Clive Branson, *Roy Jenkins: A Question of Principle?* (Moat Hall, 1982).

Vernon Bogdanor, *The People and the Party System* (Cambridge, 1981).

Ian Bradley, *Breaking the Mould? The Birth and Prospects of the Social Democratic Party* (Martin Robertson, 1981).

Samuel Brittan, *Steering the Economy: The Role of the Treasury* (Penguin, 1971).

David Butler and Michael Pinto-Duchinsky, *The British General Election of 1970* (Macmillan, 1971).

David Butler and Dennis Kavanagh, *The British General Election of February 1974* (Macmillan, 1974); *The British General Election of October 1974* (Macmillan, 1975).

David Butler and Uwe Kitzinger, *The 1975 Referendum* (Macmillan, 1976).

Barbara Castle, *The Castle Diaries, 1974–76* (Weidenfeld & Nicolson, 1980).

C.A.R. Crosland, *The Future of Socialism* (Jonathan Cape, 1956).

Susan Crosland, *Tony Crosland* (Jonathan Cape, 1982).

R.H.S. Crossman (ed.), *New Fabian Essays* (Turnstile Press, 1952).

R.H.S. Crossman and Janet Morgan (eds.), *The Backbench Diaries of Richard Crossman* (Hamish Hamilton & Jonathan Cape, 1981); *The Diaries of a Cabinet Minister* (Hamish Hamilton & Jonathan Cape, 1975, 1976, 1977).

Stephen Haseler, *The Gaitskellites: Revisionism in the British Labour Party, 1951–1964* (Macmillan, 1969); *The Tragedy of Labour* (Blackwell, 1980).

Michael Hatfield, *The House the Left Built* (Gollancz, 1978).

Simon Hoggart and David Leigh, *Michael Foot: A Portrait* (Hodder & Stoughton, 1981).

David Howell, *British Social Democracy: A Study in Development and Decay* (Croom Helm, 1976).

Robert Rhodes James, *Ambitions and Realities: British Politics, 1964–70* (Weidenfeld & Nicolson, 1972).

Douglas Jay, *Change and Fortune* (Hutchinson, 1980).

Peter Jenkins, *The Battle of Downing Street* (Knight, 1970).
Roy Jenkins, *Mr Attlee* (Heinemann, 1948);
        Fair Shares For The Rich (Tribune, 1951);
        Pursuit of Progress (Heinemann, 1953);
        Mr Balfour's Poodle (Heinemann, 1954);
        Sir Charles Dilke: A Victorian Tragedy (Collins, 1958);
        The Labour Case (Penguin, 1959);
        Asquith (Collins, 1964);
        Essays and Speeches (Collins, 1967);
        Afternoon on the Potomac (Yale, 1972);
        What Matters Now (Fontana, 1972);
        Nine Men of Power (Hamish Hamilton, 1974).
Gerald Kaufman, *How to be a Minister* (Sidgwick & Jackson, 1980).
Peter Kellner and Christopher Hitchens, *Callaghan* (Cassell, 1976).
Wayland Kennet (ed.), *The Rebirth of Britain* (Weidenfeld & Nicolson, 1982).
The Cecil King Diary, 1964–1970 (Jonathan Cape, 1972).
Uwe Kitzinger, *Diplomacy and Persuasion* (Thames & Hudson, 1973).
Sir Robert Mark, *In The Office of Constable* (Collins, 1978).
David Owen, *Face The Future* (Jonathan Cape, 1980).
Leo Pliatzky, *Getting and Spending: Public Expenditure, Employment and Inflation* (Blackwell, 1982).
William Rodgers, *The Politics of Change* (Secker & Warburg, 1982).
David Steel, *A House Divided* (Weidenfeld & Nicolson, 1980).
Hugh Stephenson, *Claret and Chips: The Rise of the SDP* (Michael Joseph, 1982).
Michael Stewart, *The Jekyll and Hyde Years* (Dent, 1977).
Dick Taverne, *The Future of the Left: Lincoln and After* (Jonathan Cape, 1974).
Alan Watkins, *Brief Lives* (Hamish Hamilton, 1982).
Philip Williams, *Hugh Gaitskell* (Jonathan Cape, 1979).
Shirley Williams, *Politics is for People* (Allen Lane/Penguin, 1981).
Harold Wilson, *The Labour Government, 1964–1970: A Personal Record* (Weidenfeld & Nicolson/Michael Joseph, 1971); *Final Term: The Labour Government, 1974–1976* (Weidenfeld & Nicolson/Michael Joseph, 1979).
Lord Windlesham, *Communication and Political Power* (Jonathan Cape, 1966).
Peter Zentner, *Social Democracy in Britain: Must Labour Lose?* (John Martin, 1982).

Index